Passionate Engines

Passionate Engines

What Emotions Reveal About
Mind and Artificial Intelligence

Craig DeLancey

OXFORD
UNIVERSITY PRESS

2002

OXFORD
UNIVERSITY PRESS

Oxford   New York
Athens   Auckland   Bangkok   Bogotá   Buenos Aires   Cape Town
Chennai   Dar es Salaam   Delhi   Florence   Hong Kong   Istanbul   Karachi
Kolkata   Kuala Lumpur   Madrid   Melbourne   Mexico City   Mumbai   Nairobi
Paris   São Paulo   Shanghai   Singapore   Taipei   Tokyo   Toronto   Warsaw

and associated companies in
Berlin   Ibadan

Library of Congress Cataloging-in-Publication Data
DeLancey, Craig, 1965–
Passionate engines : what emotions reveal about mind and artificial intelligence / Craig
DeLancey.
    p.   cm.
Includes bibliographical references.
ISBN 0-19-514271-3
1. Philosophy of mind.   2. Emotions (Philosophy)   3. Artificial intelligence.   I. Title.
BD418.3.D45 2002
128'.37—dc21   00-066903

9 8 7 6 5 4 3 2 1

Printed in the United States of America
on acid-free paper

For Lorena

Preface

Goals of the Book

This book is a survey of what basic emotions reveal about some central problems of the philosophy of mind. Given their relative importance to our mental lives, emotions remain the mental phenomena most neglected by contemporary philosophy of mind and the sciences of mind. This is not to deny that important work has been done in our time in the philosophy and science of emotions; rather, it is to note that for the traditional interests of philosophers of mind, cognitive scientists, artificial intelligence researchers, and many others, emotions remain peripheral, sometimes even a seemingly irrelevant issue. This is a glaring exception not only because emotions play such important roles, but also because the last several decades have seen a tremendous growth in our scientific understanding of emotions. In this book, I will show that a proper accounting of some of the emotions is essential to many of those aspects of the philosophy and sciences of mind heretofore considered distinct from them. Given our increased knowledge about emotions, the time is now ripe for an overview of how they reflect on some of the theoretical issues of these disciplines. This book provides such a survey for five central issues:

(1) The Affect Program Theory. Emotions are mental phenomena of intrinsic interest; the affect program theory is a compelling and powerful theory that explains what some of the emotions are. I introduce the theory, defend it against rival views, and outline some of what it can tell us about the mind.

(2) Intentionality. The basic emotions are representational states. I describe the structure of the intentionality of the basic emotions, and explore some implications of this enriched view.

(3) Rationality. Philosophers have long thought that emotions may play an important role in rational action; I describe some aspects of this relationship, and apply my findings to a core problem concerning practical reasoning.

(4) Phenomenal consciousness. Some features of phenomenal experience are particularly pressing when we consider the basic emotions. Discovering the structure of the relation between phenomenal experience and affects will be used as a way to explore the more general issue of the relation between those experiences and the body states of the organism.

(5) Artificial intelligence (hereafter "AI"). Work in AI offers us an opportunity to test hypotheses, and also helps us to question our own presuppositions. Our best understanding of the affects reveals important principles useful to the theoretical underpinnings of our attempts to engineer intelligence.

These last four issues are not necessarily related to each other except in as much as they are all core concerns of the philosophy of mind. I chose these because they are topics in the philosophy of mind about which, I believe, our understanding of the basic emotions has profound lessons to offer.

My approach to these issues is united under three themes. First, the theory that I argue for in the first section of the book—the affect program theory—is used throughout the text. To attempt an overview of all the import of all the things that we call "emotions" would be folly. Focusing on a small number of emotions and a single theory of their nature will allow me to reveal some of the important implications of these affects, instead of constantly obscuring any such lessons under difficult issues of taxonomy.

Second, I argue that the affect program theory is consistent with, and points us toward, a view of mind quite contrary to much contemporary theory of mind. I call this the *hierarchical view of mind.* This is a modular view of mind in which certain capabilities are seen as more fundamental to autonomy, and are likely to be required by other (hence, dependent) capabilities. In particular, many of our affective capabilities, and also our capabilities underlying motor control and its integration with perception (capabilities that are likely highly integrated with affect), are more fundamental than, and can and often do operate independently of, the kinds of capabilities that are typically taken to constitute "high cognition"; and in turn many cognitive abilities make use of, and may require, these other subcognitive abilities. Instead of a top-down, highly cognitive view of mind, in which language is seen as the fundamental mental capability that enables autonomy and intelligence, a proper appreciation for the role of affects in our lives reveals that we must start with a bottom-up, embodied view of mind in which motor control and its integration with perception, along with our affective capabilities, are the fundamental features of autonomy, upon which intelligence must be built. Equivalently, I argue that explaining a general conception of autonomy, and not cognition, should be the primary goal of the philosophy of mind. This is a theme that arises throughout the book.

Third is a theme that will come to the fore several times: Giving the relevant emotions their due reveals a need to reevaluate the richness of a naturalist view of mind. In contemporary philosophy of mind, almost everyone pledges allegiance to naturalism; yet we are in the ironic position that there is a widespread reaction to naturalism in contemporary analytic philosophy, often apparently motivated by the belief that naturalism is an impoverished approach to mind. This is ironic because the offered alternatives are usually stupefyingly simplistic, the most common being that all of mind and action can be explained by generic concepts of belief and desire. Since my concern in this book is with basic emotions and other motivating states, I will on several occasions discuss the inappropriateness of the philosopher's notion of desire; it is hard to overestimate the harm that this notion has done to moral psychology, action theory, and other aspects of the philosophy of mind. In contrast, far from being a source of simplistic descriptions likely to label as illusions whole swathes of our mental lives as we reduce down to some simple physics, the sciences of mind usually reveal surprising complexity (for example, there are many kinds of motivational states, but no generic one corresponding to the philosophical notion of desire) and are causes even for the introduction of new entities and thus an expansion of the relevant ontology. In this book, I do not review the literature and issues in the philosophy of science concerning naturalism, but rather I show by example that a kind of naturalism is both richer than it has been portrayed and far richer than the alternatives. Through the study of the basic emotions certain features of a mature view of mind can be clarified, and a rejection of a simplistic portrayal of naturalism is one such feature.

By saying that an account of some emotions is essential to the philosophy and science of mind, I mean at least that we cannot expect a theory of mind to be sufficient unless we have taken into account whether it is consistent with what we know about these emotions. Establishing this point is easily done when we recognize that many theories of mind, which seem quite plausible when emotions are ignored, become quite implausible when emotions are taken into account. This is the case not just because these theories fail to predict or explain emotions. After all, since many researchers in the philosophy and science of mind see emotions as something to be tacked onto a theory of mind after cognition is explained, the failure to predict or explain emotions is hardly surprising. Also, there is broad agreement that if we want to model real biological minds, we will need to model affects, since they are biological events which, in us, are nearly omnipresent. But even the kinds of things that a philosopher or scientist might want to study independently of emotions are often so highly integrated with them that treating these emotions as a kind of sideshow can only result in inadequate theory. Many of these inadequate theories are considered viable in contemporary philosophy and science of mind, and their continued pursuit results in wasted effort.

Although these negative conclusions are crucial, my task is not solely to attack inadequate approaches. Throughout, my arguments for the general and widely applicable affect program theory will prove useful in showing how our understanding of emotions can offer new approaches to understanding minds. I argue for positive theories of the nature of emotional intentionality and rationality, and of the substrates of phenomenal consciousness, that are consistent with the affect program theory, and I offer some speculations about how our understanding of emotions might help AI. At this moment in the philosophy and sciences of mind, because of the relative neglect that emotions have suffered for some time, they are a promising source for new understanding of the mind.

The Audience

Although this is a work in the philosophy of mind—tackling issues traditionally in the domain of philosophers and using methods and terminology characteristic of philosophy—I wrote this book with the hope that it could reach across disciplines and speak to anyone interested in mind and emotions. For that reason, I have provided throughout the book explanations of some technical, and mostly philosophical, terms and theories; when these explanations were quite independent of the argument, I put them either into footnotes or into boxes that run parallel to the text. The boxes aim to do two things: first, to explain some technical terms and theories in an unobtrusive way; second, to attempt to make clear why these issues are important. I also found that when I referred to a concept that I would later discuss at length, it was most convenient to delay defining the relevant terms; readers are therefore urged to check the index for reference to an unfamiliar notion and then skip ahead to find explanations. Over the last few years I have had the good fortune to work and study with psychologists, psychiatrists, neural scientists, computer scientists, electrical engineers, anthropologists, physicists, and philosophers. This has taught me that our terminologies often sound deceptively similar when they are significantly different, and that it is often difficult for workers in one discipline to understand why the concerns of those in another are of any relevance. The study of mind is an interdisciplinary undertaking, and I try to participate in this spirit by exploring issues that, although largely philosophical, span several domains of inquiry. But doing this requires that we be very explicit about what our terms mean, what our concerns and goals are, what our underlying method is or should be, and why the issue should matter to someone not directly concerned with the debate at hand.

I have also tried to approach each issue discussed in the book on its own ground; that is, in the terms and formulation of the theory in question. This is neither an endorsement of theoretical ecumenicalism nor an attempt to get around the disparate uses of terms in different disciplines, but rather is an attempt to achieve results that will stick. For example, our best scientific understanding of emotions effectively demolishes the view that all emotions are just judgments or some other kind of propositional attitude. Some views of mind and emotion are quite immune to these scientific findings, however, because they place the stuff of mind outside the reach of these results. By confronting one popular such kind of theory in its own terms, I show that it is untenable even on its own presuppositions. Similarly, artificial intelligence is the attempt to create systems that exhibit intelligent or autonomous behavior. Even if some approaches turn out to be biologically implausible, if they result in practical solutions to real-world problems, they will be gladly and rightly embraced. Thus, indifference to emotion will not likely be accepted as a problem if it means nothing more than a failure of biological modeling. But by showing that understanding affects has more to offer than just augmenting the realism of models, I will show that artificial intelligence at the engineering end of the spectrum has something to learn also. A corollary of this approach is that the overarching themes that unite my topics are not the sole purpose of the claims made here. In those arguments not solely directed at the defense of the affect program theory or of the hierarchical view of mind, my claims about both the emotions concerned and alternative theories should stand or fall on their own merits. Thus, for those wholly hostile to the affect program theory or to the view of mind I advocate, much of the material in this book should still be of interest.

The Form of the Book

The book can be divided into two parts. Part 1 introduces the affect program theory and defends it against some cognitivist and irrealist alternatives; part 2 surveys some core concerns in the philosophy of mind, and applies to them the insights that our best understanding of the basic emotions, and other affects, provides.

Chapter 1 introduces and explains the affect program theory, showing why it is compelling, given both the empirical evidence consistent with it and its explanatory power. There is still no widespread agreement about the taxonomy of emotions, and so the statement of this theory is couched in a limited discussion of taxonomy to assure the reader that the affect program theory is both a worthwhile way to understand some emotions and is actually a theory of the emotions that we refer to in our normal discourse.

Although a strong cognitive view of emotions still seems to be widely held, it has drawn a number of powerful criticisms in recent years. However, these criticisms have not touched upon two factors. First, little attention has been paid by philosophers to the vast body of neuroscientific and psychological evidence that is contrary to cognitivism about emotions. In chapter 2, I undertake this task. This will also offer an opportunity to review some of the empirical evidence for the hierarchical view of mind that is one of the primary themes of the book. Second, the implications of the failure of cognitivism about emotion for the theory of mind have not yet been explored. In chapter 3, I consider one of the most influential views of mind today, the interpretationist view advocated by Donald Davidson, Daniel

Dennett, and others, and show how it requires a cognitivist view of emotion and fails because of its inability to properly explain emotional actions. Interpretationism is an irrealist theory of mind, and so it has certain immunities to some kinds of appeal to scientific evidence. My task will be to both criticize the view on its own ground (using conceptual analysis coupled with some platitudes about action and basic emotions), and to show how basic emotions suggest that a naturalist theory of mind is a more satisfactory approach than these alternatives. Social constructionism is a view of mind consistent with interpretationism and other forms of irrealism about emotions, but immune to the problems I raise in chapter 3; thus, in chapter 4, I discuss and criticize social constructionism about basic emotions on different conceptual and empirical grounds.

Having introduced the affect program theory and defended it against both cognitivism and some forms of irrealism about the relevant emotions, I then survey the import of this view for some core issues in the philosophy of mind. Chapters 5 and 6 are concerned with intentionality. Chapter 5 describes the heterogenous structure of the intentionality of the basic emotions—a view consistent with the hierarchical view of mind. I argue that explaining the intentionality of the basic emotions is best done by reference to their role in action. This alternative view is a powerful way to explain some perplexing problems. In chapter 6, I clarify these insights and pursue an application of them by considering our common practice of emoting for imaginary events, such as those portrayed in fictions. This offers a ready counterexample to a cognitivist view of emotion and also provides an example of one of the key features of intentionality: the possible inexistence of the intentional object. The heterogenous model of intentionality developed in chapter 5 will allow me to give a proper account of our ability to emote for fictions, and will help clarify the relationship between emotional intentionality, propositional intentionality, and some instances of intentional states "directed at" nonexistent things.

Chapters 7 and 8 explore the senses in which the basic emotions can be rational and what role they may play in more general notions of rationality. Chapter 7 extends the hierarchical model of mind to explaining the rationality of the basic emotions in a way consonant with the discussion of the form of the intentionality of the basic emotions. Chapter 8 applies this approach to a core problem in the philosophy of practical action: the question of internalism.

Chapters 9 and 10 are concerned with the question of consciousness. Basic emotions have been largely neglected in this now burgeoning debate. Chapter 9 addresses some puzzles that the phenomenal experiences of some affects raise for the current debate. Chapter 10 argues that these puzzles reveal that an appropriate theory of consciousness should be consistent with a claim for strong supervenience of phenomenal experiences on the functional role of the relevant states as given in a systems-based teleofunctional theory. I provide the outlines of one such theory, and show how it solves the puzzles presented in chapter 9. This theory also is consistent with the bottom-up aspect of the hierarchical view of mind, and as such the theory provides a way to clarify the notion of autonomy.

Chapters 11 and 12 address the theoretical underpinnings of AI. Many of the general lessons of the history of AI are consistent with a view of mind that gives the basic emotions their proper place in the theory of mind; most important, the failures and limitations of AI spotlight some of the misconceptions that are common to the theory of mind and that also typify a view in which the role of affects is ignored. Thus, although AI is not a topic so much as a field of study and a collection of techniques, I discuss it here for the important empirically based view it offers, one that augments the neuroscience to which I refer throughout the book. Chapter 11 returns to the issues of intentionality and rational action, but this time in terms of the computational theory of mind. I show that some affects and their influences upon cognition stand as a counterexample to certain forms of computational functionalism. Chapter 12 is something of an indulgence: I draw some distinctions concerning the place of affects in AI and summarize some practical applications of our knowledge of affects.

In the conclusion, I review some of the theoretical implications of this knowledge and summarize the view that it suggests: the mind as passionate engine.

All academic work is open source. It is my hope to gather comments, corrections, references to new (and overlooked) relevant scientific findings, and suggested additions from readers like you. I will use these to revise and expand future editions of *Passionate Engines*. Please bring your insights to www.passionateengines.org.

Acknowledgments

I am indebted to a number of colleagues for help and support. Foremost are Nino Cocchiarella, who has been a teacher, mentor, and friend, and Adam Kovach, who has read and offered useful comments upon several chapters of this book, and has long otherwise been to me a gadfly and example. Joe Steinmetz introduced me to neuropsychology, which was the beginning of my interest in emotions, and for this I shall always be grateful; Joe also offered helpful points of clarification for my interpretations (for which he cannot be held responsible!) of neuroscientific results in chapters 1 through 5. Jonathan Mills and the other researchers at Indiana University's Adaptive Systems Lab have provided instruction, infectious enthusiasm, and much encouragement for my efforts to break into AI; Jonathan patiently tried to turn me into a "philosophical engineer," as he so aptly called it, and though I have made only small steps in that direction, I owe him much for showing me the path. I also owe thanks to Paul Griffiths, Lis Nielson, and Jaak Panksepp for valuable advice. Two anonymous reviewers for Oxford University Press offered gracious guidance. Thanks also to the other members of the Analytic Philosophy Project and of F.R.E.R. Most important, Lorena Ferrero DeLancey and Nancy Calabresi have for many years patiently supported all of my undertakings, including the long road to the research underlying this book.

Some of the work in this book was supported by a Nelson Fellowship from the department of philosophy at Indiana University, and by a summer research grant and a summer research fellowship from the Program of Cognitive Science at Indiana University. I am grateful to the department and program for their support. My work on artificial intelligence has been supported by a National Science Foundation graduate research traineeship.

Chapter 3 appeared in a slightly different version in *Philosophical Psychology* (11, no. 4 [1998]), and some of chapter 10 appeared in *Philosophical Psychology,* (10, no. 2 [1997]). I thank Carfax Publishing Limited (P.O. Box 25, Abingdon, Oxfordshire, OX14 3UE, United Kingdom) for permission to use the pieces here. Some of chapter 9 appeared in *Journal of Consciousness Studies* (3, nos. 5–6 [1996]); thanks to the journal for letting me reprint some of that article. Some of chapter 11 appeared in 1997 in *Two Sciences of Mind: Readings in Cognitive Science and Consciousness,* edited by Seán Ó'Nuallaïn, Paul McKevitt, and Eoghan Mac Aogín. Thanks also to John Benjamins, the publisher, for permission to draw upon that work.

Contents

Passionate Engines

1

Introduction

The Affect Program Theory of Emotions

There probably is no scientifically appropriate class of things referred to by our term *emotion*. Such disparate phenomena—fear, guilt, shame, melancholy, and so on—are grouped under this term that it is dubious that they share anything but a family resemblance. But particular emotions are another matter altogether. There is good reason to believe that different sciences can make quite compelling sense of a more fine-grained differentiation of affects. My task in this book is to reveal some of the important and neglected lessons of some of the emotions for the philosophy and sciences of mind, and this task can be accomplished with just a working characterization of a few of these. More important, there is a compelling theory of some emotions that has far-reaching implications for the philosophy and sciences of mind. This is the *affect program theory*. Using a version of this theory as a guide to what phenomena we will be concerned with and to the nature of these phenomena will allow us to avoid fundamental confusions and to provide richer results.

The affect program theory is the view that some emotions are pancultural syndromes enabled by inherited biological capabilities. By calling them "syndromes," we mean to point out that they are coordinated collections of complex biological responses that occur together. These emotions will be characterized by several features, including at least physiological responses, such as autonomic body responses, and stereotypical associated behaviors, such as facial expressions but also relational behaviors. I will call the emotions that are taken to fall under the affect program theory "basic emotions," just so that we have some way to refer to them.[1] This is a very general formulation of the affect program theory; however, with some small elaboration in this chapter, it will be sufficient to allow me to draw some very important lessons about the nature of mind.

This theory is meant to describe only some of the things that we might call an emotion. In part as a result of this, there is plenty of room for controversy regarding whether this is a proper theory of emotion. For example, some theorists have argued that conscious experience is a necessary element of an emotion (Clore, 1994), whereas this is not the case on the affect

3

program theory. Thus, one might argue that the affect program theory does not properly describe the emotions as the normal speaker means to refer to them. The affect program theory is an empirical theory; it is not beholden to fit exactly our folk use of affect terms, or our folk theory about affects (see Griffiths, 1997). Ultimately, the defense of the affect program theory must rest on how well it (1) usefully defines and distinguishes the various affects, and (2) explains and predicts the relevant phenomena. Defending the theory's utility to explain and predict the relevant phenomena is done throughout this book, by way of applying the theory and showing how it can offer powerful new ways to think about some of the problems of mind. Defending the theory as a useful way to categorize the affects is something I will do in this chapter and the next. My approach will be to examine some of the features of affects that other scholars have singled out as necessary or sufficient or perhaps even just important to emotions and other affects. Our best scientific understanding of these features reveals that they are either consistent with the affect program theory, or are not appropriate ways to ground a theory of affect. This will also allow me to review the scientific evidence and theoretical reasons that lay the foundations for a view of mind that is quite different from most of those that characterize contemporary philosophy of mind.

Although scientists have tended to be more careful, and usually provide sufficient operational notions of the emotions and other affective states they study, until recently (e.g., Griffiths, 1997) there has been scandalously little concern among philosophers (even philosophers of emotion) for clarifying their taxonomic presuppositions. This oversight is not innocuous, since it fosters both an extremely error-prone armchair theorizing, sometimes even armchair neuropsychology, and also vagueness and confusions that can result in question-begging and pernicious ambiguities.

Most philosophy of emotion has proceeded in one of three ways. In recent years it has been most common for emotions to be investigated through the use of emotion terms. This is an approach which is sometimes taken to an extreme by those who endorse the position that the conceptual analysis of ordinary language is all that is needed to understand emotions, or by the social constructionists, who see culture—of which they take language to be the most important and revealing element—as the creator of emotions. Paul Griffiths (1997, 21ff.) has effectively criticized the former, pointing out that ordinary language analysis approach to emotion studies has been based upon philosophical presuppositions that are now largely debunked. I will criticize a strong social constructionist approach in chapter 4. A second method for philosophizing about emotions, more revealed in the lack of an explicit method, is to take emotions as primitives open to reliable introspection; not surprisingly, this approach usually yields the view that emotions are fundamentally cognitive. But taking emotions as having properties that are somehow obvious inevitably leads to begging all the important questions; emotions are introspected to have just the qualities needed to support whatever theory is at hand. I shall review some cases that show

how psychologists and neural scientists have discovered some very surprising things about our everyday emotions, things which would certainly fail to be noticed by introspection. Introspection also results in subjective characterizations that are hard or impossible to pin down. Without some, even if rough, prior and objective (that is, third-person, open to observation) characterization of the things we are discussing, much of this work on emotions can be useless. A third approach is to simply define emotions and work with these definitions; this also has traditionally yielded cognitive approaches. Defining emotions up front in some cognitive form would be, of course, quite acceptable if this were not usually followed by sweeping generalizations that reach beyond the scope of the class of phenomena picked out by the definition. As it stands, all too often we find that a theorist starts with a definition of emotions that is strongly cognitive, then makes claims about all emotions, surreptitiously slipping in the assumption that all of what others call "emotions" fall under the definition of emotions as cognitive. We therefore either need to be extremely careful not to erroneously generalize from our definition, or we need to characterize (at least some) emotions in some sense that is guided by empirical data and allows us to formulate the core questions about emotions. I will take the latter route, beginning with a broad characterization of affects that is not by definition cognitive, and then exploring how we can build our way to a characterization of some emotions which will let us learn some lessons from them.

A General Notion of Affect

It will be useful to start with a more general characterization of affect. This will give us a chance to place the relevant emotions in relation to things like pleasure or mood. There is little agreement upon terminology for emotions and other affects in philosophy, psychology, or any other of the cognitive sciences. In general, terms like *emotion* and *affect* are used synonymously. However, for most of us (at least in the English-speaking world), paradigm emotions include fear, anger, joy, sadness, and disgust. At the same time, some people consider moods to be emotions, including thus long-term states that have motivational features very different from those of, say, terror. And philosophers will talk about the importance of emotions to rationality, seemingly grouping desire and other more general conative states together under the term "emotion." Given that such a disparate group of things can be labeled as emotions, we need to draw some distinctions among these phenomena. Here I shall try to avoid confusions by using "affect" as a general term, and desires, emotions, moods, and other states will classify as types of affects.

I still need to characterize affect in some positive way. The working definition I propose is: *Affects are body states that are motivational.* (Throughout this book, I will take body states to include neural states; when I want to draw attention to the body independent of the central nervous system, I will use the term "extended body.") This is not in itself very enlightening, since motivation is not a little mysterious. But the principal feature of these motivations is that they are internal physical states of an organism that cause it to perform an action if the organism is not inhibited by different motivations or otherwise constrained. The relation of inhibition by other motivations, and also the notion of constraint, although both intuitively clear, are very hard to specify. Without a better account of what it is to inhibit or constrain a motivation, this characterization might be too vague if we meant to explore the nature of affect *per se.* But the claim that the affects are types of body states is sufficient to distinguish this notion of affect from many of the competing notions; in particular, it commits us to a realist theory of motivations (in contrast to, for example, ascriptivist notions of desire, such as I discuss below and in chapter 3). Furthermore, this is a claim for type-identity: the body states that motivate are instances of a recognizable type. Since it will be sufficient to have a working notion of just a certain class of emotions, I will take motivation as a primitive; however, this notion, as it is involved with the basic emotions that will be my concern here, will be developed at more length in the coming chapters. In the meantime, this definition makes it clear that I link affects to actions.

Affect Is Characterized in a Functional Way

Affects include desires, pleasures, emotions, and moods. We should note that these things are quite distinct in the physiological and, in particular, neural structures that underlie their function; we should not expect to find a single brain system for all motivation. Furthermore, when they are cognitive, affects can include significant input from not only subcortical brain areas but also from cortical polymodal and supramodal areas. More simply put: a lot of the brain, including areas seemingly dedicated to more abstract thought, can (but need not) become involved in the affect. Thus, as occurs with many biological functions, we should expect some of the brain and body substrates of affects to be distributed. All of these distinctions reveal that this notion of affects is a functional characterization that may not in any simple way reduce to a physical one.[2] We may indeed find that the neural underpinnings, for example, of some particular affects can be quite clearly mapped out; but the concept of affects in general is unlikely to have such a common characterization.

Two other things should be noted about this characterization of affects. First, although I believe that they are necessarily motivational, pains are often understood in neuroscience as somatosensory phenomena that activate a motivational system. We could use "pain" in a broader sense to include the activation of the motivational systems that neuroscientists take the somatosensory aspects of pain to activate; but, given that nothing here depends on it, I will instead avoid expending effort on what could be a contentious issue. I will not require that pains be counted as affects. Second, moods pose special difficulties; since moods will only be a passing concern here, I will not try to characterize them at more length. As a working notion, we can think of moods as long-term affective states, perhaps even long-term emotions; as such, their motivational aspect is revealed more as a long-term and consistent alteration in motivation (relative to the subject when not in that mood).

Affects Are Not All Bivalent/Monodimensional States

Many have suggested that affects are states that are either negative or positive appraisals (of something, such as the organism's situation). It is extremely common in psychology to group emotions into groups with "negative" and "positive" valence. Similarly, some philosophers have defined emotions as belief states coupled with some bivalent feature or one-dimensional magnitude meant to capture the affective aspect of the emotion; Patricia Greenspan (1988) uses comfort/discomfort as this feature, while many others (e.g., Marks, 1982) assume desire is this feature. I will not respect these uses of the term "affect" because they are ultimately unhelpful; although they may be valuable when used to describe some affects, they fail as broad characterizations of all affects. For example, the notion that an appraisal or state is "positive" is too vague. What makes an appraisal positive? Ultimately, if the notion of a positive or negative appraisal is not to be vacuous, it must either yield some measurable feature of the body, or, better yet, it must reveal something about the kind of behavior that such an appraisal results in (such as approach or avoidance). One supposes that joy, for example, is positive (as per colloquial usage of "positive") and that it leads to approach (in some sense). But what about anger and fear? Colloquial usage would make them negative; but one can lead to approach of the emotion's object (in attack), the other to retreat from it (in flight). Given such distinct behaviors, the categories just do not explain anything. Similarly for comfort and discomfort. Suppose anger and fear are uncomfortable. What does this tell us about the behaviors that would result? That we seek to avoid them? But it seems, at least prima facie, that we sometimes seek these emotions, through art (revenge films include bad guys who are there specifically to raise our ire, and frightening movies garner audiences because they are frightening) or activities (like seeking fights or riding a roller coaster). Or does it mean that once we have the emotion we seek to get out of it? But, again, if a movie-goer or a mountain climber is even partly motivated by the thrill of fear, their behavior is inconsistent with such a supposition (they stay in the theater, or they keep climbing). Pleasure/displeasure, comfort/discomfort, positive/negative, and various degrees of satisfaction of a desire are all too crude to tell us anything interesting about many of the emotions and the behaviors that typify them.

Note that I am not arguing here against the use, by neuroscientists and others, of activation and inhibition (and cognate notions) of behaviors as general explanatory posits (e.g., Gray 1991); I am rejecting the use of (usually far more general) one-dimensional measures for taxonomizing emotions and other affects into, say, the positive group or the negative group. Another way of making the same point is to note that such monodimensional categorizing threatens to be far too impoverished for explaining data. It can result in such a reductive simplification that effects of the phenomena involved can be lost as they are pressed onto a single measure.[3] One solution to this kind of simplification is to introduce a host of bivalent appraisals for each emotion; this is a strategy taken by Andrew Ortony, Gerald Clore, and Allan Collins (1988) in their discussion of the cognitive origins or causes of emotions. They argue (18) that emotions are bivalent reactions concerned with three aspects of the world: events, agents, or objects. But, of course, multiplying the number of dimensions in a model can distinguish any number of states; so before we accept a complex of bivalent appraisals or monodimensional features, we need some independent reason to accept the dimensions that are being offered. Here, we shall see that dropping the very notion of bivalent appraisals and related notions loses us nothing. The term *affect* will be used in a way that does not presuppose bivalent or monodimensional measures of this sort.

Affects Are Occurrent States, Not Dispositions

Affect terms can all be used in a dispositional sense. If we say that Tony desires chocolate, or that Eric is angry at his landlord, we could mean at least two things in each case. We could mean that the person in question is in a particular body state, or we could mean that he tends to be in that body state, given the right conditions. The former I will call an *occurrent affect,* and the latter a *disposition to affect.*[4] Thus, in ordinary discourse a sentence like "Eric is an angry person" can be ambiguous; it could mean that Eric is angry right now, or that Eric is the kind of person who is often angry. Similarly, one might say that Eric has been angry at his landlord for years, but of course it is not the case that anyone can be in an occurrent state of anger for that long a period of time. Instead, we mean that when reminded of his landlord or confronted with his landlord, Eric usually becomes angry. We might also mean that the beliefs and values Eric holds that cause him to be angry at his landlord—say, the belief that his landlord is charging him too much money, and the high value he places on being treated justly, and so on—are still held by Eric, which should have as a consequence that when he attends to these things he has an occurrent state of anger as a result. Or Tony can be said to have a disposition to desire chocolate if he desires chocolate often, or if he desires chocolate whenever he sees it. But Tony has only an occurrent desire for chocolate if he is actually in a state of desiring chocolate. Disposition to emotions and other affects are of particular importance to our normal discourse because we use them in attributions of temperament[5] and other affective personality traits: a sybaritic person may be someone who has a disposition to desire to ingest chocolates and to pursue the experience of various other pleasures; a choleric person is someone who has a disposition to be angry. However, the concept of disposition to affects is (at least as I am using the term here) derived from the concept of occurrent affect, and does not admit of many of the features that occurrent emotions have (for example, there is no sense in arguing whether a disposition to affect is a propositional attitude—this could at best mean that the occurrent affect for which one has a disposition is itself a propositional attitude). I shall hereafter mean an occurrent affect by any affect term.

Affects Are Real Physical States, Not Ascribed Explanations

There is a related notion of affect which can be held by someone who denies that there are occurrent affects, and holds that talk about affects and about disposition to affects are both just a convenient gloss for dispositions to behavior. On such a view, attributions of affects may not correspond to an actual body state but rather might just be a kind of logical construction relating actions and beliefs.[6] Say, Adam always ascend the steps to his front door in a single leap. It may be that there is no significant sense in which Adam has a kind of body state that corresponds to the desire to leap up to the door; rather, he may just do it out of habit, without any need to choose between this option and the option of taking the steps one at a time. However, one might still say that Adam "desires" to leap the three steps in a single bound and simply mean by this that Adam believes (if he were queried) that he can get to the door that way, and furthermore he does get to the door that way. We then might understand the "desire" as a kind of relation between the relevant belief or beliefs and the relevant action. One who is very skeptical about affects being actual body states in any significant sense might advocate the view that all or many such affects are just kinds of logical attributions. There are measurable occurrent states that seem to correspond to instances of desirelike states (though it is dubious that there is any generic motivational state like the philosopher's notion of desire), but I need not defend this claim here, since my goal is to develop a theory of some of the emotions—emotions for which it is uncontroversial that there are strongly related physiological and brain states. We need only note, then, that affect terms as they are used here will not be meant as mere logical relations between belief and action or between any other mental states or actions; what they stand for must necessarily include actual (in principle measurable) body states that are best identified as states resulting from or constituting the affect.

Distinguishing Features of Affects

Ultimately, we shall do best to fix a theory of basic emotions and other affects on a developed scientific understanding of the neural systems that enable those affects. Thus, our best criteria to identify affects will include those such as Jaak Panksepp (1998) uses. He writes: "The most compelling evidence for the existence of such systems is our ability to evoke discrete emotional behaviors and states using localized electrical and chemical stimulation of the brain" (52). Such evidence often reveals quite definite neural structures, some of which offer very compelling neuroanatomical evidence in favor of the affect program theory. I shall refer to some of the relevant neuroscientific evidence throughout my discussions of the basic emotions and other affects. However, since my task here is in part to relate the affect program theory to commonsense notions of emotion, including the kinds of features that have traditionally come in for much conceptual analysis and therefore have been of concern to philosophers, I will begin with a number of observable or introspectable features; these features are also a good starting place because some of them are likely essentially linked to the functional role of the relevant affects.

Such possible distinguishing features of occurrent affects that have interested scientists and philosophers are their physiological state, conscious experience, associated actions, and relations to cognitive content.[7] We might also add to this list the relative temporal duration of the affect: Generally, it seems that affects that are not moods or emotions do not last as long as emotions, and that emotions last less long than moods. One might hold that two affects can be indistinguishable as to their physiology, but can be distinguished according to duration (sadness and depression, for example, might be such a case). There is a significant body of literature on stress that is concerned with duration of some affects. For my purposes here, however, this research will not be taken to be sufficient to characterize the emotions.[8] Here I will remain agnostic about all the possible meanings of differences in duration. Instead, I will turn next to the first three of these four features. Since in the next chapter I will discuss the cognitivist theories of emotion (the view that emotions are in some part constituted by, or at least require, beliefs or other propositional attitudes), I will leave a discussion about cognitive content for that chapter.

Physiological State

Affects, especially some emotions, have noticeable and measurable physiological correlates. For example, a large body of research reveals that some forms of decision making (and thus, presumably, very basic forms of affects) result in often very subtle autonomic changes measurable by electrodermal recordings of skin conductance (e.g., Damasio, 1994). For emotions, many more measurable physiological changes occur. Depending upon the intensity of the emotion, these can include changes in autonomic functions, such as heart rate, blood pressure, respiration, sweating, trembling, and other features; hormonal changes; changes in body temperature; and of course changes in neural function as measurable by EEG (Frijda, 1986, pp. 124–175).

For a long time, it has been controversial to suppose that some of these changes were distinct for particular emotions. It has often been seen as an important element of a cognitive theory of emotion to hold that the physiological changes accompanying an emotion amount to a kind of undifferentiated excitation, and that cognitive contents were needed to distinguish anger from fear, happiness from sadness, and so on (a source often cited in support of this view is Schachter & Singer, 1962).[9] However, much of the previous failure to clearly establish distinguishing physiological profiles for emotions or other affects appear now to largely have arisen because of the inadequacy of past measuring techniques. Although the claim remains controversial, evidence is growing for the view that autonomic activity distinguishes among at least some emotions. Paul Ekman, Robert Levenson, and Wallace Friesen have found, for example, that discrimination of a number of emotions (fear, anger, sadness, disgust, surprise, and happiness) was possible just by observing temperature and heart rate changes from baseline measurements (that is, measurements of the subject when presumably not experiencing the emotion). Since these are measurements from a baseline, this study (1983) does not establish that we can actually identify one of these emotions in a subject on first observation, but it does at least show that we can distinguish the emotion from some others when several measurements are available. These experiments were done with actors, but later found to work with normal subjects (Levenson, Ekman, & Friesen 1990). They also worked not only for directed facial action (asking subjects to form the expression of an emotion) but for reliving (that is, recalling, thinking through) an emotional experience; and results from many other researchers is consistent with these findings (see Levenson 1992 and 1994 for a review). More research is needed in this area as some outstanding questions remain,[10] and the experimental difficulties are great (generating fear, sadness, joy and so on in laboratory conditions is not easy), but these results are substantial and encouraging: they show that a significant number of the emotions may be distinguishable from each other by these autonomic features alone.

These results do not yet allow us to identify emotions by their physiological effects or constituents. But these kinds of investigations at least provide compelling evidence that there are reliable physiological changes that accompany some affects. For the emotions that we will be concerned with here, there is sufficient evidence that these affects necessarily include physiological responses such as changes in temperature, heart rate, and other features—even when the subject is having a relatively weak emotional experience, and even when the subject may be unaware of any such changes. Many cognitivists will deny that emotions necessarily have these correlates. In such a case, we can just be disagreeing about the semantics of our terms: these cognitivists take emotions to be mental contents, perhaps social relations, and these other features are incidental. But, as I will show in the next chapter, such a position is inconsistent with the scientific evidence, and it leaves us unable to distinguish emotions from other kinds of mental states. The claim that measurable physiological changes are necessary—leaving open whether they are sufficient to identify the relevant emotions—is important because such changes are sufficient to distinguish emotions from some other states with which some like to conflate emotion, such as belief. Furthermore, the autonomic patterns and related physiological changes are surely part of the phenomenal experience of some emotions. And these physiological responses are probably also essentially connected to relational actions and other affective behaviors. At the very least, we must explain or take into consideration these physiological features if we are to have a satisfactory theory of emotions.

If the physiological changes accompanying an emotion are necessary but perhaps not sufficient to identify that emotion, we must turn next to the three features of conscious experience, associated actions, and relations to content in order to get a more complete understanding.

Conscious Experience of Affects

Affects like anger, fear, despair, pleasure, and many others can have distinct conscious experiences. It might then seem that affects all are necessarily accompanied by a conscious experience; and many scientists and philosophers assert that emotions must be conscious. There is ambiguity in the term *conscious* here, one that has recently come under much analysis by philosophers (I will return to this in chapter 9). However, in this section I am concerned with the notions of consciousness that scientists tend to use; intuitively, a process is conscious if the subject is aware of it, in some sense reflecting upon it, and can use that awareness in directing or performing some action. I will call this sense of consciousness *working consciousness* whenever there is a threat of ambiguity.[11] What it is to be aware of a state is not clear, and there certainly are mental states of which the subject is not aware but which influence working-conscious action. This lack of clarity alone casts grave doubts upon the idea that we can gain any definitive understanding of emotions by asserting that they are conscious, or by otherwise finding a role for consciousness in them. Thus, in order to try to ground my discussion of consciousness and emotions, I will have to find some criteria for something's being conscious. One sign of working consciousness is that the agent can, barring any deficiencies (such as brain damage that makes speech impossible, etc.), report on the state. This criterion is too-strong, and it does not get to what the notion of working consciousness seems to be aiming for (that is, I grant that the ability to report on a state is not the same as being aware of it). However, it is at least relatively clear. Furthermore, it comes close to capturing what I believe is really motivating many who insist that emotions must be working conscious: a notion that emotions play a part in our rational and deliberative control of our activities. So for the sake of clarity, I shall use in this section the very strong criterion that a process is working conscious if a subject can report upon that process (I am leaving vague what counts as a report; this should be acceptable since the examples discussed below are clearly instances of inability to give different kinds of report).

If we are to retain the idea that motivation is the quintessential feature of affects, then not all affects are working conscious. Instead, we have strong evidence that there are affective states which are effectively motivating but of which the agent is not able to report—not even indirectly. One of the most interesting examples is found in the mere exposure effect, as primarily championed by R. B. Zajonc. Much research has established that people tend to prefer familiar stimuli, even when they fail to properly recognize those stimuli (see Zajonc 1968, 1980). What Zajonc and his colleague found was that subjects could form preferences for certain stimuli to which they were subjected for extremely short durations (e.g., tens of milliseconds), making it extremely unlikely that they performed the kind of complex cognitive processing necessary for categorizing and memorizing the stimuli for later recognition of a kind sufficient for a declarative report (Kunst-Wilson and Zajonc 1980). When subjects were shown pictures of shapes, then were asked to pick out, among a number of shapes, those they had seen before, they chose randomly. When asked to choose the shapes they preferred, however, they showed a significant preference for the stimuli to which they had first been exposed. Mere exposure effects on preferences can also be shown for some nonhuman mammals (Hill 1978).

An everyday example with similar import might be the use of polygraph machines, the so-called lie detectors. Lie detectors measure skin conductance response, which changes as a result of activity in sweat glands and which appears to be well correlated with other physiological changes. As we have noted, physiological body activity, including autonomic activity, is one of the distinctive features of at least some affects. What is interesting is that normal subjects show measurable galvanic skin conductance changes to certain kinds of plausibly affective situations—such as to a situation in which they want to deceive and be undetected and are, perhaps as a result of their awareness of their potential loss from being detected, experiencing some affective reaction of which they need not be conscious nor over which they have any conscious control.

But one might argue that the affective states seen in mere exposure and in subtle skin conductance differences are not emotions, and that although some affects can fail to be conscious, emotions are always conscious. However, it seems possible that emotions are capable of being unconscious. First, an emotion might be unconscious in the sense that one has an impaired ability to understand or describe the emotion. Such seems to occur in some cases of alexithymia (Sifneos 1972). Alexithymics show an impairment in both the verbal and nonverbal recognition of emotions (Lane et al. 1996), and this impairment can extend to their own emotions. Sometimes these subjects report that they are experiencing some kind of an emotion, show some of the stereotypical behavior of an emotion (e.g., weeping), but are unable to say what caused the behavior (Nemiah and Sifneos 1970) or to properly categorize it. There is also some evidence that some alexithymics can have abnormally large autonomic responses to emotion-generating stimuli (Martin and Pihl 1985; Papciak, Feuerstein, and Spiegel 1985). The best explanations of alexithymia are of the form that an emotion is occurring, but that the individual is not properly aware of it (perhaps in a way analogous to blindsight; see Lane et al. 1997) or is unable to properly categorize it (perhaps because of a failure to have developed a cognitive skill to recognize emotions; see Lane and Schwartz 1987).[12] If by an emotion being conscious we mean that the subject can recognize and properly categorize the occurrence of an emotion in herself, then the alexithymic subject has an unconscious emotion.

Second, there is evidence supporting the hypothesis that some phobias arise because some individuals have an inherited predisposition to fear certain stimuli (including concrete objects), and that this predisposition allows for fear reactions that are unconscious (see Seligman 1971). Thus, results similar to the mere exposure effect have been found for fear by Arne Öhman (1988) and his colleagues (Öhman, Dimberg, and Esteves 1989; Öhman and Soares 1993, 1994). In these experiments, subjects have demonstrated skin conductance responses for fear-conditioned stimuli that are presented so quickly, and with masking, that they are not consciously recognized. For example, in Öhman and Soares 1993, subjects were tested with fear-relevant images (snakes and spiders), along with neutral images (flowers or mushrooms), and some of each were used in fear conditioning; following the conditioning, these stimuli were shown for short durations and followed with a mask (a neutral stimulus which interferes with any conscious memory of the initial stimulus); skin conductance responses were then shown to be strong only for the conditioned fearful stimuli. This strongly suggests that unconscious processing of some kind is sufficient to cause fear responses. These results were also shown to be independent of where in the visual field the stimulus was presented, which is consistent with the process being subcortical since no lateralization (as occurs with many cognitive, cortical processes) of the ability is observed. Similar results were found with images of angry or happy faces, using aversive conditioning only for the former (Esteves, Dimberg, and Öhman 1994) (attention can have effects on these results, but the subjects are not conscious of

---

FEAR CONDITIONING

In fear conditioning, a *conditioned stimulus* (for example, a sound) is paired with an *unconditioned stimulus* (such as a painful shock), and after some short training period, fear reactions (such as autonomic changes, and a startle) are shown for the conditioned stimulus alone. In most organisms, once fear conditioning has occurred, the response can be suppressed but apparently never unlearned; it can spontaneously reappear, or reappear under stress, or be retrained in significantly less time.

the stimuli in that they cannot identify, even in forced-choice tests, the stimuli after exposure). These results provide strong evidence for at least fear conditioning and for fearful or phobic responses occurring unconsciously.

Third, there is a significant body of psychoanalytic literature dedicated to the idea that emotions can be unconscious, and that they can still play an important role in shaping actions by, and in the psychoanalytic explanation of the behavior of, the subject. It is unclear, however, to what degree and in what senses these emotions are unconscious. Are they dispositions to emotions, which lead to occasional occurrent emotions of which the subject is unaware? Are they, as Freud apparently held, not emotions but emotionally relevant unconscious beliefs? Or is it that the subject sometimes has occurrent emotions and it is the cause of these that he or she is unaware of? It will not be my place to try to answer these questions here, but only to note that some of these kinds of explanations require that unconscious emotions be possible. If any proves to be a powerful explanatory tool, that is reason to posit unconscious emotions.

Fourth, for some theorists, the underlying notion of an emotion being working conscious seems to be that we somehow know *why* we are having the emotion, that we are aware not only of the emotion but also of its cause or at least its object (and, on some views, its cause should be its object). We can refine our criterion in such a case to include that the subjects can report not only that he is having an emotion, but also why he is having it; or at least that when having an emotion the subject is aware of the object and cause of it. If this is required for one's notion of what it is for an emotion to be conscious, then the view that emotions can be unconscious has some valuable supporting evidence to be found in neuropsychology. Working with split-brain patients in the 1970s, Michael Gazzaniga and Joseph LeDoux were able to show a very clear sense in which emotions were not, in this sense, conscious. These split-brain patients are people who have had a commissurotomy, a surgical procedure to cut the commissure, a bundle of nerves that connects the two neocortical hemispheres of the brain. This procedure is used as a last resort treatment for some forms of epilepsy. But neuropsychologists have long known that the two hemispheres of the brain have specialized functions. What happens if you separate one of the primary links between them? Gazzaniga was able to show that subtle deficits can be revealed under controlled conditions. A stimulus can be shown to one side of the brain, leaving the other side of the brain in some senses unaware. For example, the language centers of most people are in the left hemisphere. Showing a figure just to the right side of the brain (done by placing it only in the left-hand side of the field of vision) can result in the object being (in some senses, defined in the respective experiments) recognized, but with the split-brain subject being unable to say what the thing is. LeDoux and Gazzaniga used this same approach to study affects. They could show the right side of the brain an affective stimulus. Though the subject was unable to verbally identify the stimulus, the affective import of the stimulus seemed to somehow "leak" to the left neocortex. The subject, wholly unconscious of what the stimulus had been (in the sense of being unable to report on it), could properly categorize it under some value terms as "bad" and "good." This at least shows that affective characterizations or related value judgments can be made in a way that is unavailable for report. In one case, for example, a word was shown to the right hemisphere and the subject was told to perform the action described by the word. Gazzaniga and Le Doux report:

> His reaction to the word *kiss* proved revealing. Although the left hemisphere of this adolescent boy did not see the word, immediately after *kiss* was exposed to the mute right hemisphere, the left blurted out, "Hey, no way, no way. You've got to be kidding." When asked what it was that he was not going to do, he was unable to tell us. Later, we presented *kiss* to the left hemisphere and a similar response occurred: "No way. I'm not going to kiss you guys." However, this time the speaking half-brain knew what the word was. In both instances, the command *kiss* elicited an emotional reaction that was detected by the verbal system of the left hemisphere, and the overt verbal response of the left hemisphere was basically the same, regardless of whether the command was presented to the right or left half-brain. (1978, 151)

The researchers conclude that this result "is inconsistent with the currently accepted cognitive theory of emotion" because "the left hemisphere appeared to have experienced a directionally specific emotion in the absence of a cognition" (152). That is, the affective reaction was significantly directed—it resulted in or was a withdrawal from a suggested course of action—and the subject is clearly aware of something. However, the subject is not aware of the affect in a way that enables him to identify its cause or object; it would appear, at least, that the kind of conscious awareness that a cognitive theory of emotion requires was not present. Using my terminology, the behavior here is not necessarily revealing a basic emotion: it may require only what we are calling "affect." But it does at least show that some strong affective reactions, plausibly related to emotions, are unconscious in this sense. The next case is more relevant to emotions.

Gazzaniga also found spontaneous emotional reactions of laughter unavailable to report. In the following passage, "the machine" is the apparatus used to ensure that visual stimuli are seen only in one side of the visual field and thus get only to the opposite hemisphere:

> When a pin-up was flashed without warning to the right hemisphere of [the subject], amongst a series of more routine stimuli, she first said, upon being asked by the examiner, that she saw nothing, but then broke into a hearty grin and chuckle. When queried as to what was funny, she said that she didn't know, that the "machine was funny, or something." When the picture was flashed at the left hemisphere she laughed too,

and quickly reported the picture as being a nude woman. Using a different modality (olfaction), Gordon and Sperry (1968) recently confirmed this kind of result.

Neither hemisphere in [another subject] found the nude overtly funny (he was 51 at the time of testing), but did find other testing situations humorous. In one test of tactile learning capacity, using the left hand, [this subject] broke out laughing when feeling one member of the stimulus pair. The particular stimulus consisted of a tack nailed into the middle of a wooden square block. Every time he felt it, he would pick it up and twirl the block about the axis and would chuckle heartily when doing so. When asked what was funny he would say, "I don't know, something in my left hand I guess." (1970, 105–106)

If laughter is properly an expression of an emotion, then that emotion is occurrent but unavailable to the relevant kind of introspection for these patients. Note that I do not endorse, and these observations do not require us to conclude, that emotions are cortical (that is, that the neural centers that underlie their function are in the neocortex) and lateralized (that is, that the underlying neocortical center is specific to one side of the brain); rather, for my concerns here the point is that the kinds of capabilities that constitute working consciousness in this stronger sense, or at least that offer criteria for its existence, *are* cortical and lateralized phenomena. These split-brain studies show failures in working consciousness that differentiate some of its features from emotions or other affects.

Defining affects in terms of their conscious role is therefore unlikely to be a strategy that succeeds well in identifying them or otherwise helping us to understand them, since some of them can be unconscious and still have behavioral effects other than conscious reports. Nonetheless, given that some affects are sometimes not working conscious, it remains that certain affects seem distinguishable from other affects by the nature of their phenomenal experience when there is such a working-conscious awareness of the experience. This is particularly true of the common emotions: rage, joy, sadness, fear, and shame—to pick just a few examples—seem to have feelings (when they are conscious) specific to the emotion (or, at least, specific enough to distinguish the emotion from other kinds of states, like belief), so that we may find it convenient to use their conscious experience as one of their distinguishing features. Should we then define some affects, such as emotions, in terms of their phenomenal experience? This strategy has several stumbling blocks. There is the problem, already observed, that some affects can be unconscious. But, supposedly the suppressed affect has effects on the subject, and these are usually the kind of effects one would expect of that affect. If we are able to identify unconscious occurrent anger with a working-conscious instance of occurrent anger, or any suppressed affect with its working-conscious counterpart, then the common element must be something other than the phenomenal experience of the affect, since those properties per se are just freely spinning wheels without the working-conscious awareness of them. If there are unconscious emotions we thus cannot have as a defining feature of affects their phenomenal features alone. Another problem is that, like the "feeling theory of affect" which has long been in disrepute, treating emotions as conscious states characterized by one's awareness of the experience does not explain much. Ultimately, philosophers and scientists want to understand how emotions relate to behavior, and what role they play in our mental lives, and specifying how they "feel" does little to further this goal. A related problem is that reference to phenomenal experience does not give us any objective (that is, third-person) criteria with which to distinguish these emotions. But we certainly do properly recognize emotions in others, and if we are to study affects in a scientific way we will need some objective criteria with which to work.

The conscious experience of an affect, although important, cannot be a fundamental feature used to define emotions.

Associated Actions

Another approach to understanding and categorizing emotions is to look at the kinds of behaviors that they cause, or with which they are associated. This is not to say that emotion concepts are nothing but useful ways of grouping together disparate classes of behaviors; on the contrary, looking at emotional behavior has also provided evidence that many of them are highly associated with stereotypical, pancultural behaviors; and this in turn should be viewed as evidence that the behaviors are caused by biologically based, inheritable capabilities.

Some of the most compelling evidence for pancultural human emotions has come from studies of facial expression. It was Darwin who first argued at length that facial expressions of emotions are evolved emotion-expressing behaviors. In more recent times strong evidence has been gathered that Darwin was correct. Irenäus Eibl-Eibesfeldt studied the facial expressions of children born deaf and blind, some with extensive brain damage. He discovered that these children showed spontaneous signs of emotions such as smiling when playing or sitting in the sun, laughing when playing, and crying when in an unfamiliar environment (1973; see also Fulcher 1942). Some of these children had severe cognitive deficits, and none was able to see or hear the emotional expressions of others, so it is highly implausible that they learned these behaviors.

Cross-cultural studies of facial expressions have found evidence of high cross-cultural correlations. These kinds of studies were made in a thorough manner by Ekman and colleagues (Ekman, Sorenson, and Friesen 1969), who sought to get as pure a cross-cultural study as was possible. They created a set of thirty photographs of facial expressions that they felt expressed six emotions that other psychologists had proposed as basic (happiness, surprise, fear, anger, disgust, and sadness). They then showed the photographs to college students in the United States, Brazil, and Japan, and to volunteers in New Guinea and Borneo. The six emotion terms were translated into the appropriate languages and then the subjects were asked to group the pictures under the terms. A very significant degree of agreement was usually found—higher for some emotions than others, and for some cultures than for others, but in general there was an unmistakably significant degree of agreement. Ekman and Friesen re-created this experiment (1971) working with the Fore of New Guinea, a cultural group relatively isolated from the rest of the world, and found agreements again ranging from 64 percent (for fear) to 92 percent (for happiness). This work and related work (Izard 1971) support the view that human facial expression of some emotions is pancultural.

These results have some interesting supporting evidence in neuroanatomy. There are two distinct neural pathways that control facial movements. One is through the pyramidal tract, and the other through the phylogenetically older extrapyramidal tract. It seems that emotional facial expressions are controlled by the older, extrapyramidal tract. This is evident when damage to the motor cortex that impairs motor control of the face (as often occurs in hemiparalysis) is sometimes (when the damage is localized to the motor control area) spontaneously overcome in the expression of emotion by the unfortunate subject. For example, a stroke victim might be unable to smile on the paralyzed side of the face when so commanded, but might smile involuntarily and normally at a joke. Conversely, damage to the extrapyramidal tract could leave voluntary control intact but result in the loss of all spontaneous emotional facial expression (Rinn 1984).

These findings suggest that emotional facial expression is pancultural because of inheritable, evolved neural structures that are shared by all, or at least many, human beings. There is also interesting evidence available for this view in studies of nonhuman primates. Research by R. E. Miller, W. F. Caul, and I. R. Mirsky has shown that the facial expressions of rhesus monkeys can transmit significant information to other monkeys, and though monkeys raised in isolation do not recognize the meaning of the facial cues of other monkeys as readily as do the monkeys raised in a social setting, these isolated monkeys show facial affective cues that other monkeys recognize and properly understand (1971). This research is consistent with the view that our near evolutionary cousins share with us the having of innate facial expressions of affect, and that the innate expressions are therefore highly likely to have evolved in a common ancestor.[13]

These results all find surprising support in some of the studies by Ekman of facial expressions among Japanese and American college students (1980). In the experiments, each student was left alone to watch films, some of which were stressful, and some of which were not. Their facial expressions were recorded, and these recordings measured by researchers who did not know what films the subjects were watching. When the students were alone, both Japanese and American students showed significantly similar facial expressions. In some cases, however, someone dressed in a lab coat was put into the room with the subjects. In these cases, as expected, Japanese students altered their expressions much more, smiling more and showing less stress. This is consistent with facial expressions being pan-cultural but amenable to different display rules. Even when researchers were in the room with the subjects, the pancultural element was not wholly eliminated: "Examining these videotapes in slow motion it was possible to observe sometimes the actual sequencing in which one movement (a smile, for example) would be superimposed over another muscle action (such as a nose wrinkle, or lower lip depressor)" (94). In other words, the evidence suggests that the pancultural facial expression is being generated but then promptly suppressed. Note that this is also very suggestive of a two-track view of these emotional expressions: a potentially subcognitive emotion causes the facial expression, perhaps primarily through the extrapyramidal tract, and a slower, secondary, cognitive appraisal suppresses it.

This is consistent with the use of surface electromyographic recordings (EMGs) in studies of emotion (see Tassinary and Cacioppo 1992). Such recordings measure muscle action potentials in, for example, the face— that is, neural stimulation of facial muscles. They can detect these muscle action potentials even if they fail to result in any change in facial expres-sion, for example if they are too weak or too short in duration to cause a muscular action. This technology provides a tool for psychophysiologists to measure facial reactions to emotion-eliciting stimuli even when no ob-servable change in facial expression occurs. The underlying method is guided by the belief that emotions can cause muscle action potentials that are not under conscious control or awareness of the subject.

Emotional behaviors are much more than just facial expressions. Perhaps one of the most compelling accounts of the use of emotion concepts is found in D. O. Hebb's classic 1946 article on the recognition of emotion. Hebb reviews an experiment at a primate laboratory where for two years the scientists working with the primates were not allowed to use emotion terms to describe the animals' behaviors. Instead, they had to keep records which described only what the animals did at one time or another. What Hebb discovered is that describing different chimpanzees without using emotion terms left people unable to really convey the sense of the character of the different primates. One could not tell, just from looking over the records of past events—described painstakingly without "anthropomorphic terms"— what the animal was like or how it would behave:

> All that resulted was an almost endless series of specific acts in which no order or meaning could be found. On the other hand, by the use of frankly anthropomorphic concepts of emotion and attitude one could quickly and easily describe the peculiarities of the individual animals, and with this information a newcomer to the staff could handle the animals as he could not safely otherwise. Whatever the anthropomor-phic terminology may seem to imply about conscious states in the chimpanzee, it provides *an intelligible and practical guide to behavior.*

The objective categorization therefore missed something in the behavior of the chimpanzees that the ill-defined categories of emotion and the like did not—some order, or relationship between the isolated acts that is essential to comprehension of the behavior. (88)

A pragmatist should be satisfied on this observation alone that emotions are genuine scientific entities. Someone of a more realistic bent might rightly argue that Hebb's conclusion is true because some emotions lead to, or are in some way linked to, actions that are specific to and explicable by these emotions.

Hebb's observations should remind us of the strategy of the ethologist. The ethologist looks to find patterns of behavior in animals. If there are patterns that occur again and again, and if these patterns can be found in isolated groups and even in closely related but different species, then this is some evidence for a homologous behavior. The ethologist is not therefore much distinct from the evolutionary biologist, utilizing the concept of homology for behaviors as well as for anatomical structures (where homologous behaviors would presumably arise from, and ultimately be explained by reference to, homologous structures). The ethologist's method applies to humans as well (see Eibl-Eibesfeldt 1989). Evidence that some emotional expressions are pancultural, that the structures allowing for the expression are inheritable, and that certain patterns of reoccurring behavior are inexplicable (not regularly predictable) without emotion concepts all point toward the primary thesis that some emotions can be identified via their homologous associated actions.

This makes sense of the presence of emotions in other nonhuman animals. Our primary means of recognizing fear in a rat, anger in a dog, surprise in a cat, and so on, is through the behaviors that they show in such states. Scientists regularly use these criteria (and others, such as autonomic responses) to study emotions in nonhuman animals. It is difficult to see how else we are going to understand these claims except through the identification of shared kinds of behavior.

Some cognitivists about emotion have argued that observations of behavior fail to provide any evidence for emotions in nonhuman animals, and therefore fail to support theories like the affect program theory. Ortony, Clore, and Collins have claimed:

It is tempting to suppose that animals experience fear. However, such attributions are typically based on observations of *behaviors* (aggressive behavior or avoidance behavior), which turn out to be dissociated from the emotional states to which they are presumed to be linked. . . . It would be a relatively straightforward matter to program a robot to exhibit aggressive or avoidance behavior toward certain objects or classes of objects, yet, if having done so one were to claim that one had produced the emotions of anger or fear in the machine, one would be scoffed at by the scientific community, and rightly so. (1988: 27–28)

There are at least two errors in this argument. First, it is not the case that we posit that there are emotions in nonhuman animals just because we observe simple behaviors. An ethologist who sees a bird leaving a branch to fly to another is not about to claim it fled the oak in fear in order to attack a maple out of anger. We posit that there are emotions in nonhuman animals because it is the best explanation for a very large body of evidence. This evidence includes, but is not limited to, behavioral patterns which are in particular ways both flexible and inflexible, so that they reveal the pursuit of a kind of action (see chapter 3); which are observed again and again; which can be best described as fulfilling the functions that we suppose in our theories that these emotions fulfill, or even that we ascertain the emotions in ourselves fulfill; which can reliably be described as being elicited by conditions consistent with that function; which are reliably accompanied by expressive behaviors; which include autonomic and other physiological changes that are special to the emotion and perhaps even shared by us; and which (most important!) in some animals are caused or constituted by neural structures which have homologs in the human neuroanatomy of emotion. Thus, behavior is a crucial element, but it does not stand alone.

Second, to say that it is a "straightforward matter to program a robot to exhibit aggressive or avoidance behavior toward certain objects or classes of objects" is a patent falsehood. It is a major accomplishment to get a robot to navigate a small, unchanging, and extremely simplified environment. To get a robot to actually recognize, effectively track, and pursue a resistant (say, a moving or even fleeing) object so that the robot could effectively attack it is truly the kind of engineering beyond, or at least at the very limit of, contemporary AI and robotics. Of course, it is a straightforward matter to program a robot that on a flat surface in a featureless environment moves toward or away from a light, for example (the kind of "behaviors" sometimes referred to as "Braitenberg behaviors"; see Braitenberg 1984). But this cannot be the kind of thing that is meant by "aggressive or avoidance behavior," because the very thing at issue here is the attribution to nonhuman animals of emotions had by humans; and so no respectable argument for the presence of these emotions in nonhuman animals would depend on counting such simplistic "behaviors" as examples of aggression or avoidance (and, as noted, the attack or avoidance behaviors of most animals are *extremely* sophisticated). Furthermore, this kind of reasoning may well be backward; to program a robot that can exhibit effective behaviors like aggression and avoidance with the kind of flexibility that even a relatively simpler animal (such as an insect) reveals—to actually engineer an autonomous agent—may best be accomplished by working with a robust theory of affects and then attempting to engineer an affective agent (I shall indulge in some speculations in this direction in chapter 12). Finally, to suppose that it is a simple matter to program these behaviors may be an instance of a common fallacy—what I will call the *cognitive autonomy fallacy*—that what is not cognitive is simple and inflexible, while what is cognitive is complex and flexible and the wellspring of autonomy. I will return to this point several times.

The view that some emotions can be identified through the actions with which they are associated is perhaps merely a consequence of my definition: since affects are motivations, then the principal method we have for discerning and distinguishing them is through the behavior they motivate. We can always keep in mind, however, a realist (as a philosopher would call it) criterion: when we identify an affect, we are identifying a genuine physical state of an individual organism, and if it later turns out that there is no such significant (that is, measurable) state, or the behavior was best explained in some other way, then we were wrong to so identify the state. In the cases of things like preferences, the motivation is very general (let us assume, for a moment, that there is a state corresponding to "preference"). If a subject S prefers to do some action A, then we are saying little more than that S is in a motivational state which has as an effect that she will A, *ceteris paribus* (when it is possible, when she is not constrained, and when there is no stronger motivation to do something inconsistent with A). But other affective states are much more structured. We can understand fear by supposing that if subject S fears some object O, then S will flee from O—with the same *ceteris paribus* clause. Some emotions, it seems, are characterized specifically by the complex behavior that they have as a consequence— what psychologists sometimes call "relational actions," since they are explicitly concerned with relations to other things (Frijda 1986, 14–24).

The Affect Program Theory

Some of the things that we call emotions appear to be a collection of things: physiological responses, stereotypical actions, and perhaps even normal cognitive roles. Instead of reductively explaining these emotions in terms of one of these features, I will adopt the naturalistic theory that tries to respect all of them: the affect program theory. This theory is not favored by philosophers or by psychologists who work on the social end of their discipline, but in various forms it is quite common to psychobiologists, neuropsychologists, and others who concern themselves with the biology of emotion. I adapt the notion from Ekman, who took the term from Silvan Tomkins:

> For there to be such complexity and organization in various response systems, there must be some central direction. The term *affect program* refers to a mechanism that stores the patterns for these complex organized responses, and which when set off directs their occurrence. . . . The organization of response systems dictated by the affect program has a genetic basis but is influenced also by experience. The skeletal, facial, vocal, autonomic, and central nervous system changes that oc-

cur initially and quickly for one or another emotion, we presume to be in largest part given, not acquired. (Ekman 1980; 82)

By "affect program," Ekman means to refer to only some aspects of the emotions in question. He argues that an emotion is made of an affect program along with a response system, an appraiser, and elicitors (86–87). In a sense, this is of course correct, and a weak form of cognitivism about emotions is tantamount to the view that all of these things are normally present in emotions but they need not all be. I will therefore here just use the term "affect program theory" to refer to the whole syndrome, recognizing that the cognitive elements are in humans quite common, but unnecessary, and that the physiological and behavioral consequences are necessary.

The idea of emotions as affect programs best explained by reference to our evolutionary heritage is perhaps most indebted to the research of Paul MacLean. MacLean introduced the "triune brain" hypothesis (1990), in which the brain is seen as having three systems, hierarchically arranged, each of which is to some degree independent of the others and which corresponds to a definite stage of evolutionary development. These systems are the "reptilian brain," the paleomammalian or limbic brain, and the neomammalian neocortex. On this model, many affects are reptilian or limbic system adaptive programs that in humans can operate to varying degrees independently of our neocortical systems.

The neuroscientist Jaak Panksepp also offers a compelling approach to the basic emotions that is consistent with the affect program theory. He has offered six criteria that distinguish the basic emotional systems:

1. The underlying circuits are genetically predetermined and designed to respond unconditionally to stimuli arising from major life-challenging circumstances.
2. These circuits organize diverse behaviors by activating or inhibiting motor subroutines and concurrent autonomic-hormonal changes that have proved adaptive in the face of such life-challenging circumstances during the evolutionary history of the species.
3. Emotive circuits change the sensitivities of sensory systems that are relevant for the behavioral sequences that have been aroused.
4. Neural activity of emotive systems outlasts the precipitating circumstances.
5. Emotive circuits can come under the conditional control of emotionally neutral environmental stimuli.
6. Emotive circuits have reciprocal interactions with the brain mechanisms that elaborate higher decision-making processes and consciousness. (1998, 49)

What these various approaches share is a common recognition that some emotions are complex, coordinated events that include motor programs or

subroutines, that evolved and are recognizable in homologous form in related organisms, and that are fundamentally enabled in neural circuits. For
my purposes here, one of the most fruitful features of the basic emotions, as
understood in the affect program theory, is the action or motor programs
that in part constitute some of them.

The Central Role of Action and the Parsimony of the Affect Program Theory

The linking of emotions to actions is widely accepted. Nico H. Frijda writes,
"Emotions are changes in readiness for action as such . . . or changes in
cognitive readiness . . . or changes in readiness for modifying or establishing relationships with the environment . . . or changes in readiness for specific concern-satisfying activities" (1986, 466). More strongly, he says: "It
will be clear that 'action tendency' and 'emotion' are one and the same
thing" (71). The psychobiologist Robert Plutchik has argued that "an emotion is a patterned bodily reaction of either protection, destruction, reproduction, deprivation, incorporation, rejection, exploration or orientation,
or some combination of these, which is brought about by a stimulus" (1980,
12). More recently, he added that "emotions are complex chains of events
with stabilizing loops that tend to produce some kind of behavioral homeostasis. . . . [The] physiological changes [that accompany an emotion] have
the character of anticipatory reactions associated with various types of ex-
ertions or impulses, such as the urge to explore, to attack, to retreat, or to
mate" (1994, 100). So that

> From an evolutionary point of view one can conceptualize emotions
> as certain types of adaptive behaviors that can be identified in lower
> animals as well as in human. These adaptive patterns have evolved to
> deal with basic survival issues in all organisms, such as dealing with
> prey and predator, potential mate and stranger, nourishing objects and
> toxins. Such patterns involve approach or avoidance reactions, fight
> and flight reactions, attachment and loss reactions, and riddance or
> ejection reactions. (229)

Silvan Tomkins claims that emotions are innately patterned responses and
that these affect programs are stored in subcortical brain centers (1962,
1963). Richard Lazarus argues that emotions result from primary appraisal
of a situation, and a secondary appraisal results in a coping action (1991).
And, as noted above, Panksepp advocates a psychobiological theory of
some emotions in which they arise from neural circuits and enable adaptive
behaviors; these neural circuits "are genetically hard-wired and designed
to respond unconditionally to stimuli arising from major life-challenging
circumstances" and they "organize behavior by activating or inhibiting
classes of related actions (and concurrent autonomic/hormonal changes)
that have proved adaptive in the face of those types of life-challenging

circumstances during the evolutionary history of the species" (1982, 411). Howard Leventhal has presented a perceptual motor theory of emotions, in which "there is a basic set of stimulus-sensitive expressive-motor templates, each of which generates a different emotional experience and expressive-motor behavior" (1984, 127). I advocate, and will assume here, the hypothesis that basic emotions have as an essential element a motor program.

What is the motor program that is part of the affect program of some emotions? This is an empirical question, but here I can clarify the notion, draw some likely conclusions about its evolution, and warn off likely misunderstandings of the term "program." The program need only be functionally specified for my purposes, but it surely is (primarily) instantiated in a neural system. Once activated, this action program will, if not actively inhibited, result in the emotional behavior. Strictly speaking, the functional definition of the action program therefore has the action as a consequence— much as a functional definition of motor cortex activity, for example, can have motor activity as a consequence.[14] Thus, on this view, given an occurrent basic emotion, it is not the emotional action but the common lack of it, or the modification of it, that requires additional theoretical posits. This is all consistent with the compelling working hypothesis that some emotions evolved from innate behavioral responses—that is, what ultimately amounts to motor programs—in ancestors of the emoting agent. The term "program" is perhaps unfortunate, but I use it because I know of no clear alternative. The motor program is not meant to be a simplistically deterministic list of discrete symbolic instructions, such as a computer program written in Java, for example. It is rather a dynamic capability. A rat running from a fearful stimulus might take a different path each time it flees—but it still may always consistently flee. Many brain systems are perhaps best thought of as dynamical systems (see Port and van Gelder 1995), and like many dynamical systems result in output that is most conveniently described in terms of a range of possible continuous trajectories moving through a state space—which, compared to a computer program, has the flavor of a kind of qualitative, as opposed to quantitative, description.

With this general notion of motor programs in place, the affect program theory yields a bonus of increased parsimony in our theorizing. As we saw, many theories of emotion (including some cognitive theories) share the supposition that an essential feature of emotions is that they have some kind of significant relation to action; the most widespread agreement is that the emotions are at least some kind of disposition or tendency. Although "disposition" takes on the sound of a substantial and well-placed primitive concept in much action theory, it is a mysterious entity and provides not a proper part of a theory but rather a debt to be discharged. Present understanding of the human mind and brain are not sufficient to expect a successful theory of all our disposition talk, and many or most of our disposition concepts and related concepts are merely placeholders for the possibility of the relevant action. However, I have suggested an inversion of the usual explanations: we should take the emotional action as primary, and either the failure to act, or the cognitive guidance of action, as secondary. Since we do have general theories of how inhibitions can work,[15] and since cognition is already a problem, there is some theoretical gain in this approach. Every debt we can pay off is, after all, a net gain in our theoretical finances.

Evolution, Innateness, and Inheritability

The affect program theory will ultimately be verified and fully developed as the relevant neural systems are identified and understood. However, from a functional and from a psychoevolutionary perspective, the most distinguishing feature of an affect program is the behavior that, at least in part, constitutes it. Presumably, like the facial expressions that accompany and express some basic emotions, the more complex relational action patterns that characterize some basic emotions started as motor programs that evolved into inheritable patterns of behavior. As some of the species having these motor programs evolved ("toward" us, for example), some of these behaviors remained, although they became subject to alteration and inhibition via new capabilities that accrued to the species involved. In ourselves, these action programs can be occurrent—one might say, "running"— but result in diverse or even no overt behavior. Thus, the program that makes up an occurrent basic emotion, I claim, is in part the occurrence of the relevant behaviors (in the broad neuroscientific sense); and for at least some of the basic emotions, this includes some relational action. The relational action of a basic emotion is a consequence of the occurrent action program if the action program is not inhibited. Similarly, most other features of an affect program can also best be explained by reference to their role in the behavior of the emotion.

But I have been rough with the evolutionary claim about the affect program. This is partly because the conclusions I aim to draw in this book are largely independent of the variations that I gloss over. Thus, how "universal" the relevant affects are is a concern I hope to pass over in the interest of avoiding a set of important but distinct philosophical problems. For my purposes here, any significant portion of the relevant populations having some of these features is going to be sufficient. Thus, I will hold only that the basic emotions are biologically based capabilities (that is, the structures which allow them to occur can be described by a biological science—above all, neuroscience), that they are pancultural (that they arise in every culture, even if not in every individual), and that they are inheritable (the reason they occur in individuals in every culture is because some people inherit this capability). Maintaining only these presuppositions should allow me to avoid such issues as, for example, the degree to which the inheritability of the basic emotions is "innate" or a result of the inheritance of common environments. It is fair to say that no feature of our neuroanatomy is not shaped by learning, and I certainly would deny a claim that basic emotions come prepackaged at birth. But whether affect programs are so very determined by inherited characteristics that they would occur in a recognizable form in radically different environments, or whether instead a significant degree of their inheritability arises because certain environmental features are pancultural and these help determine the program, is (though very interesting) not relevant to the discussions that follow. Similarly, whether the elements of the emotion syndromes are generated and coordinated by a central neural program, or whether they just occur together because of reliable environmental conditions (and thus, for example, could be controlled by several neural systems that could potentially operate individually, were certain unusual environmental conditions to occur), need not be answered here. I do believe that the affect programs arise from centralized neural programs, but otherwise the issue is one I leave to future empirical research. (For a discussion of these issues, see Griffiths 1997.)

Which Emotions Are Basic?

I will call all and only the emotions that are pancultural and that fall under the affect program theory the *basic emotions*. But there remains disagreement about what these emotions are. Ekman and others involved in facial studies have included fear, anger, joy, sadness, and disgust (Ekman and Friesen 1971). Panksepp doubts that disgust is a basic emotion; he believes that the basic emotions include at least seeking, fear, rage, and panic (a social distress system), lust, care, and play (Panksepp capitalizes all these terms to draw attention to the fact that these are technical terms related to, but still potentially distinct from, our usual uses of these terms; see Panksepp 1998). Some have also found preliminary evidence that there are pancultural expressions of contempt (Ekman 1988), and embarrassment and shame (Keltner 1995). But since fear and anger are in the intersection of all such lists (such as also Izard 1971, Plutchik 1980; see Kemper 1987 for a review of such attempted lists), for my purposes in this book I shall ensure that each argument regarding the import of basic emotions can be made with this subset alone. We can otherwise remain agnostic about the exact set of basic emotions. For the record, I opine that the union of both Ekman's and Panksepp's lists identify (not necessarily all) basic emotions: fear, anger, joy, sadness, disgust, seeking/curiosity, social distress, lust, care, and play.

Some Hypotheses Concerning Function and Eliciting Conditions

In arguing that some basic emotions are in part constituted by action programs, I have endorsed a view that these basic emotions have specifiable functions. That is, for example, if part of fear is the action program of flight, then flight is a function of fear; and if part of anger is the action program to attack, then attack is a function of anger. Although it will not be necessary for many of the arguments that follow in this book, it will at times be useful to refer to both potential roles and also eliciting conditions of the basic emotions. These are separate issues, strictly speaking; and yet, one should expect that functions that are type-specific to a basic emotion have eliciting conditions that are also type-specific. Thus, if a function of fear is to motivate flight from a dangerous object, then we expect that a dangerous object would be a typical eliciting condition.

There is growing evidence that there are some universal eliciting conditions for basic emotions, and for other affects (Boucher and Brandt 1981; Scherer and Walbott 1986; Scherer, Walbott, and Summerfield 1986). The general patterns revealed in these and other studies are quite familiar. Ekman and Friesen (1975) identify an actual or a threat of harm as an elicitor for fear; loss of an object for sadness; something repulsive for disgust; and frustration, a physical threat, insult, a violation of one's values, or someone's anger directed at oneself being causes of anger. Lazarus (1991) offers a taxonomy of "Core Relational Themes" for various emotions; these help define both function and eliciting conditions. They include a demeaning offense against me and mine for anger; facing an immediate, concrete, and overwhelming physical danger for fear; having experienced an irrevocable loss for sadness; taking in or being too close to an indigestible object or idea (metaphorically speaking) for disgust; making reasonable progress toward the realization of a goal for happiness (122).

These and other accounts suggest that, for some of the basic emotions, an abstract characterization of function and eliciting conditions is possible that will be consistent with many of the contemporary theories. Since I will work only with fear and anger as typical emotions, I suggest the following:

Fear functions to motivate flight from a threat, and is elicited by the perception of a threat.

Anger functions to motivate an attack against a defeasible enemy, and is elicited by the perception that a defeasible enemy has harmed or intends to harm the organism or something the organism values.

This list is obviously short; I could attempt an account of the functions and elicitors for many other affects (e.g., disgust functions to motivate the expelling of, or withdrawal from, potential toxins or pathogens, and is elicited by the perception that something is both potentially ingestible and is a toxin or pathogen). But the actual function and universal eliciting conditions of basic emotions and other affects is an empirical matter, and will require additional empirical investigation. This partial list will suffice to allow me to make a few points regarding function and eliciting conditions in later chapters, and so I will end with the hypothesis that these two accounts are correct.[16]

2

The Case Against Cognitivism

In chapter 1, I observed that one thing that might distinguish affects is their cognitive contents (or perhaps their relations to these contents). This would be an approach that is consistent with the various cognitivist theories of emotion. My purpose in this chapter is to address cognitivism and show that it is an untenable view of the basic emotions if it is meant to define them or otherwise explain their necessary nature. In recent years, many criticisms of cognitivism about emotions have been made (see Deigh 1994; de Sousa 1987; Gordon 1987; Griffiths 1989, 1997; Stocker 1987; Stocker and Hegeman 1996). These various criticisms have not, however, touched upon the important scientific evidence, especially from neural science, that is inconsistent with cognitivism about emotions. In this chapter, I use a sampling of this evidence to explore why cognitivism is inadequate. This will also, as in chapter 1, provide an opportunity to support my overarching themes: the affect program theory, a hierarchical and bottom-up view of mind, and an enriched naturalism.

Cognitivism about emotions presumably arises from the observation that affects can be about something: they can be representational states, even propositional attitudes. Some scholars have attempted to reduce affects to propositional attitudes like belief or judgment, or at least to claim that affects require these kind of states. In philosophy, the most common attempts at reduction of affects have generally been made for emotions, although some have also attempted to so reduce desire. Here I will criticize only theories that reduce the basic emotions to, or posit that they require, beliefs or other propositional attitudes (for criticism of attempts to reduce desire to belief, see, for example, Lewis 1988, 1996).

A Note about "Cognitivism"

Theories that claim emotions require or are made of beliefs have been, at least in philosophy, called "cognitive" theories of emotions. This is an unfortunate term. In contemporary cognitive science, for example, researchers freely posit mixtures of unconscious and even simple processes together with complex conscious processes into explanations of the kind of skills that would normally be called "cognitive." There is, in other words, no clear demarcation between cognitive processes and complex but noncognitive processes; rather, the only things that would clearly be noncognitive processes would be things like very simple reflexes or activities that are not neural, such as digestion. However, in theories about emotions, the notion of "cognitive" tends to be much stronger; and subcognitivism about emotions might correspondingly involve processes much more complex than simple reflexes.

Thus, what makes some theories of emotions "cognitive" is sometimes not clear for philosophers or scientists. However, although scientists have had their own debates regarding cognitive theories of emotion (one classic debate was held between Lazarus and Zajonc; see Scherer and Ekman 1984, 221–270), a lack of clarity is sometimes not as pressing a practical problem for the scientific study of emotions since such studies often need not be explicit about what is necessary and sufficient for a process to be cognitive. This is because if a theory posits a process that is widely granted by other scientists to be cognitive, and the existence of the process can be demonstrated in experiments, then more conceptual clarification may be unnecessary. For example, if someone believes that emotions require appraisals which are by definition cognitive, and appraisals are granted to be demonstrated by the answers of subjects to certain questions, then the otherwise somewhat mysterious notion of an appraisal may not need further analysis for a hypothesis to be defended or a limited theory to be posed. Since my goals here require conceptual clarity, I will focus upon several theories that are cognitive insofar as they contain claims that one can reduce emotions to, or that emotions require, beliefs or closely related kinds of propositional attitudes. This too may suffer from serious ambiguities; for example, it could be that one kind of brain state is sometimes acting as a constituent of a propositional attitude or otherwise being used as one, and at other times it is not, so that the very idea of a state *being* a propositional attitude would be deceptive. However, since my goal is to criticize cognitive theories and not to endorse them or any theory of propositional attitudes, I can avoid clearing up these ambiguities any more than is necessary to provide counterexamples. That is, often a cognitive theory of emotions is stated in a way (e.g., that emotions require particular kinds of judgments or beliefs) that can be refuted without providing more clarification about the necessary and sufficient conditions for a process to be cognitive. In this regard, we can best address cognitivism by examining philosophical theories of emotions that offer clear statements of some features of such positions.

Paul Griffiths, in his criticism of some cognitivist theories of emotions (1997), has used the term "propositional attitude theory" to describe those philosophical theories that hold that these affects require, or are, propositional attitudes. This is a useful clarification, and it also touches upon related issues that I aim to criticize (such as particular views about the role in

---

WHAT IS A PROPOSITIONAL ATTITUDE?

Propositional attitude is the philosopher's term for any mental state that is directed at, or has, a proposition. Any mental state that is best described as relating to a proposition is prima facie a propositional attitude: "Karen believes that it is raining," "Eric is angry that his landlord did not fix the water heater," or "Adam fears that he may not pass the exam." In these cases *it is raining, his landlord did not fix the water heater*, and *he may not pass the exam* are propositions "had by" the attitudes of belief, anger, and fear, respectively.

From a naturalist perspective, the notion of a propositional attitude presents at least two challenges. First, propositional attitudes have as yet no clear place in scientific theories of mind, and so we should not complacently assume that they somehow represent the fundamental form of thoughts. Second, there is a possible ambiguity between a mental state warranting the title "propositional attitude," and the ability to formulate explicitly and reflect upon the kind of contents that are objects in a propositional attitude. In the former case, we might say that a cat tracking a mouse "believes that the mouse is behind the bookshelf." This might be a correct attribution of a propositional attitude if by such an attribution one merely wants to predict in a robust way the cat's behavior. But philosophers who grant special status to propositional attitudes and to their role in behavior tend to be concerned with the role of such attitudes in deliberative reasoning, such as in inference. In such a case, it seems likely that nonhuman animals do not have them. Often, what appear to be at issue (and what shall be my primary concern in this book) are the abilities that humans have to actually, in some sense, reflect upon cognitive contents; the ability to not only believe that the mouse is behind the bookcase, but also such abilities as to understand that "the mouse is behind the bookcase" is a proposition, to be able to express it as one in a language, to be able to draw logical inferences based upon it, or at the very least to be able to recognize some of the conditions that must obtain in order for the proposition to be true. All of these seem to be capabilities that accompany adult language use, and so the ability to use language provides a sufficient condition for the ability to have propositional attitudes.

---

mind of certain forms of rationality). In most of this book I will take cognitivism about emotions to be the view that the relevant affects are, are in part constituted by, or require, propositional attitudes. However, I will continue to use the term "cognitive." The primary reason is that the term is already established as a label for these propositional attitude philosophical theories. But another reason is that there are some approaches that attempt to explain affects by reference to the kind of states that we might call high-level cognitive states, but which are not based on propositional attitudes. In chapter 11, I will criticize the idea that emotions can be explained by symbolic models of the kind that have typified classical AI, and one might well call these kinds of theories cognitive. Thus, I eventually aim to expand the notion of cognitive to include both propositional attitude theories and symbolic computational functionalism (and I do not claim to show that any other notion of cognitive is inappropriate for the basic emotions or any other affects).

I suspect that one might, eventually, find an even broader characterization of the cognitive that is demonstrably not a necessary condition for basic emotions. Thus, I am criticizing philosophical theories in this chapter, and in chapters 3 and 6, as my target cognitivist theories, but the results here will generalize to many of the cognitive theories of emotion held by many scientists (particularly psychologists), even though they are using the term "cognitive" in a way usually divorced from any conception of propositional attitudes. For example, in their book on the cognitive origins of emotions, Andrew Ortony, Gerald Clore, and Allan Collins have argued that emotions are *"valenced reactions to events, agents, or objects, with their particular nature being determined by the way in which the eliciting situation is construed"* (1988, 13). If we were to understand this to be either a definition of emotion, or otherwise as a statement of the necessary conditions of any emotion, then this might be a theory which implies that emotions require mental states, like beliefs, that are propositional attitudes or are at least of similar complexity. This is because the notion of how a situation is construed could require all kinds of abilities to recognize and categorize situations, to recall other situations, to draw inferences about them based upon our beliefs, and so on. Thus, if a certain form of the propositional attitude theory fails, then this reading of Ortony and his colleagues might also fail. Similar conclusions can be drawn for a host of other cognitive theories of emotion; I will not be undertaking a literature review of these theories, but I will be arguing for a view of emotions and of minds that is antithetical to some of the presuppositions common to some of these theories, and so it is important to recognize that the arguments against certain forms of cognitivism are meant to outline a general objection to some of these presuppositions. In this regard, it is sometimes useful (especially in building a case against the cognitive autonomy fallacy) to keep an admittedly vague contrast between cognitive processes that are typically involved in our conceptual abilities, especially language, and that perhaps arise primarily from neocortical neural circuits, on the one hand; and potentially subcognitive processes that are typically involved in perceptuomotor control and integration, and in affect, and which perhaps arise primarily from subcortical neural circuits, on the other hand. Nonetheless, let me reiterate that the general use of *cognitive* in the sciences of mind is definitively not the defining feature of the philosophical cognitive theories of emotion that are my present targets; a cognitive theory of emotion is here understood to be a propositional attitude theory (or, in chapter 11, also a symbolic computational functionalist theory).

I will thus use the following terminology. A *representation* is (in the kind of organisms that are my concern here) a brain state that stands for another (not necessarily real) state or object. Representations need not be discrete (i.e., they can be magnitudes), but they must play a role in a representational system (that is, although I do not endorse holism and so do not require that each representation requires others, each representation must be part of a system that "consumes" that representation appropriately). I grant that affects use or are constituted in part by representations, and so have no objection to those theories (which, in some contexts, might be called cognitive theories) that take affects to use representations. *Symbols* are discrete representations that function in a representational system in a way that can be properly modeled by a combinatorial syntactic system. An example of a symbolic system is a natural language. *Propositional attitudes* are representations of events or states of affairs, and they have the special property that they are normally true or false (thus, these mental states can play a role in logical inference that a proposition can play—this is important when I discuss matters of rationality), and they are articulate representations formed of symbols or other representations. Thus on this terminology a cognitive state, or a cognitive system, is one that requires propositional attitudes—although, as stated, I shall later weaken this to include complexes of symbols, and argue that we can also reject this weaker form of cognitivism.

In recognition that the term *cognitive* is difficult to pin down, and also that the line between cognitive and other representational processes is likely not clear (there is probably no clear line between symbols and nonsymbolic representations, for example), I will use the term *subcognitive* instead of *noncognitive* for those processes that are not propositional attitudes or complex symbolic representations. Subcognitive processes may be conscious but do not need to be so; and they can be representationally rich but are not propositional attitudes or otherwise propositions, and they do not all require language. Evidence that a kind of process is potentially subcognitive will include any of the following: it is shared by nonhuman animals of presumably simpler mental abilities (e.g., rats); it develops in humans before language and other complex cognitive abilities; it does not have to be learned; it happens or is elicited very quickly (e.g., in a few tens of milliseconds); it is enabled by neural wiring that is subcortical or otherwise can operate independently of the kind of neural structures that enable abilities like language. Also, a process may be suspected to be subcognitive if it is the case that assuming the process is a propositional attitude explains nothing more than would assuming it to be a more basic representation; if assuming the process is a complex of symbols explains nothing more than would assuming it to be a more basic representation; or if the agent is unable to report accurately or at all on the process or its object or cause.

Two Kinds of Cognitivism: Reductive and Doxastic

Philosophical theories that associate emotions with cognitive states like beliefs are usually of two kinds. Some identify emotions with other propositional attitudes; I will call these *reductive cognitive theories*. Others may not identify an emotion with these other mental states but claim that emotions require beliefs of particular kinds; I will call these *doxastic cognitive theories*. The claim that the beliefs need be of certain kinds is necessary. Most of us, for example, might think that human minds must have some beliefs, and since human emotions are mental states they would require beliefs in this sense. But the doxastic cognitivist means something stronger than this; what is of importance in the doxastic theories is that emotions require beliefs which are instances of particular kinds specific to the emotion. This requirement will be made clear for each doxastic theory as needed. The reductive cognitive theories are usually trivially doxastic cognitive theories, but doxastic cognitivism need not be reductive. In the rest of this chapter, I shall show that these theories, when construed as universal claims about all instances of basic emotions, are false.

Reductive cognitive theories generally have similar presuppositions, and here we can get a sufficient characterization of them by reviewing just a few of these presuppositions. Most of the reductive cognitivist theories in philosophy are of two general kinds:

(1) Judgment theories. Robert Solomon claims that "an emotion is a *judgment* (or a set of judgments)" (1977, 185). Not all such judgments result in emotions, but rather, "Emotions are self-involved and relatively *intense* evaluative judgments. . . . The judgments and objects that constitute our emotions are those which are especially important to us, meaningful to us, concerning matters in which we have invested ourselves" (187). Martha Nussbaum reconstructs, and endorses a version of, the view of the stoic Chrysipus that emotions are judgments of value concerning something that is essentially related to the *eudaimonia*—the well-being—of the subject. Nussbaum writes, an "emotion is itself identical with the full acceptance of, or recognition of, a belief" (1990, 292). This phrasing makes it seem that Nussbaum has a second-order theory (where emotion is a belief about belief), but as I understand her, the actual formation of the relevant belief is the emotion (albeit the belief may be one we resist, and so second-order epistemic matters are involved).

(2) Reduction to belief and desire. Joel Marks proposes that emotions "are belief/desire sets . . . characterized by strong desire" (1982, 227), and thus "emotion reduces to belief plus strong desire" (240). Ronald Alan Nash gives a slightly more sophisticated version of this in a theory he calls the "new pure cognitive theory" (1989). He holds that beliefs and desires give rise to a dispositional state that results in a desire upon which the subject has an unusual degree of focused attention and (potentially obsessive) overvaluation. The emotion is this state of having and focusing upon an overvalued desire (or perhaps desires).

We can, without loss of accuracy, group these views if we recognize that the cognitive element is the formation of the right kind of beliefs given certain desires. There are many situations in which we form or assent to some belief (that is, in which we make a judgment) but do not feel an emotion (such as, forming beliefs unconcerned with our self-esteem or *eudaimonia*). Clearly the particular kinds of beliefs, not the act of judging, is the operative notion.

Doxastic cognitive theories are more homogenous, and can be treated as of one kind:

(3) Doxastic cognitivism. Radford (1975), Walton (1978), Shaffer (1983), and many others hold that emotions are caused by certain beliefs and desires. Shaffer gives an example: "I am driving around a curve and see a log across the road. . . . I turn pale, my heart beats faster, I feel my stomach tighten. . . . I slam on the brakes and stop before I hit the log. I acknowledge that when I saw the log I felt afraid" (161). In his analysis, an emotion is "a complex of physiological processes and sensations caused by certain beliefs and desires. Thus, seeing the log, I *believed* that bodily harm was likely and I *desired* not to be harmed." (161)

This view is quite similar to that of Marks and Nash, but the two kinds are distinct in that doxastic cognitivists take other bodily responses to be essential to the emotion—even to *be* the emotion—whereas Marks, Nash, and the other reductive belief/desire views take the physiological response to be an inessential consequence.

Empirical Evidence against Reductive and Doxastic Cognitivism

In chapters 3 and 6 I introduce arguments against both reductive and doxastic cognitivism that appeal to philosophical notions of rational action and to common platitudes about emotional behavior. These approaches are important, since philosophical differences about the import of scientific results can mean that the vast empirical evidence available to us is moot. Here, however, I will go straight to the scientific evidence, which, for at least the basic emotions, effectively demolishes both views. I will review 6 objections here.

1. *The confusion of cognition with affect.* One problem with reductive cognitivism is that it does not capture what is specific about affects and separates them from other cognitive states like beliefs or merely entertained ideas. For example, basic emotions are characterized by autonomic body changes (one can of course deny this, and may have to, in order to defend a reductive cognitive theory of emotion). But judgments or beliefs are not so

characterized. For Marks, these body changes are just features of desire: for him it turns out that an emotion is not just a combination of beliefs and desires, but of beliefs and "strong" desires. This is perhaps nothing more than a terminological difference from the kind of taxonomy I introduced here: whereas I doubt that there is anything like desire, and so I separate basic emotions from desires, Marks would group desires and basic emotions together, calling the latter "strong desires," and then construct cognitive emotions out of beliefs and the strong desires. Much the same could be said about Solomon's notion that the judgments that constitute an emotion are "intense." But if all that was intended were a terminological change, such an approach could at best be called misleading, since: (1) there is surely something distinct about anger and desire, or anger and judgment, as these are usually understood; (2) emotions do not operate like desires are supposed to do (see chapter 3); and (3) this would make it impossible to distinguish the different emotions, since they would all be instances of a generic notion of desire; so that (4) this would make the position merely a form of doxastic cognitivism, since it would presumably be the beliefs which distinguish the emotions. Nash, on the other hand, is explicit: emotions normally have but do not need their physiological correlates. "What I deny is that bodily changes *constitute* being emotionally upset or perturbed, or are even necessary to such a state" (1989, 497). Nash's theory sounds like a cognitivist theory that reduces emotions to more than just beliefs and desires, since it introduces these elements of focus and overevaluation. However, since presumably one can be focused upon other things and value other things without having an emotion, these are not sufficient to have an emotion; and as for their being necessary, there appears to be no way to distinguish desires that one is focused upon and values highly from other desires, except of course to call the former "emotions" (a parallel to the problem discussed below regarding Marks's "strong desires" and normal desires).

Even if we avoid talk about beliefs, and instead reduce emotions to judgments, the result is similarly problematic. What separates judgments that are emotions from other kinds of judgments? The answer is the content of the judgment: the belief that is formed. In Solomon, emotions arise when we are making judgments about ourselves, the content of which matters to our self-esteem. For Nussbaum's Stoic, they arise when we are making judgments about things we value. This characterization could be circular, given that much moral theory attempts to explain value—or at least valuing—in terms of emotion; if we were to accept such claims and then argue that emotions are judgments about what we value, the theory would be quite vacuous. But these theories fail on more explicit grounds. Since emotions are identified with judgments, the relevant judgments should always be accompanied by the proper emotions, but they are not. This has been shown by, to pick just one example, Antonio Damasio's studies of prefrontal cortex damaged patients who show no measurable loss of cognitive skills but who have, as a result of their brain damage, emotional defects. One such subject, EVR, was studied extensively (Damasio, Tranel, and Damasio 1990). This subject has an IQ of 135, and passes all the usual neuropsychological tests like a normal. But he came to the attention of Damasio and his colleagues because he showed deficits in rational decision making. In one experiment, EVR was shown pictures of disturbing and provocative scenes. These pictures cause in normals a skin conductance response—a clear measure of the autonomic signs of affect. But EVR showed no significant response—he literally flatlined on his polygraph when he merely looked at the pictures and was not asked to describe them. This subject even reported after the test that he had noticed that he did not have the kind of feeling that he thought he ought to have for some of the pictures. He has the cognitive ability to recognize and describe the phenomena, but he does not have the appropriate emotional responses to them. Damasio's explanation of EVR's lack of reaction, and of his impaired rationality, is his own somatic marker hypothesis: Damasio argues that the bodily reaction that a normal subject has for the affect-evoking stimuli acts as a marker of that stimuli, and we sometimes depend upon this marker in making rational decisions. But regardless of whether the somatic marker hypothesis is true, EVR is a clear counterexample to reductive cognitivism, and perhaps even to doxastic cognitivism. He has intelligent, seemingly rational judgment-making abilities, makes the correct kinds of judgments, and not only has little or no affects in some of these cases, but in his everyday life performs so many irrational tasks that he is essentially disabled.

2. *The inexplicability of direct neural stimulation and of abnormal cases.* Other kinds of evidence of basic emotions without the kind of content as constituent or cause that cognitivism requires include the generation of basic emotions through direct stimulation of the brain by electrodes, or by what is believed to be direct stimulation from defects like epilepsy. Direct electrical stimulation of particular subcortical areas of the brain can yield affective states in humans and nonhuman animals (see King 1961, Gloor 1990; Fish et al. 1993; for review, see Frijda 1986, 381–386). Recall also that (as we saw in chapter 1), the neuroscientist Jaak Panksepp has argued that the basic emotions are identifiable by the criterion that they can be generated by direct electrical stimulation of the brain (1998, 52). Also, brain damage can result in spontaneous and excessive affect. Specific emotional reactions often accompany the onset of seizures for epileptics (Ervin and Martin 1986). It has long been known that lesions in parts of the hypothalamus can cause rage in human and nonhuman animals. The classic studies of decorticate cats also first led to such observations (Cannon and Britton 1924; Bazzett and Penfield 1922; see also Bard 1928). To sustain a reductive or doxastic cognitive theory given such observations one must either deny that these are real emotions, contrary to all the behavioral evidence that is available; or somehow claim that these lesions and direct stimulation first,

or at least simultaneously, generate the required beliefs of the organism. This is possible but implausible; at least, the burden of proof is surely with these cognitivists.

A related and noteworthy fact is that some emotions seem to be more easily triggered by features which are not in any relevant way beliefs. For example, R. B. Zajonc has argued that failure to cool the brain properly (which can happen, for example, if your sinuses are very severely clogged) can cause anger (Zajonc, Murphy, and Inglehart 1989). And we recognize that things like being too hot, loud noises, an uncomfortable chair, and other environmental factors can predispose us to certain emotions.

3. *The problem of homology.* If we accept evolutionary theory, we should expect there to be homologs of many capabilities between organisms, where more nearly "related" organisms share more common features. Thus, we should expect affects to most likely exist in other species of animals, and to be more similar to our own affects as those animals are more closely related to ourselves. And we do in general talk this way, and most scientific understanding of emotions has these states as being present in many species of nonhuman animals. We do not usually attribute fear to worms, but we do usefully attribute fear and a host of other emotions to cats and dogs; and many scientists readily study fear by using cats or rats or other organisms as models. Are we mistaken to do this? It would seem on a doxastic or reductive cognitive theory of emotions that we are, since presumably a cat or rat does not have the kind of cognitive capabilities necessary for an emotion on such a view. As already observed, we can weaken the sense of emotions being cognitive, so that a cat's fear is said to be merely representational. The cat is afraid of an approaching dog because undoubtedly it recognizes and categorizes the dog as a threat. But such a weakening of the requirements of what will make an emotion cognitive will fail to satisfy some of the goals of having a doxastic or reductive cognitive theory of emotion. One of the principal motivations for a doxastic or reductive cognitive theory of emotions has been to make emotions a part of rational action by having each relevant emotion be a state with content that itself can be part of a rational "belief-desire system"; a foremost feature of this is the formation of propositions and some minimal proper logical procedures upon them (drawing inferences, expunging contradictions). Presumably mere representations, which are not part of reflectively propositional contents, do not qualify: mere representations are not true or false, for example, so cannot be consistent or inconsistent; they cannot alone play the same kind of role in an inferential system that propositions can; we cannot revise them in the same way; and so on. Similar problems arise for emotional evaluation. At the very least, doxastic or reductive cognitivism is going to have to be supplemented with a powerful theory of representation if it is going to explain how both rats and humans can have emotions that are to be reductively or doxastically construed.

Even setting aside these concerns, it seems clear that some nonhuman animals emote and do not have the same kinds of content that we do when we have what is purportedly the same kind of emotion. Since the state of the "fearing" cat can share many of the physiological and behavioral features that our own emotions do, we are again confronted with the question of why we would take the cognitive aspects of the emotion as more important than these other features. Taking evolution seriously suggests that the other features should be primary, such as the kind of behavioral responses (in this case, flight) shared by these animals. Finally, our growing understanding of some of the neural circuitry enabling some emotions and other affects often includes the identification of crucial roles for subcortical structures that are widely shared across mammals, and some of which may even have homologs in more distantly related species.

4. *The problem of early development of the emotions.* Human beings show a development of some emotional capabilities from infancy (see Scherer and Ekman 1984, 73ff) to mature adulthood, and some affective capabilities develop prior to our cognitive abilities. An infant can show some of the facial expressions of emotions, and after only a few weeks exhibits many of the behavioral features of some emotions—signs of anger at being frustrated, or fear when confronted with strange stimuli, or pleasure when they see a mother's face. Surely such infants do not have the developed cognitive skills, however, to allow them to have the attitudes like belief and desire that a doxastic or reductive cognitive theory require (and consider also Eibl-Eibesfeldt's research discussed in chapter 1). Our best understanding of development suggests that affects like the basic emotions are capabilities that are inherited, and which can be changed by learning, including eventually being directed or caused by propositional attitudes. This is a view contradictory to reductive or doxastic cognitivism, in which the abilities to entertain propositional attitudes of the relevant kind would have to precede the ability to have the relevant emotions.

5. *The problem of neuroanatonomical differentiation.* There are structural distinctions in the neuroanatomy underlying basic emotions and some other affects that are not consistent with cognitivism. This is a point well illustrated, for example, by recent research by Joseph LeDoux, who has worked to map out the neural pathways of fear and show that there is functional and anatomical separation between affective and cognitive processing systems (for an overview see 1996). LeDoux has shown that there are neural pathways involved in fear conditioning which link to both cortical and subcortical areas. In particular, using fear potentiation studies of rats, he found that the aural cortex could be ablated and the fear-conditioned response could still be shown, working through the subcortical pathways. What was lost when the aural cortex was ablated was tone discrimination: a rat would show fear response to any tone, where before it could discrimi-

nate the tone to which it had been conditioned. In human beings there are also a host of complex pathways that operate for basic emotions, including connections between the amygdala and other subcortical structures believed to be essential to basic emotions, and also connections to various cortical areas, including polymodal and supramodal areas. The proper picture of the relation between affects and content therefore seems to be that affects can have varying degrees of cortical contribution. If any one of these cortical areas that was connected to the amygdala and other relevant subcortical structures was lost, we can expect that an affective ability could in some specific way be impaired, but that it would still remain.

The subcortical pathway that LeDoux identified for fear (and presumably such pathways could be present for other basic emotions) is similar to the kind of system that is suggested by Zajonc's research on the mere exposure effect. The affective results of these pathways are not best called cognitive, or at the very least they are surely not best identified as operating by way of generating propositional attitudes: they are faster than high-level cognition, less discriminating, and not open to report. LeDoux's subcortical pathway is also consistent with the findings of Arne Öhman and Joaquin Soares (1993), discussed in the last chapter, which provide some evidence for the theory of M. E. P. Seligman (1971) that some subjects are biologically predisposed for fear conditioning for some stimuli, such as snakes. Also, since Öhman and Soares's findings were shown to be independent of lateralization, and since many cognitive functions, and especially language, are highly lateralized, this suggests that the relevant fear conditioning or recognition in question is subcortical.

6. *Displacement.* Finally, there is a phenomenon that has in part been studied by scientists in terms of generalization and second-order conditioning (and which may also have an analogue in theories of emotional congruence in perception and attention; see Niedenthal and Kitayama 1994), and that is part of our folk preconception of emotions. It is common folk psychology that an emotion can, as it were, go searching for an object. Eric can start out angry at his landlord, and end up angry at his boss for reasons that at some other time would not make him angry at his boss. Our common understanding of such events is that Eric is in a state of anger, caused by beliefs about his landlord, and this state can take different objects. But if reductive cognitivism were true, then such displacement should be impossible; instead, in having two different sets of beliefs or judgments, we would have two unrelated emotion events. And similarly for doxastic cognitivism: if an emotion requires a belief, then either we have two emotions here (because two different beliefs) or we have one emotion with two different beliefs. If the latter were the case, we could rightly ask what in the emotion is shared between these two doxastic states, and this unchanging element would seem to be more essential to the emotion than the fungible beliefs that are said to be required. The former case is ruled out by the conditions of the thought experiment: we supposed that the displacement results in an emo-

tion in cases that otherwise would not give rise to the emotion. If Eric's belief that his landlord is charging him too much money is necessary for Eric to be angry at his landlord, how can it then be that Eric ends up angry at his boss for reasons that normally would not cause him to be angry? The anger in the latter case would seem to be better explained not by the beliefs involved, since these can sometimes fail to cause an emotion, but by some other factors. Thus, if emotional displacement of this kind occurs, it poses a counterexample to both doxastic and reductive cognitivism.

Weak Cognitivism

In arguing against doxastic or reductive cognitivism, I do not deny that, in humans, a basic emotion might often have some kind of belief or propositional content accompanying it; all evidence indicates that emotions in humans often are guided by propositional contents in a way that merits being called "cognitive." It is also possible that doxastic cognitivism could be true of some of the things we call "emotions"; that is, some of the things that we call "emotions" may be distinguished, by reference to related beliefs, from affects which on any other scientific measures of the individual are relevantly of the same kind; such a thing might even be because social standards play a role in the concept of what that emotion is (I return to this theme at the end of chapter 4). Also, as already stated, given a weak sense of "cognitive"—so that, for example, a mental process is cognitive if it is representational—then all emotions might come to be necessarily "cognitive." Finally, of course, one is free to chose any taxonomy she desires; so we could strengthen our definition of basic emotions to make something like doxastic cognitivism true.

As we have seen, however, one reason for choosing against doxastic and reductive cognitivism is that they fail to distinguish basic emotions from other kinds of cognitive states. Our goal should be an understanding of basic emotions that is as broad and as rich as possible, and doing this requires that we look not for what is normal for, but rather for what is necessary for (or at least, most common to), the relevant emotions.

These cognitive theories are perhaps most compelling when they are used to account for those features of emotion that ally them with what would normally be called cognitive features. These include the intentionality of emotions (the fact that they are often in some sense "about" something), their evaluative nature (they are often like judgments, which can be seen as evaluations made by the subject), and their interesting connections to rationality (some see emotions as necessary to rationality, others see them as antithetical to rationality, but most see them as having a complex and significant relation to rationality). These are all features for which any theory of emotion should account, and a doxastic or reductive cognitive theory can make a quick and plausible job of this by making emotions into judgments or having them require beliefs. Beliefs are by definition intentional, and they can be evaluations; on most accounts of rationality these are going to be the elements of rational thought. In chapters 5 through 8, I shall show that there are other equally plausible explanations for these features of some emotions—explanations that have more explanatory power.

Finally, these observations are not meant to be arguments that there is no place for a cognitive theory of emotions. In fact (as I will argue again in chapter 12), if our goal is to understand the cognitive structure of emotions, then one approach should be to study emotions directly in terms of their cognitive causes and their cognitive structure. That is, the denial of strong forms of cognitivism like doxastic and reductive cognitivism does not entail that any study of emotions in terms solely of beliefs and similar kinds of cognitive states is erroneous. Given how incomplete our present understanding of the brain and mind is, one might make little or no progress near term in understanding the cognitive structure of emotions by any other method. Again: I do not reject the goal of understanding the cognitive structure of emotions in terms of their cognitive contents, nor even the claim that emotions are often cognitive in some robust sense; rather, it is the separate claim that the basic emotions necessarily are cognitive in a strong sense such as, for example, we find in reductive or doxastic cognitivism, that is false.

An alternative to doxastic and reductive cognitivism is a view I will call *weak cognitivism:* the hypothesis that the occurrent instances of relevant emotions are for humans often, but not necessarily, highly integrated with cognitive states (including propositional attitudes). This integration can include beliefs and other cognitive states causing, determining the expression, the eliciting conditions, or the intensity of, the relevant basic emotion. I endorse a form of weak cognitivism (but, as I will show in chapter 6, we need to weaken this even further by explicitly disavowing that beliefs are even normally necessary for cognitive instances of emotions). Weak cognitivism is consistent with the affect program theory.

Summary: The Hierarchical Model of Mind

If I am going to review what lessons some of the emotions can hold for the problems of intentionality, rationality, and consciousness, and for AI, it will be sufficient to stop the taxonomic investigations here with the notion of the basic emotions. This is hardly the last word on emotions—it leaves most of those things we call emotions uncategorized, and it raises as many questions as answers—but it is enough to start some explorations that will reveal much about the importance of the basic emotions and the views of mind with which this understanding is consistent.

I have been concerned to describe occurrent affects, and have proposed the thesis that they are motivational states. Affects can be characterized by such properties as their duration, physiological correlates, conscious experience, behavioral correlates, and content. All of these elements play an important role in our understanding of emotions, but of these only physiological and behavioral correlates appear to be potentially sufficient to identify and distinguish an emotion. Given that there is a class of affective states that appear to be pancultural, based in inherited biological capabilities and characterized by recognizable behaviors, I concluded that these are the basic emotions. These basic emotions include at least fear and anger, and probably many other affects. These are the emotions described by the affect program theory.

The affect program theory is consistent with or explains all of the objections raised in this chapter against doxastic and reductive cognitivist theories of emotion. Cognitivism is understood as the view that emotions are constituted by or otherwise require beliefs or other propositional attitudes (and subcognitive states are therefore any representational states that are not propositional attitudes); this terminology is standard to much philosophy of emotion, but not to the sciences, so we must be careful to remember that *cognitive* here is used in this strong sense. The basic emotions are clearly distinct from beliefs and other cognitive contents in a fundamental way. Thus no problem arises from those abnormal cases of spontaneous emotions or the direct stimulation of the brain; we should expect it to be possible to stimulate the neural substrates of the affect programs directly, without having to stimulate the cognitive centers that would often be responsible for their elicitation. Nonhuman animals show these behaviors because the affect programs evolved and so likely have homologs in other related species. The development of the affect programs is also no problem. Blind children, even blind children who are retarded, need not learn, but already have, these programs. The existence of subcortical emotional pathways and the extrapyramidal enervation of affective facial expression is consistent with this, and actually suggests that it is because the affect programs of the basic emotions are phylogenetically older than our cognitive abilities that they are in part independent of these abilities. Finally, displacement of emotions is at least potentially explicable, since the affect program itself does not depend for its actual existence upon a single intentional object of the relevant kind.

These findings provide us with a powerful way to view the human mind, when affects are properly accounted for: the human mind has a hierarchy of differentiable systems. These are not only modular systems, in J. A. Fodor's sense (1983; see also Griffiths 1990, and 1997, 91–97); some of them are also more fundamental in that they are required for, and constitute part of, the function of many other systems. Thus, for example, a basic emotion that has propositional content will require capabilities that underlie the possibility of instances of that basic emotion without the cognitive content. Echoing Howard Leventhal, who hypothesizes that two distinct but parallel systems are involved in affect (1984), I can in a preliminary way illustrate the feature of a hiearchical view of mind that is important to my goals here by making a simplified, but very useful, distinction between two gross supersystems. On the one hand, there are the subcognitive affective systems (among many other subcognitive systems, such as primary perceptuomotor control systems) which include the capabilities that constitute the basic emotions, and which can operate independently of many or most of the capabilities that typify "high cognition." In terms of Paul MacLean's distinctions, this would include both the "reptilian" and the limbic systems; for Leventhal, this is the emotional or affect control system. These subcognitive systems function faster than most instances of deliberative reasoning; need not be available to report (and thus are not, in this sense, necessarily conscious or cognitive); do not require intentional content sufficient for propositional attitudes; and are intimately related to homeostatic and motor control systems (such as maintaining set points in body states, and motivating actions, including the emotional actions). On the other hand, sitting (perhaps literally, in a neuroanatomical sense) above these systems are the cognitive systems, some of which may be able to operate independently of the subcognitive systems but many of which appear to need them to function properly. These are the systems that constitute the capabilities that typify "high cognition": language, the ability to plan, the ability to report on one's deliberations, and so on. Leventhal calls this the "problem control" system.

It is also tempting to assume that the affective systems are largely or wholly subcortical, and the cognitive ones largely or wholly cortical. Although there is perhaps some truth in this, it is not necessary to assume this, since the distinction is primarily a functional one; and even some phylogenetically ancient functions have been "rewired" in primates to involve neocortical structures. The functional notion of subcognitive capabilities need not correpond to this basic anatomical distinction.

This two-tier distinction is too simple: a mature science of mind will find it more useful to refer to many systems, not easily grouped into two sets, but nonetheless clearly hierarchically arranged. However, even roughly hewn into two groups, the hierarchical view of mind is useful for drawing out a number of issues. First, it points us toward a very different way of thinking about mind, and therefore a very different kind of theory of mind, than is typical in contemporary philosophy, where critical issues are often framed in relation to propositional contents or lack thereof. The basic emotions and many other affects are clearly able to operate independently of many cognitive skills, and the neural circuits that constitute some of them appear to be centered in subcortical regions or in brain structures that are functionally independent of the kind of abilities that enable propositional attitudes. Furthermore, our evolutionary understanding of the basic emotions is encouraged by the observation that other mammals, which share with us strikingly similar subcortical anatomies, also exhibit many of the same affects, including some of the basic emotions. This is all consistent with a bottom-up view of mind, in which affects and perceptuomotor abilities are understood to be phylogenetically and functionally prior to, and likely necessary for, cognition.

Second, this simplified perspective on the hierarchical view of mind also helps us to clarify where disagreements about the taxonomy of affects are, and are not, substantial. There is a great deal of implicit agreement among many scientists for the essential features of the affect program theory. Disagreements tend to arise about how much we need to add to get a full-bodied "emotion." Roughly, and using again the simplistic two-tier idealization, it may be that for some basic emotions we could outline two kinds of definitions, or identity criteria. The first, of the kind I use here, would refer primarily to the subcognitive systems to identify the capabilities and neural circuits that constitute the basic emotions. It would expect the exercise of those emotions not to require the kind of cognitive skills that are special to humans, since homologs of these emotions exist in other animals. The second kind of definition would refer also to cognitive systems, and thereby make use of a broad, or "thick," notion of the basic emotions, perhaps construing them as necessarily conscious, or necessarily propositional attitudes. Which kind of definition one should use is not an issue we need spend much time debating; I have argued that something quite like the former is a richer notion, which avoids the fundamental confusions encouraged by the latter. But the latter notion is wholly consistent with the substantive claims made throughout this book, as long as it is recognized that affective systems that are not necessarily propositional attitudes are *necessary* to the emotion in the thick sense. Given this, I hold no disagreements with anyone who accepts that the kind of things that happen in the affect program theory are necessary to the relevant basic emotion, but then defines that emotion in a cognitive way or even a necessarily social way. Disagreements arise, instead, with those who either (1) deny that the subcognitive elements on the hierarchy are necessary, or (2) define the basic emotions as cognitive and then use such a definition in too general a way. (The first disagreement is what we saw in reductive cognitivism: the view that the beliefs and other kinds of cognitive states are alone necessary, and the other features picked out by the affect program theory are unnecessary.) Given this understanding, a very great deal of agreement should be possible between what is said here and the majority of views on the relevant emotions.

3

Interpretationism

In this chapter I want to accomplish two things. First, to give an example of how the failure of cognitivism about emotions can be important for contemporary theories of mind. Second, to argue against a potential form of cognitivism that is resistant to the criticisms raised in chapter 2. There, we learned that much scientific evidence is not consistent with a doxastic or reductive cognitivist theory of the basic emotions. However, this kind of evidence is compelling only if a theory of mind is open to it, and there are a number of extremely influential theories of mind to which this scientific evidence would arguably not apply. The most prominent of these are the various interpretationist views.

Interpretationism and functionalism have been the most favored alternatives to the kind of simple reductive naturalism that has long been out of favor in philosophy; in chapter 11 I discuss one form of functionalism, and in chapter 13 I briefly discuss why the conception of naturalism shared by much contemporary philosophy of mind is erroneous. In this chapter, I will consider interpretationism and draw out its relation to basic emotions by considering some emotional actions. These emotional actions raise special problems for theories of mind and action. Ultimately, I will show that the affect program theory better explains these actions. This advantage in explaining behavior is evidence in favor of the affect program theory as the best account of the relevant emotions. By way of contrast, I will show that these leading irrealist theories of mind fail to adequately explain these actions. This provides strong evidence that these theories fail to account for the nature of these emotions. It also shows that these are not appropriate theories of mind.

Because interpretationism takes cognitive states to be ascribed, it entails an irrealism, and in practice a reductive cognitivism, about emotion that can be particularly difficult for a naturalist to counter. This is because the scientific evidence can often be pushed aside since it supposedly tells us nothing about the mental states that the interpretationist claims we ascribe (and where an emotion is either a new one of these states or reducible to some of these). My strategy in this chapter therefore is to build the case for

---

REALISM, IRREALISM, NATURALISM, INTERPRETATIONISM

Realism will be used here in the following way: a theory is realist if the kinds of things referred to in that theory exist and play the relevant roles in our theories independently of the existence of that theory, of what we know about those things, or of what kinds of evidence are available to us about those things. Thus, if I were a realist about astronomy, I might believe that there is a fact of the matter about what happens inside a black hole, and that this fact of the matter would obtain even if there were no astronomers, and even if there were no way to verify what happens inside the black hole. In contrast, we can understand *irrealism* to be the view that for some things the truth of a claim depends on the existence of the theory in which those things play a role, or depends upon what we can know about those things and how we know about them.

Note that you can be a realist about some things, and an irrealist about others. I take naturalism to be a form of realism, and to be at least the view that empirical scientific methods are sound, and that we should seek to have our theories cohere with the best findings of our sciences. To use this philosophical terminology, we can call the affect program theory a naturalist theory about emotion. As such, the distinguishing features of the view are that some affects are taken to be objective and scientifically measurable events: states of the body which can be partly described using a theoretical vocabulary such as that of neurophysiology. This view stands in opposition to irrealism about emotion. One kind of irrealism about emotion is interpretationism, the view that some mental states are dependent upon the stance or perspective of an observer.

---

a naturalist theory of emotions by confronting what I take to be the most resistant alternative (interpretationism) by primarily using conceptual arguments and commonsense examples (both of which should be admissible by the interpretationist).

First, I will introduce a special class of emotional actions. Then, I will discuss Daniel Dennett's intentional systems theory and show that Dennett's irrealist position is unable to account for these actions. Considering both these actions and other problems, I will then discuss the more difficult case of the interpretationism of Donald Davidson. Throughout, I will show how their respective versions of interpretationism about belief and desire require that they be reductive cognitivists about emotion. In conclusion, I will return to some of the relevant scientific evidence for the affect program theory, and show how that theory is best suited to account for the actions introduced in this chapter.

WHY BE AN INTERPRETATIONIST?

The interpretationists are motivated by a belief that a proper understanding of mind should be consistent with the physical sciences; but they also, for various reasons, believe that the physical sciences do not and will not ever speak about certain kinds of mental entities. That is, the interpretationist believes that the naturalist view does not and will not have a place for such mental entities as beliefs, concepts, fears or desires; instead, the natural sciences of mind will have room only for neurons and ion channels and electrical potentials and similar kinds of physical entities. If this were true, one would seem to be confronted with the dilemma of rejecting naturalism or rejecting ("eliminating," as it is usually called) the supposed referents of these mental terms. Interpretationists struck upon a novel way of doing the latter without seeming to do it. They argue that mental "entities" are not real entities at all. Instead, they are just posits, clever ways of talking about and understanding such complex systems as humans. Mental talk, such as one's description of her own or her friend's motivations, is just a convenient kind of game-theoretic fiction. Things get complicated in that some interpretationists can, and do, argue that this interpreting of complex systems by way of ascribing mental states to them is sufficient for one to be able to say that mental states "really do exist" in some sense. But, setting aside this unfruitful line of debate, the general outline of the position is clear: for the interpretationist, the natural world has no place for the mental, and our talk about mental states is merely a tool we use to interpret, and thus understand and predict, the behavior of ourselves and others. This view can also be tempting to some scientists, such as ethologists, since it can endorse the liberal use of mental terms (such as talking about what rats believe, what cats imagine, what spiders want) without incurring any costs for it.

Emotional Actions

In this chapter, I will use "emotional actions" as a nontechnical term to label those actions that can be explained (not necessarily exclusively) by citing a basic emotion as their cause. Emotional actions are most clearly identified when contrasted with a belief-desire account of action. In such an account, a volitional[17] action is explicable via the beliefs and desires supposedly held by a minimally rational agent. This is a useful starting point because the interpretationists assume that our mental states are sufficiently explained via belief and desire. In contrast, emotional actions are normally described as being the product of emotions.

We can identify at least three ways in which the commonsense explanation of an action will relate to a belief-desire explanation of the same action by distinguishing between four kinds of emotional actions. I call these kinds of actions B-D consistent actions, B-D inconsistent actions, B-D independent actions, and B-D postfunctional actions.

(1) An emotional action is *B-D consistent* just in case the action is what would be predicted by a belief-desire account.

Suppose that Eric runs away from a rabid dog. It may be true both that Eric ran because he was afraid of the rabid dog;[18] and also that Eric ran away because he believed the rabid dog would bite him, and he desired not to be bitten. These are the kinds of cases in which emotion poses no challenge to belief-desire psychology; such cases also provide the most plausible supporting evidence for the reduction of emotion to belief and desire (e.g., Marks 1982).

(2) An emotional action is *B-D inconsistent* just in case the action is inconsistent with what would be predicted by a belief-desire account.

These are actions that not only would not be predicted or posited on the belief-desire account but would be predicted or posited *not* to occur or are at least incompatible with the kind of action predicted or posited. An example: Karen is afraid of dentists and so avoids them, although she believes that a dentist will do more help than harm to her teeth, and she desires that her teeth be helped, and so on.[19]

Unlike B-D consistent emotional actions, which pose no problem to our irrealist, B-D inconsistent emotional actions are counterexamples to the view that emotions are reducible to belief and desire, and provide some strong evidence in favor of a naturalist theory of emotions. However, B-D inconsistent actions (at least of the kind of which I am aware) make problematic counterexamples for a number of reasons—for example, some philosophers deny that such actions are even possible. We can therefore make the case against interpretationism more simply by focusing upon specific cases of B-D independent emotional actions.

(3) An emotional action is *B-D independent* just in case there is no plausible B-D account of that action.

The most obvious such actions are purely expressive actions, such as kicking a tree when mad at your boss, or jumping for joy upon getting some good news. Such actions simply have no plausible B-D account. However, these expressive actions are open to the criticism that they are automatic behaviors, like digestion or a reflex jerk of the knee, and thus of no interest to a B-D account. We need to focus upon a special kind of B-D independent action to sidestep this moot point: B-D postfunctional actions.

(4) An emotional action is *B-D postfunctional* just in case the action continues beyond the satisfaction of any of the agent's relevant desires.

Although not inconsistent with a belief-desire account, these actions result in an explanatory gap for such an account. Consider the following plausible story of a B-D postfunctional action:

> **Case A:** Eric is terrified of the rabid dog that is before him. He also believes that it will bite him, he desires not to be bitten by it, and he believes that by running into his house and closing the door he will not be bitten (because he knows that the dog cannot get through the door, cannot turn a doorknob, etc.). These are all of Eric's relevant beliefs and desires.[20] Eric runs into the house, frantic; once inside, he not only locks the door but runs upstairs and into another room. He closes and locks that door, and then he moves into a corner: the place in the room farthest from where he believes the dog is.

I propose that the case as supposed is possible—indeed, that there is nothing extraordinary about such a case (especially if we imagine that Eric is young, or, better yet, the kind of person we might call fearful). But the action of Eric *after* he is already in the house with the door closed now continues beyond the scope of the belief-desire explanation of his action. His desire not to be bitten was satisfied when he got inside and closed the door. From the perspective of the belief-desire account, everything else that he does is extraneous. I have set up this case so that the action of closing and locking the second door is plausibly a continuous extension of, and of a kind with, the closing of the first door; so that there is one continuous action that extends beyond the realization of the relevant desire.

We can imagine any number of such cases, involving different emotions. Consider the following supposition:

> **Case B:** Tim is furious at a rabid dog that has attacked his daughter. He desires to kill the dog, and he believes that by shooting it with his gun he can do so (again, these are all of his relevant beliefs and desires). He decides to shoot it, hurriedly finds and loads his gun, chooses the best approach to the dog, sneaks up on the growling canine, and shoots it. On the first shot the dog falls down, obviously dead (and Tim at this moment knows that it is dead). Tim fires all the rest of the rounds in the gun into the body of the dog.

How can we understand Tim's action? To most of us, there is nothing mysterious about it: Tim was enraged, and his behavior would be explained, even predicted, given that observation. But by supposition his desires were satisfied with the first shot. Again, his continuation of the action of firing is, from the perspective of a belief-desire account, postfunctional.

Intentional Systems Theory

Postfunctional emotional actions pose a special problem for the interpretationist theory of mind. There are many types of interpretationism (see
Dennett 1993c for an overview); I will focus upon Dennett's intentional
systems theory as the most basic example. Intentional systems theory is
irrealist because it maintains that intentional states are the products of
interpretation. They are ascribed to an agent by an interpreter but are not
natural states to be found and measured by natural sciences. Intentional
terms like "desire" therefore are used for the interpretation of behavior and
are not genuine scientific descriptions of the mental.

To use intentional systems theory to explain behavior and mental states,
we understand actions of a complex system by attributing to it beliefs and
desires, and then making predictions based upon those attributions. The
procedure is to:

1. treat the object whose behavior is to be predicted as a rational agent;
2. figure out what beliefs the object ought to have; and
3. figure out what desires the object ought to have.
4. Assume the object reasons through (2) and (3) (via the rational abilities granted by (1)), and derive a course of action for the object; this
   is the course of action that we as observers predict. (Dennett 1993a,
   17).

This is the *intentional strategy,* and to look at something in this way is to
take the *intentional stance* toward it. If we see a human being (the object) in
a room that catches fire, we might attribute to him the desire to survive; and
attribute to him the beliefs that the room is on fire, that fire can kill him, and
that fleeing the fire would prevent the fire from killing him; and finally
predict that he will run out of the room to flee the fire. If he does run out of
the room, we have made a successful prediction, and we take this as showing the object is rational and has these beliefs and desires, and actually did
undertake the predicted action. Prediction plays the role of making this a
theory that is, in some sense, appropriately scientific because falsifiable.
Without this, intentional systems theory is nothing more than an attribution of actions and mental states, and is unenlightening, since any behavior
can be labeled as the product of any of endless different combinations of
beliefs and desires.

One of the features of this strategy is that the intentional states, and the
actions these states are to explain, are tightly connected. A belief is the kind
of thing that explains why some action followed some desire (our agent
believed the room was on fire, since he fled the room and desired to avoid
being killed by the fire); a desire explains why some action followed some
belief (our agent desires to survive, since he believed the room was on fire,
believed that fire could kill him, believed fleeing the room would prevent
that, and fled the room); and what makes a behavior one kind of action

rather than another is the beliefs and desires attributed to the acting object (our agent fled the room—as opposed to running out into the hall in order to, say, get home more quickly—because his desire was to survive, and he believed the room was on fire, believed that fire could kill him, and believed that fleeing the room would prevent that). Being a rational agent is at least making the appropriate inferences from ascribed beliefs in order to satisfy desires. We can thus also use this stance to understand actions that have occurred, and to understand what a belief or a desire is, and all of this is encompassed by *intentional systems theory*. To quote Dennett on belief: "*All there is* to being a true believer is being a system whose behavior is reliably predictable via the intentional strategy, and hence *all there is* to really and truly believing that *p* (for any proposition *p*) is being an intentional system for which *p* occurs as a belief in the best (most predictive) interpretation" (1993e: 29). The theory entails the same thing for desires: all there is to being a true desirer is to be a system whose behavior is reliably predictable via the intentional strategy when the desire in question is so ascribed and this ascription yields the most predictive interpretation.

In this scheme, emotion must fit as some form or combination of beliefs or desires. Dennett has not discussed emotion in his works except to sometimes mention them as intentional states to be ascribed via intentional systems theory (e.g., 1971, 87), but his own explication of intentional systems theory requires a reductive cognitivist theory of emotions. This is because the intentional stance aims to explain volitional behavior by ascribing beliefs and desires, and, in this way, provide a reduction of folk psychology. Here we must recognize that in intentional systems theory, "belief" and "desire" are not merely the folk psychological terms (and so should not be taken to be *prima facie* distinct from emotional terms) but rather are derived, technical terms. When he gives intentional systems theory in its most general form, Dennett writes,

> One predicts behavior [from the intentional stance] by ascribing to the system *the possession of certain information* and supposing it to be *directed by certain goals,* and then working out the most reasonable or appropriate action on the basis of these ascriptions and suppositions. It is a small step to calling the information possessed the computer's *beliefs,* its goals and subgoals its *desires.* (1971, 90)

Like some forms of decision theory and game theory—which Dennett recognizes as intentional systems theory's "close kin" (1993d, 58)—the theory takes these two things as the sole primitives and aims to analyze all actions with them. Emotional actions, therefore, have to be so explained. The intentional systems theorist has left himself no choice but to be a reductive cognitivist about emotion.

We are now in a position to consider whether intentional systems theory can explain the postfunctional emotional actions. On an intentional systems theory account of case B, we must first ascribe to Tim the beliefs and desires he ought to have. Presumably the most important of these—the beliefs and desires relevant in this case—are Tim's belief that the dog is rabid, that it attacked his daughter, that it might attack Tim or someone else, that killing it would render it unable to attack another; the desires include wanting no one to be hurt by the dog and to kill the dog. But on these most plausible ascriptions of beliefs and desires, Tim's action after the first shot is absurd.

We can attribute to Tim further desires like the desire to hurt the dog, but even assuming we can justify the claim that this is the kind of desire that Tim ought to have, Tim presumably knows that the dead feel no pain, and therefore that the additional shots are not satisfying such a desire. Similarly, we can attribute to Tim the desire to shoot the dog until he is out of ammunition, or to shoot the dog when it is dead, and so on. But Dennett wants his belief-desire psychology to be more than a vacuous interpretation, so he needs there to be something more robust to desire than just a relation between ascribed actions and beliefs. Recall that the intentional stance is supposed to yield predictions, and before we make the prediction we are to ascribe to the agent those desires which it should have. But the most plausible desires, the desires that Tim ought to have, and those that would be consistent with the other desires that Tim has (the desire to secure the safety of his daughter, etc.) are not desires like emptying the magazine into the dog regardless of whether it is already dead. There is no reason, given that Tim believes dead dogs feel no pain, that they don't attack people, and so on, that Tim ought to desire to shoot the dog when it is already dead. This is not to deny that desires (should there be a general motivation state that deserves this nomination) may accompany or be the product of an emotion; there may even be a sense in which some understand desire such that Tim does desire to shoot the dead dog. But if the emotion causes or is accompanied by another desire, one that falls outside the usual ascription of desires the agent should have, then we have not reduced emotion but rather introduced it as an additional thing.

If we suppose that Tim's desires are those listed above, then the action is post-functional: there is a continuity between what happens up to and including the first shot of the rifle, and what happens after this. This is one action, and it continues beyond the satisfaction of the most plausibly attributed desires. Since the action continues after the satisfaction of these desires, the whole action is unpredictable on the intentional stance. This claim that all the shooting is one continuous action is an important one: it is meant to stand in denial of the possible claim that the intentional stance explains everything up to and including the first shot, but then what follows is irrational. Such a move would be an ad hoc division of actions into the rational and irrational based on their predictability; I elaborate this objection below.

Case A poses the same kind of problems for intentional systems theory. By supposition, Eric knows that getting past the first door will prove sufficient impediment to the dog, were it to attack him. His additional behavior is inexplicable from any credible attribution of beliefs and desires, and hence would not be predictable from the intentional stance. The relevant desires that Eric can reasonably be said to have or which he should have—in this case, primarily to get safely distant from the dog—are satisfied once he is through the door. Running upstairs and closing another door is a continuation of the action, and this continuation cannot be said to satisfy that desire or any other desire that could be reasonably attributed on the intentional stance account.

Intentional systems theory is not meant to be an analysis alone but a predictive framework. To rephrase these cases in the form of an objection to the intentional stance, then, is to recognize that from the intentional stance B-D postfunctional emotional actions will not be predicted. The intentional stance predictions depend upon some action being expected to satisfy a desire of the agent, given beliefs held by the agent. We know, however, that B-D postfunctional emotional actions like those in the examples above go beyond the satisfaction of the relevant desires that can plausibly be attributed via the intentional stance—the desire to kill the rabid dog, or to get away from the dog—so that on the theory the B-D postfunctional emotional action either should not occur or will at least be unpredictable. We also know that these individual tales are not unique, and that emotional behaviors are common behaviors, and we recognize actions like those in the cases above as being possible instances of significant types of human behavior. This shows that the intentional stance fails to predict, and so explain, the B-D postfunctional emotional actions, and therefore is *prima facie* inferior to any theory of the relevant emotions that does explain these kinds of actions.

But there are some potential objections the intentional systems theorist can raise, and I will consider these now. The goal of intentional systems theory is to provide a reduction of mental states to a more manageable domain: "The claim that every mental phenomenon alluded to in folk psychology is *intentional-stance-characterizable* would, if true, provide a reduction of the mental . . . to a clearly defined domain of entities whose principles of organization are familiar, relatively formal and systematic" (Dennett, 1993d, 68). Presumably the intentional systems theory reduction does not need to be total; rather, as Dennett aptly puts it, "A prospect worth exploring . . . is that folk psychology (more precisely, the part of folk psychology worth caring about) reduces—conceptually—to intentional system theory" (66). Granting that emotions of the kind we describe here are worth caring about, the intentional systems theorist might still object that the B-D postfunctional actions are not significant. One might deny that the emotional postfunctional actions are actions, and instead call them mere behaviors—something like a blink or a sneeze, although admittedly more complicated. What reason could be given to call them mere behaviors? The most likely course might be to say that they are not volitional or that they are arational (outside the scope of rationality, just as is digestion or blood flow) or irrational (contrary to rationality).

Although volitional behaviors are clearly actions (nonphilosophers need to note that, in this context, "action" is a technical term for philosophers, meaning something like events caused by a thinking agent as a consequence of [not necessarily conscious] thoughts, usually best described as propositional attitudes), on some definitions of "volitional" there can be actions that are not volitional. The notion of volitional action is very problematic,[21] and different intuitions and working definitions abound. However, one philosophical standard is to hold that volitional actions are those actions that fulfill a plan. This standard is rather strong, and therefore it is safe to take it as at least sufficient for an action to be volitional.

The examples used above were special in that the actions undertaken accomplish a goal, but the actions then continue beyond the realization of that goal; part of the behavior is postfunctional, from the point of view of the most plausible belief-desire account. Indeed, there are other kinds of emotional behavior, such as B-D inconsistent behaviors, that we regularly see, but which so clearly fail to satisfy any plausible desire that they are open to the challenge that they are wholly irrational. There are also emotional actions that are purely expressive, such as if Karen were to kick a tree because she was mad at her boss, or if Adam pulls his hair because of his grief over some loved one's death. These kinds of behaviors also pose a problem for a belief-desire account because there is no belief-desire explanation of such actions; but since they might be said not to accomplish a specific goal on the belief-desire attributions, they might be dismissed as not volitional behaviors. Such mere behaviors could be shouldered off as needing explanation only from a "low-level," nonintentional design-stance view. I don't think that this strategy will work, but these cases require a much more complex defense. In contrast, the postfunctional actions of the kind given in the examples are actions because they accomplish a goal, and do so by exploiting and fulfilling a plan (finding the gun, loading it, choosing and utilizing the best approach for attack; or fleeing on the most direct course to the door). And again, these cases are plausible and common enough in form for us to generalize that they represent instances of common kinds of behavior. As such, the kind would be volitional, B-D postfunctional emotional actions.

Another objection might be that emotional actions are arational or irrational; that the action was rational until it accomplished its goal, then became otherwise as it continued past that accomplishment. It could thus be argued that intentional system theory is meant to predict only rational action, and so should not be expected to account for emotional actions. But this line of argument would also beg the question. Dennett rightly observes that it is difficult to get a precise characterization of what rationality is; and that, nonetheless, many of us still proceed to make claims about rationality, or to use it in our theories (1993b, 98). But whereas it may be permissible to use an intuitive notion of rationality either as a starting point for trying to understand rationality or as an evaluation of behaviors as rational or irrational, Dennett is using his intuitive notion of rationality as part of a predictive theory in which it plays a crucial role. This would not matter so much if we were able to assess the predictions of intentional systems theory, since successful predictions could provide us with some reason to believe that the notion of rationality in use was adequate. But, it is difficult to assess the explanatory or predictive success people could achieve by using intentional systems theory, because no one has yet conducted the relevant experiments. And even prima facie, it is not clear to what extent we actually do predict each other's behavior by taking the intentional stance. Dennett offers imagined examples of successful prediction of each other's actions; for example, when we drive our cars and successfully negotiate traffic by in part predicting the actions of the other drivers. But it is not obvious that such are typical cases of how we predict behavior (as opposed to being chosen because they fit the theory). Nor is it clear that our ordinary predictive success in such cases really depends upon our assuming that other drivers are rational, and ascribing beliefs and desires to them, as Dennett claims we do (for example, we may also ascribe emotions to them, based upon their facial expressions, or posit that they are drunk, based upon the way they are driving, and so on). So we have no reason to believe that intentional systems theory's working and admittedly imprecise notion of rationality is providing useful predictions, and so is an adequate working notion of rationality. Unless there is some principled way to single out emotional actions as, in contrast, arational or irrational, to come along after the fact and call emotional actions arational or irrational behaviors would be ad hoc.

Thus, these B-D postfunctional emotional actions should count as actions of the same significance as the other kinds supposedly predicted by the intentional stance. These actions are not directly a problem for any intentional-stance predictions (except when they contradict or exclude those predictions) since they are not about to be predicted. However, the claim that the intentional stance explains all or a significant portion of our mental lives is a separate claim. The stories about Eric and Tim are not incredible, and if we were there and knew something about the situations we might very well have predicted—where the intentional stance cannot— that Tim would shoot the dog several times, or that Eric would run farther than necessary to protect himself from the dog. These kinds of action fall outside the explanatory ability of intentional systems theory, but well within the domain of folk psychology. We have thus observed that there are significant kinds of emotional actions that the intentional systems theorist will fail to predict, and that therefore the theory cannot reduce or explain the emotions that caused these actions. Another kind of explanation is needed if we are to account for these emotions and the actions that they can motivate.

Davidson's Interpretationism

B-D postfunctional emotional actions raise problems for Donald Davidson's interpretationism similar to those we have seen for Dennett's intentional systems theory. However, the case is slightly more difficult to formulate because Davidson's action theory does not use prediction as a justification mechanism. What we can do, however, is show that problems with Davidsonian interpretationism raise doubts that his analysis of the relevant mental states is successful; more important, we can show that there is a better alternative. In this section I will take the first tack; in the next, the latter.

For Davidson, states like belief and desire are ascribed to agents when we radically interpret their activities and language. When confronted with an agent I want to radically interpret, I start by assuming that most of what the agent believes must be true, and I work to create an interpretation which makes the agent maximally consistent both with itself and with my own language and beliefs (Davidson is not claiming that we actually ever are in the situation of radically interpreting anyone; rather, the notion is a conceptual tool, a kind of description of the nature of meaning and action at an idealized limit). Actions, in turn, are both rationalized, and said to be caused, by *primary reasons*. Primary reasons are pairs of beliefs and *pro-attitudes*. For Davidson, pro-attitudes are essentially what would normally be called "desires" or "wants"; nothing more is needed to explain actions:

> Fortunately, it is not necessary to classify and analyse the many varieties of emotions, sentiments, moods, motives, passions, and hungers whose mention may answer the question, "Why did you do it?" in order to see how, when such mention rationalizes the action, a primary reason is involved. Claustrophobia gives a man's reason for leaving a cocktail party because we know people want to avoid, escape from, be safe from, put distance between themselves and what they fear. Jealousy is the motive in a poisoning because, among other things, the poisoner believes his action will harm his rival, removes the cause of his agony, or redress an injustice, and these are the sorts of things a jealous man wants to do. (1963, 689)

Thus, like the intentional-stance theorist, the Davidsonian interpretationist has only recourse to belief and desire to explain actions, including emotional actions.

This is borne out by Davidson's analysis of pride. In reconstructing Hume's view of pride, Davidson endorses a judgmentalist theory of emotion in which affects play no essential role. Recall that judgmentalism (which, as we already saw, in slightly different forms has been advocated by Solomon 1977 and Nussbaum 1987, 1990) is the view that an emotion is a kind of judgment that includes or contains some evaluative element. Thus Davidson writes, "The theory that I have constructed identifies the state someone is in if he is proud that *p* with his having the attitude of approving of himself because of *p*, and this in turn (following Hume) I have not distinguished from judging or holding that one is praiseworthy because of *p*" (1976: 753). What is of interest is that Davidson, in revising Hume, rejects that part of Hume most consistent with the naturalist view. Hume recognized that beliefs could not alone motivate and that some affective passion must be involved for there to be a rousing to action. But Davidson rejects the necessity of such an affective element:

> Hume surely did often, and characteristically, assert that a pleasant feeling, or a feeling of pleasure of a certain sort, was essential to pride, whereas no such feeling is essential; and, more important, such an element does not help in analysing an attitude of approval, or judgement. (1976, 754)

Davidson also claims that "what Hume called the passion has no place in the pattern" of elements Hume used to explain the nature of passions and the actions they motivate (754). Thus, the evaluative element of pride is not essentially affective for Davidson except in that it may require some pro-attitude(s), and so there is nothing distinguishing such an emotion as a kind from other kinds of intentional states like belief and desire, except their particular logical form. Judgmentalism, for the Davidsonian interpretationist, is a propositional attitude–based cognitivist theory of emotion. It is clearly at least doxastic cognitivism, since for Davidson "belief is central to all kinds of thoughts" (1984, 156), including fears and presumably all other basic emotions. The view is technically not reductive cognitivism, but the difference is merely formal; since the pro-attitudes are essentially just desires or wants, this cognitivism is very close to being a species of belief-desire reductivism, where the evaluative dimension of an evaluative judgment can be glossed as a desire of some kind. For example, being afraid that a dog will bite you will amount to something like a belief that the dog is likely to bite you, and the evaluative judgment that being bitten would be very unpleasant or bad; this evaluative judgment in turn amounts to nothing more than the belief that being bitten would cause pain or scarring and so on, and the desire to avoid pain or scarring or etc. What separates Davidson from the belief-desire reductionist is only his claim that emotions will have logical structures not reducible to the logical structures of belief and desire (1984, 156); otherwise, the failure of such a reduction lies not in any differences in the relevant kinds of natural states, such as the physiological changes accompanying an emotion, since these are inessential to the emotion.

Davidsonian interpretationism faces the same problem as does the intentional systems theorist when attempting to explain a postfunctional emotional action. Surely Eric and Tim can avow to their beliefs and desires; but then we have again the problem of explaining, in a belief-desire account, why they act as they do. Davidsonian interpretationism stumbles over postfunctional actions for the very same reasons intentional systems theory failed: the B-D postfunctional actions continue beyond the satisfaction of the pro-attitudes the agents could reasonably be ascribed.

Ultimately, Davidsonian interpretationism is inadequate to the task of explaining these actions because the elements of folk psychology which interpretationism aims to save are insufficient to explain some emotional actions. We were able to locate the failure of intentional systems theory by observing that it cannot predict or explain these kinds of emotional actions. For Davidsonian interpretationism, explanation does not rely upon prediction; instead, we can locate the failure of the explanation in Davidson's posit that the agent interpreted is rational in a special sense. This rationality basically amounts to an idealized ability to reason logically, which we might think of as an application of decision theory.

> The cogency of teleological explanation rests . . . on its ability to discover a coherent pattern in the behaviour of an agent. Coherence here includes the idea of rationality both in the sense that the action to be explained must be reasonable in the light of the assigned desires and beliefs, but also in the sense that the assigned desires and beliefs must fit with one another. (1984, 159)

And:

> To the extent that we can see the actions of an agent as falling into a consistent (rational) pattern of a certain sort, we can explain those actions in terms of a system of quantified beliefs and desires. (1984, 160)

Presumably, to be rational the agent must be able to draw some inferences from its belief set, and some inferences regarding its desires, sufficient for it to be able to act in order to sometimes satisfy some desires; it must also demonstrate some consistency in its beliefs. Let us call this B-D rationality. To be B-D rational is to satisfy, to some degree, standards regarding one's beliefs and one's actions in light of one's desires and those beliefs. Such standards are usually stated as ideals: being fully consistent, making all the useful inferences, taking all the actions that will satisfy one's desires given one's beliefs, and so on (see Cherniak 1986 for an overview and criticism). The problem that some emotions pose for Davidson's interpretationism— including the emotions that motivate B-D postfunctional actions—is that these emotions are normally attributed to the agent even if they result in actions that fail to be B-D rational.

It seems unlikely that Davidson could revise his interpretationism to include, along with pro-attitudes, the appropriate kinds of emotions— those that can motivate B-D postfunctional actions. First, as we have observed, if the radical interpreter adds emotion to the interpretive tool kit, and then claims that emotions motivated these actions, she must explain in what sense emotions could motivate the actions. But Davidson provides no tools other than pro-attitudes to explain motivation to actions. Adding emotion would require a revised action theory. Second, if we introduce an emotion not as a natural entity but as an explanatory posit, there is a problem concerning how it will it fit into Davidson's brand of rationality. Davidson admits that "where one constellation of beliefs and desires will rationalize an action, it is always possible to find a quite different constellation that will do as well. Even a generous sample of actions threatens to leave open an unacceptably large number of alternative explanations" (1984, 160).

Davidson believes we can avoid this explosion of explanations by adhering to his decision theory brand of rationality. This gains some plausibility because in decision theory beliefs and desires are simple primitives that play irreducibly simple roles for the theory. Having one basic kind of doxastic state, and one basic kind of motivational state, seems a sparing theory— there is nothing here to shear away with Ockham's razor. But emotions are not a similarly simple primitive. They are certainly a complication to the theory, leading to actions that are inexplicable via belief and desire. But then, if we reach beyond the cut of his B-D rationality, there is no reason to add emotions into the theory instead of any other of infinitely many posits. For example, one might posit mental kind state P which causes you to act as if some desire was not satisfied even when it is satisfied. The naturalist posits instead basic emotions because she believes basic emotions are natural, observer-independent states that can motivate actions. The interpretationist cannot hold this, and so the problem of unacceptably large numbers of alternatives rises again.

Finally, the Davidsonian interpretationist should not be allowed recourse to suppose that the agents have additional beliefs and desires to which they did not, perhaps even cannot, avow (e.g., the desire to flee as far as possible, the desire to shoot all the bullets into the dog). Such a strategy underlies Davidson's explanation of akrasia (1980b).[22] This is not a strategy that Davidson has used to explain emotions; in his discussion of akrasia, Davidson wants to avoid the cases of emotional akratic actions and focus on the far more difficult cases of unemotional actions that are akratic. Still, the strategy would seem to generalize. The problem, however, is that it too would not cohere with the rest of Davidson's interpretationism. We must interpret agents in the most charitable way, trying to make them maximally consistent, and taking their own claims about their mental states as mostly right. We can posit desires that are hidden from the agent or which the agent fails to describe properly, but only by explaining how this is going to maximize coherence in the whole interpretation. We would not have this here: the emotional actions in our cases are of a type both common and commonly understood and described. There is no reason why adding new beliefs and desires would be more suitable than the explanation that refers instead to the emotion not as a judgment but as a natural motivating state.

I can summarize by restating the problem for Davidsonian interpretationism in a more problematic, but intuitively more compelling, way. We have already seen that basic emotions are not reducible to belief and desire, and Davidson agrees with this to the extent that he claims their logical forms are different from the logical forms of other ascribed states (1984, 156). Granting this, suppose that there was an intelligent organism which lacked emotions, and had only beliefs and desires. It would be a kind of belief-desire decision-theory thinker; popular culture examples include the character of Data.[23] Now, suppose that this thinker radically interprets the actions of humans. Using only radical interpretation, it would be unable to explain the postfunctional emotional action. The best interpretation of the mental states held—and one consistent with the agent's reports, the agent's behavior in other contexts, and so on—is the one we have given and to which the agents can attest (after all, on the belief-desire psychology view, "People are in general right about the mental causes of their emotions, intentions, and actions because as interpreters we interpret them so as to make them so" [Davidson 1976, 757]), and it includes reference to emotions. (This same problem would arise for any projective version of interpretationism: if I have no emotions and I must simulate a model of the agent by ascribing my kinds of mental states, then I should fail to explain the postfunctional actions.) Of course, the radical interpreter (or the pure belief-desire projector) is free to study ethology and other sciences and raise a hypothesis about emotions. Such a study would lead to the discovery of basic emotions in humans and other related animals, and also hypotheses about how these function, why they evolved, and so on. But these hypotheses now include scientific claims; we have moved into the domain of naturalism, and posited this additional, scientifically specifiable thing: the basic emotion.

The Naturalist Approach

I have shown that some emotions are motivational in a way that is potentially—although not always—distinguishable from the relevant intentional states that participate in and are constrained by B-D rationality. And this is tantamount to common sense. Examples from folk psychology include classifying some crimes as "crimes of passion" (which I take to mean motivated by passion). This view is not only evident in our normal discourse, but we have even institutionalized it: someone who kills in rage is treated by the law and by opinion as somewhat less culpable than someone who planned and committed a murder without anger. Here is evidenced our long tradition of treating emotions as sometimes causing actions which are somewhat independent of the control of (B-D) reason. But the leniency of the law and common opinion in these matters does not run so far as to remove all culpability; killing in rage is not like, for example, killing someone in a car accident when your brakes fail through no fault of your own. We do not treat emotions as brute and completely involuntary forces; in normal discourse we recognize varying degrees and kinds of voluntary control. This is consistent with emotions being part of our mental lives, giving rise to volitional actions, but sometimes resulting in actions that fail to meet standards of B-D rationality.

I reviewed in chapters 1 and 2 some of the vast and varied scientific evidence that coheres with this view. This evidence convincingly shows that some emotions potentially—even if not normally—are able to occur independently of the kind of cognitive skills necessary for B-D rationality. For Davidson and Dennett, a mental state is not the kind of thing that is directly observable, but rather is inferred from patterns of behavior. This is why both interpretationists are able to espouse versions of naturalism and still hold an irrealist belief-desire psychology. But a basic emotion is not observable only in patterns of action. That an agent is experiencing a motivating affective state is directly observable both via scientific measurements and via expressive behaviors that are not the behavior in question. Although we may not yet have sufficient understanding of basic emotions to identify an emotional state by its autonomic or other physiological features, we can identify that an agent is experiencing some kind of affective excitation by observing such measures as galvanic skin response, blood pressure, adrenaline levels, and many other features. We are thus able at least to know, by such measurements alone, that some kind of affective state is present. I also reviewed some evidence that pancultural expressive behaviors include facial expressions (Eibl-Eibesfeldt 1973; Ekman, Sorenson, and Friesen 1969; Ekman and Friesen 1971; Ekman 1993) and that some of these can be involuntary and operate independently of voluntary motor control (Rinn 1984). Recognizing this does not require us to interpret the action in question that results from the emotion: I can see fear expressed on Eric's face, and this is a distinct behavior from the flight that he undertakes. And this observability extends to nonhuman animals; people learn to recognize expressive features of fear in dogs, for example, and take this as a sign of a state of the dog which is not a logical construct out of behaviors but rather a potential cause of some behaviors (recalling Hebb 1946).

That we can identify emotions in nonhuman animals of many kinds is consistent with the presupposition that our emotional capabilities evolved and as such have homologs in other animal species. Depending on how thinly one defines fear, for example, some scientists will include not only larger, more complex animals in the set of things that have the ability to fear, but even such small and relatively less complex animals as some insects (see LeDoux 1996). But many, if not all, of the nonhuman animals in question lack the kinds of capabilities, like language, that would be necessary for B-D rational thought. For Davidson, there is no fact of the matter about whether a dog has beliefs (1984, 163–164). But there can be convincing scientific evidence that a dog is in fear. The evidence surely depends upon science that began with the observation of behavior, but it extends to hypotheses about brain structures underlying fear, the evolution of fear, and substantive scientific hypothesis about the actual physiological state of being in fear. And it is these kinds of hypotheses that allow us to identify fear as a kind of capability shared by many animals. This is, in itself, not an objection to interpretationism; Dennett, who grants that the intentional stance can lead us to treat thermostats as minds, would perhaps be willing to say that flies have beliefs; and Davidson can stick to his dodge that there is no interesting fact of the matter about these issues. But this observation provides evidence that our emotional capabilities evolved in part separately from some of the relevant cognitive capabilities.

How can the affect program theory of emotion do better than the interpretationist in explaining B-D postfunctional actions? Note that on the affect program theory, certain emotions (including those in our examples) can motivate an agent *to undertake a kind of activity specific to the emotion.* Eric's fear motivates him to the action of flight; fear motivates him not just to get safely away but it also motivates the action of fleeing itself (fear, to be even more precise, *is* in part the fleeing itself). Similarly, Tim's anger motivates him to attack. He may (in some sense) desire to kill the dog, and he does just that, but his continued action is part of the attack.[24] The principal characterizing feature of this realist position is that specific kinds of actions are essentially related to the emotions in question: anger is not anger that does not effect or encourage attack, fear is not fear that does not cause flight or the preparation and motivation for flight. But it is the action, and not some particular goal, which is motivated. It may be right, and probably is, to say that some emotions evolved to satisfy some broad class of goals: it seems likely that fear probably evolved as a capability to motivate us to flee perceived threats, anger as a capability to motivate us to attack defeasible threats. But this level of explanation is distinct from that pursued in the kind of irrealist theory implicit in intentional systems theory or in various kinds of interpretationism: an emotion is not a goal-directed state in the way that a desire is.

The potential independence of basic emotions from some cognitive processes does not amount to a denial that emotions might always require or be open to something like a representational description. But the simplicity of the representational level that might be said to be required to describe flight or attack is not sufficient to integrate with the interpretationist program. A weakly representational description of emotions will in no way depend upon the notions of rationality that interpretationism utilizes as its principal explanatory constraint. The interpretationist needs basic emotions to be essentially related to beliefs and desires to capture emotion in the web of B-D rationality.

Does it then follow that emotional actions, even postfunctional ones, are arational or irrational (a distinction which can be coherently formulated once we accept that basic emotions are natural entities independent of intentional ascriptions)? If we suppose the interpretationist standards of B-D rationality, there is a sense in which we might grant that they can lead to action which is arational or irrational. Step back, however, and include in our appraisal of an agent's rationality a scientific theory of evolution and of the role of emotions, and we might see emotional actions as very useful (as heuristics, for example) and therefore as satisfying some compelling rational standards. The hypotheses regarding the function of fear and anger given at the end of chapter 1 are examples of such functions, which are answerable to specific standards of rationality. I return to these issues in chapter 7. The upshot here is that, again, examining emotions in a naturalist light reveals that an irrealist view like interpretationism is too impoverished.

A Closing Note: Does Interpretationism Still Explain Content?

The primary concern of the interpretationists has been to explain belief and mental content, and not emotions per se. I have shown that their approach fails to explain some emotional actions and that therefore it fails to explain the relevant basic emotions. In the conclusion (chapter 13), I will further argue that this failure reveals both that the presuppositions underlying the nonreductive physicalism favored by the interpretationists is a largely misguided view of natural sciences and naturalism, and that the interpretationists are accepting a ubiquitous fallacy concerning the importance and explanatory power of cognitive skills. However, I have not explained, nor do I claim to have any theory of, propositional content. Could an interpretationist view still be a proper explanation of propositional content, even if not of emotional actions? I do not believe that it can. Davidsonian interpretationism, to consider what I take to be the most carefully worked-out version of interpretationism, is a tightly interconnected set of claims that includes a kind of explanation of behavior which I have here shown is, at least in part, erroneous; it also includes the claim that psychophysical laws are impossible, but this is erroneous for the same reasons. It remains to be seen what theory of content could be salvaged out of interpretationism or other "nonreductive" views (for example, the inferential role approach of Brandom 1994), considering that we have emotional actions being explained by what will be (when fully fleshed out) a type-physicalist theory (e.g., the affect program theory), and which therefore provides a strong psychophysical relation between the representations guiding relational emotional actions and measurable physical body states that constitute these emotions. One possible approach may be that some propositional contents can indeed be type identified in some limited form in individual organisms, but that certain richer notions of content that remain significant for human beings require also that social criteria, or other criteria that cannot be given a ready, local type-physicalist explanation, be brought to bear. The issue must await much future philosophical analysis.

4

Social Constructionism and the Contribution of Culture to Emotion

In chapter 3 I showed that interpretationism fails as a form of cognitivism about emotions, and I argued that it is inadequate as a theory of mind because it fails to account for some emotional actions and their related emotions. Some emotions point us toward a more naturalistic theory of mind, a result that is unsurprising given our common conception of emotions. But there is a view of emotions in some ways very similar to interpretationism that is not vulnerable to the arguments I raised. This is *social constructionism,* the view that emotions are (in some sense) created by culture. For the social constructionist, the postfunctional actions could have been pursued because the individuals belong to a culture in which that kind of behavior is what one is expected to do:

> The experience of passivity may be treated as a kind of illusion. Emotions are not something which just happen to an individual; rather they are acts which a person performs. In the case of emotion, however, the individual is unwilling or unable to accept responsibility for his actions; the initiation of the response is therefore dissociated from consciousness. (Averill 1974, 182)

On this view, Tim would have been taught that anger requires of him that he shoot the rifle until it is empty, and Eric would have been well socialized to know that the proper expression of fear would have him run farther than necessary from a threat. The explanation of the postfunctional actions, and presumably any other features of emotions that appear to fail to fit a reductive cognitive theory of mind, could be found in the culture and socialization of the agent. If a strong form of social constructionism were true, then the postfunctional emotional actions would not be the expressions of emotions that are natural states, but instead they would be socially constructed ways of behaving. An interpretationist, or one who held one of the many other kinds of irrealism about basic emotions or other mental states, could be a social constructionist about the relevant emotions and thus escape the criticisms I raised. Thus, social constructionism is also potentially a form of irrealism about emotions: it offers an alternative to the affect program theory in the form of a theory in which cultural factors are used to explain what is just a construction, a kind of role, of a society.

My task in this chapter is thus to confront social constructionism, and show that it is not, at least for the basic emotions, a viable alternative to the affect program theory or any other naturalistic theory of the emotions. The research and ideas that have gone into social constructionist theory have much to offer, and some of the claims that accompany it are likely true. Furthermore, much of it is wholly consistent with the affect program theory. But if it is to be taken as a theory of what the basic emotions are, and a denial of any naturalistic theory of the basic emotions, it is false.

The Problem of Coherence for Strong Social Constructionism

It is difficult to know if social constructionism is a thesis about emotions or about our understanding of emotions and the social role of emotions. For example, in an influential ethnography, Catherine Lutz claims that "emotional meaning is fundamentally structured by particular cultural systems" (1988b, 5). She describes her method as one of paying close attention to emotion terms, arguing, "The complex meaning of each emotion word is the result of the important role those words play in articulating the full range of a people's cultural values, social relations, and economic circumstances" (6). There is nothing in this that the adherent to the affect program theory cannot embrace: the affect program theory is wholly consistent with the cultural diversity of cognitive causes and the expression of basic emotions, and with the claim that in some cultures some emotions are going to receive a great deal of attention and play important roles while in other cultures these same emotions can be suppressed until they seem almost not to exist. And surely it goes without saying that the emotion concepts, the meanings of emotions, and the social roles these emotions play all require a proper placing of the emotion in its culture. Many naturalists today believe that concepts and meaning are constructed by or depend upon the society in which they play a role; and even those who think that meaning is "in the head" will accept that meanings are transmitted and maintained by cultures, and that they play social roles.

But there is a stronger sense in which social constructionism can be understood. Lutz argues that "emotional experience is not precultural but pre*eminently* cultural" (1988b, 5), and that "emotions are cultural concepts" (1988a, 413). Rom Harré claims that "the bulk of mankind live within systems of thought and feeling that bear little but superficial resemblances to one another" (1986a, 12), and so emotions in one culture are only superficially like emotions in another. And James Averill argues that "most standard emotional reactions transcend any biological imperatives related to self- or species-preservation. They are based instead on human capabilities above the animal level and, in particular, on the ability of man to create symbolic systems of thought and behavior (i.e., culture)" (1974, 181). These approaches suggest that emotions are *only* constructs of cultures, not at all the kind of thing that a naturalist approach that draws upon, for example, the neural sciences and the biological history of a species can ever rightly describe. I shall use the term *strong social constructionism* for the view that the basic emotions are socially constructed and that there are no pancultural features of any of these emotions of the kind biology or another physical science would properly describe.

It is not clear how many of the social constructionists about emotions are actually strong social constructionists; the position of social constructionism about emotions is usually stated as a negation of theories which are not widely, if at all, held, such as the view that all emotions are just feelings, that all the things that we might call emotions are of the same few innate kinds, that all emotions are constructed out of combinations of a small set of simple innate emotions, or that those emotions which are innate are somehow just simple rigid programs akin to reflexes. Thus, although one might get the impression that many social constructionists intend to claim that *no* emotions are pancultural, this is not usually explicit (of the researchers listed above, it would seem that only Averill explicitly endorses this). But even if no one were to hold strong social constructionism, the work in this chapter will serve both to clarify the consequences of the ambiguities of social constructionism, and to preserve the affect program theory and related kinds of naturalism about affects from one possible interpretation of social constructionism—an interpretation that is quite strongly suggested by most social constructionists at some time or other.

The Problem of Cross-Cultural Evidence

The most compelling evidence for strong social constructionism is found in ethnographic studies of other cultures where supposedly there are emotions with no ready analogue in our (let us say, in the English-speaking world's) emotions. But there is in these approaches an unexamined problem fundamental to strong social constructionism. This is, quite simply, *how does the anthropologist recognize emotions in the other culture?*

Consider Lutz's intriguing study *Unnatural Emotions: Everyday Sentiments on a Micronesian Atoll and Their Challenge to Western Theory.* In this ethnographic study of the Ifaluk people, Lutz analyzes our own and the Ifaluk concepts of emotions, and although she criticizes what she considers a typical scientific view of emotions, Lutz never gives explicit identity criteria for emotions. This exposes the incoherence of strong social constructionism. The problem is nothing less than this: if emotions were entirely socially constructed, and none of the emotions (as we refer to them) were pancultural, then what could it mean to investigate the emotions of other cultures? Why presume they even have emotions?

Lutz's approach includes working with rough translations into the Ifaluk language of English emotion terms, and then discovering the different eliciting conditions, acceptable forms of expression, and social roles of the analogues among the Ifaluk. But differences in any of these things do not indicate that there is nothing shared for any of the emotions under discussion. In fact, the method is wholly consistent with what one would use if we expected some of the emotions to be, or rely upon, inheritable structures that are amendable via learning, and are used in socially specific ways. Lutz's own accounts are always surprisingly unsurprising:

> In each cultural community, there will be one or more "scenes" identified as prototypic or classic or best examples of particular emotions. Thus, on Ifaluk the prototypic scene evoked by the concept of *metagu* (fear/anxiety) might be the encounter with a spirit, a flight from the encounter, and the recounting of that episode to sympathetic others. (1988b, 211)

This prototypic scene would be quite natural for a contemporary American, if we replace spirit with a growling dog or a man with a gun. A similar emotion had by the Ifaluk is *rus,* which Lutz translates as panic. Both *rus* and *metagu* quite recognizably satisfy our own conception of fear:

> The two emotions are also conceptualized [by the Ifaluk] as similar in creating flight or avoidance reactions in those who experience them. People may run away from the dangerous object in each case, but *rus* is often described as freezing its victim in their tracks or causing them to run about in a confused and crazy way. (186)

Not only is this just what we would expect from fear and panic in our own culture, but it is common to other mammals. A scientist studying fear in rats, for example, expects, and can generate reliably, both behaviors—flight and freezing—again and again, by just the kind of stimuli (e.g., the threat of pain) one would expect!

Lutz is concerned to ensure that a naturalistic view of fear gives proper place to the social roles of fear; but she also tries to argue that fear for the Ifaluk is primarily social because it primarily concerns social relations. This is consistent with the affect program theory. But it is also not established by her own evidence. She grants that the Ifaluk can have "*rus* (panic/ fright) in the face of an approaching typhoon," but unconvincingly suggests that this is not an exception to *rus* being primarily concerned with social relations by noting that the Ifaluk talk about it: "Emotion is surely also experienced in response to overtly non-social events. . . . In most of the cases, however, it can be argued that the social world plays a significant part" (212). But no one could deny this; *anything* can be discussed and can play a significant social role.

The picture that we get from Lutz's study of the Ifaluk is that the Ifaluk have the same basic emotions we have, but that these emotions play different social roles, have different specific eliciting conditions, and have different expressions. We learn that the Ifaluk have emotions like *song* (justifiable anger), *rus* (panic/fear), and *metagu* (fear/anxiety). It is difficult to understand why such results are not taken to be good evidence that some pancultural, and therefore probably inheritable and biologically based, elements underlie a rich cultural diversity. The Ifaluk are surely quite different from us—they admire fearfulness, they believe strongly in active spirits—but they also share much with us.

Other often-cited ethnographies, although always fascinating, fail to establish a lack of, or radical difference in, the basic emotions. Michelle Rosaldo (1980) has studied the Ilongot people of the Philippines. The Ilongot are undoubtedly very strikingly different from us. From our perspective, they seem obsessed with anger and killing. Males are considered immature and unprepared for adulthood if they do not murder someone, preferably an outsider, and decapitate the body. But the very motivation given for this behavior is anger, *liget*. There is perhaps something special about the importance and role of anger in this society, but it is hardly surprising that anger is seen as a motivator for a murderous attack.

Another advocate of social constructionism is Rom Harré. Harré argues that emotions are properly understood through the "proper understanding of how various emotion vocabularies are used" (1986a, 5). He explicitly attempts to give some identity conditions for the use of emotion terms:

1. Many emotion words are called for only if there is some bodily agitation. . . .
2. All emotions are intentional—that is, they are "about" something, in a very general sense. . . .
3. Finally, the involvement of the local moral order, both in the differentiation of the emotions and in the situationally relative pre- and proscription of the emotions, includes that there is a third set of conditions for the use of emotion words—namely, local systems of rights, obligations, duties and conventions of evaluation. (8)

Unfortunately, Harré also adds that not all conditions must be met; thus, what we have here are just loose guides, since not all of them, nor any one of them, is claimed to be necessary. But, taken independently, none of these criteria is either sufficient or noncircular for even our own English emotion terms. First, we have plenty of bodily agitation (and I shall grant some intuitive notion of "bodily agitation") which are not emotions. Stomachaches, headaches, illness, exhaustion, and many other bodily states would seem to be agitations and yet are not on the usual lists of emotion that a native speaker of English would form. Second, without a theory of intentionality being given, it is difficult to know what is not intentional; but, regardless, there are lots of things that are intentional but that we do not call emotions; belief is one of them. Third, many philosophers and some social scientists believe that emotions are necessary for the existence or force of moral codes (for example, some hold that emotions are necessary in order for us to make evaluations). Unless this is denied in some way, then observing that emotions are associated with the moral order threatens to be circular. And, just as with intentionality, there are nonemotional states (as I use the terms) that are also involved in the moral order. These include beliefs about the law.

Harré and Grant Gillett more recently emended Harré's previous list of potential identity criteria. They claim that the " 'rules' for the correct use of an emotion word fall naturally into four groups": a felt bodily disturbance, a characteristic display, a judgment that is expressed, and illocutionary force or an intended result of the emotion word's use (1994, 149). And, though they assume that "these four conditions exhaust the rules for the use of emotion words," these conditions do not, they argue, tell us what the "components" of emotion are: "One can't just say that the obtaining of these four conditions constitutes the having or being of an emotion. Emotions are brought into being in the interaction between actual or imagined persons in well-structured episodes and in specific historical conditions" (150). Thus again, the criteria are mere guidelines, and we must wonder what emotions are supposed to be.

The social constructionist James Averill does offer a definition of emotions: *"An emotion is a transitory social role (a socially constituted syndrome) that includes an individual's appraisal of the situation and that is interpreted as a passion rather than as an action"* (1980a, 312). However, here again, the problem of cross-cultural identification arises. For example, Averill cites a behavior by the Gururumba, a people living in New Guinea, as an example of "an emotionlike syndrome" (1980b, 44). The behavior in question is called by the Gururumba "being a wild pig," and typically occurs in young men. For a short while, they loot, shoot arrows at bystanders, and perform other aggressive acts. This behavior either ends spontaneously, or a kind of re-domestication is undertaken by the tribe.

Averill claims that " 'being a wild pig' and related syndromes are not emotions in the ordinary sense; nevertheless they exhibit many of the features of standard emotional reactions. For example, these behaviors are experienced passively" (1980b, 46). Averill's point here is that there is a behavior which is claimed to be experienced passively, but which from our perspective is a kind of social role and not some kind of necessary (say, from a biological perspective) behavior. However, even if we grant this, it does not establish that emotions are just social roles. That there are pseudo-passive states does not in any way establish that all purportedly passive states are actually pseudo-passive, any more than that some claims are lies establishes that all claims are lies. Furthermore, there are many passive experiences which we don't consider emotions. Suppose that the Gururumba have a disease that they conceptualize in a way similar to how we conceptualize disease: namely, as a thing that overcomes its victim. Since they are experienced passively, why are not diseases emotions? In other words, it is again unclear how we are to distinguish emotions from other kinds of behaviors. Averill does add, "Every emotional reaction is a function of a particular kind of appraisal" (1980b, 64), but interestingly he gives different kinds of appraisals that could underlie the "being a wild pig" behavior; these include the appraisal that the social expectations on the individual are too great, or that quarreling with a person who then dies leaves behind a terrible guilt. If appraisal were necessary to make the (seemingly) passive experience an emotion, one would expect that not just any appraisal would do.

The weakness of these many conditions points to the central problem in the use of cross-cultural evidence for strong social constructionism: on what grounds can we identify in another culture a term as an emotion term or a behavior as emotional behavior? This problem even reappears *within* a culture. It is striking that Harré makes claims about what in our own language is an emotion and what isn't. Here is a sample passage:

> But reliance on unexamined common sense can have an unfortunate effect on research methods which the linguistic turn can help to prevent. . . . For example, one well known textbook mentions only depression, anxiety, lust and anger [as paradigm cases of emotions]. Lust and depression are not emotions. Depression is a mood and lust a bodily agitation. (1986b, 5)

How does the linguistic turn settle this issue? How does it entitle Harré to criticize other native speakers of English? We are not told. I grant that many people in our culture would call depression a mood (I would; and my reasons would be that our normal usage pegs depression as an affective state that is longer lasting than, say, anger). Studies have been made of how such terms are used in our own culture, and they reveal much variation, but they also reveal some normal uses (for review see Plutchik 1994, 45–73). But if this is the method to settle such questions, it cannot allow us to criticize our own emotion concepts, nor can it allow for cross-cultural generalizations about emotions.

Strong social constructionism faces a dilemma. Either emotions are just social constructs of our own culture, amounting to nothing more than a tradition like baseball or voting; or the social constructionists need to explain how it is that they identify emotions in other cultures in any sense other than just identifying analogous traditions. The irony is that the cross-cultural evidence is usually taken as the primary evidence for social constructionism. But without some criteria aside from our own use for the emotion terms for identifying any of the emotions, we should well ask what a social constructionist could mean by claiming that other cultures even have emotions. Why do not the categories of Ifaluk emotion, for example, include what we would call illnesses? These are bodily disturbances, and, since they can be caused by evil spirits, they may have some important connections to the moral order, satisfying two of Harré's criteria; and they are passive, satisfying one of Averill's criteria. Why is it that instead we find striking evidence of quite similar emotions in these cross-cultural studies?

The one consistent alternative is that we can start with our own emotional categories, find analogues in other cultures, and then observe how those analogues fit or fail to fit with our own. But several things must be noticed about this possible approach. First, it is not clear why the strong social constructionist should then expect to find emotions in other cultures. We don't expect to find significantly similar analogues to bond trading among the Ifaluk, or backgammon tournaments among the Ilongot. Why should we find fear or anger, if these too are just social constructs? Second, this is not what the social constructionists claim to be doing. They freely talk about the emotions of other cultures, and not about the analogues of our emotions. Third, suppose that Averill or Harré and Gillett give some rough identity criteria such that one could actually find analogues of our emotions in other cultures, while denying any form of "essentialism"; but then why are the criteria so surprising? On such a view, the criteria would be the distillations of our own native speaker proficiencies. But not only is this prima facie inconsistent with the criticism of our own cultural concepts of emotions, which are ubiquitous in social constructionist literature; it is also a complete mystery why the criteria are so unlike our folk psychology. That is, how is it that conceptual analysis finds that our emotions are just social constructs, while at the same time the typical view of our own culture, as the social constructionists are eager to point out, sees them as pancultural and inheritable biologically based capabilities? This is at best a very fragile position. It would amount to simultaneously criticizing, amending, and reporting our own views. In order to do this, we need some reason to doubt our own emotion concepts: that is, we need some reason to reject what our immediate conceptual analysis will find that our folk psychology supposes emotions to be (biologically based, pancultural capabilities). More important, we will ultimately need some reason to doubt our scientific account of the relevant affects. The only reason that the social constructionists have offered for taking such a position is to refer to cross-cultural evidence that supposedly establishes that there is little like our own emotions in other cultures, and thereby supposedly casts doubt on the idea that these emotions are anything like what our folk psychology tells us they are. But, as we have seen, the cross-cultural evidence fails to establish this.

The Social Constructionist Critique of Naturalism

The instability of this position is revealed by the claims made in common by Lutz, Harré and Gillett, and Harré that the opposition to social constructionism has been misled by their use of emotion terms. Naturalists are said to naively assume that since we have the terms, there must be a kind of object that is the referent to the terms.

Two aspects of the Western approach to language—as something which primarily *refers to* or even *is* a series of things—act together to predispose us toward a particular view of the words used to talk about emotion, such as "anger," "fear," "happiness," or "emotion" itself. At best, these words are seen as labels for emotion "things"; at worst, the words *become* the things themselves rather than human, cultural, and historical inventions for viewing self and relations with others.
    The problem of the referential and reified view of language is found in even more extreme form in the domain of emotion words than it is elsewhere in language. This is so because the Western approach to language reinforces the already existing view of emotions as primarily physical things. "Anger," "fear," and "happiness" are treated, through the process of reification, not as concepts used to do certain kinds of things in the world but as labels for concretized psychophysical states or objectivized internal "event-things." (Lutz 1988b, 9)

Similarly, Harré:

Psychologists have always had to struggle against a persistent illusion that in such studies as those of the emotions there is something *there,* the emotion, of which the emotion word is a mere representation. This ontological illusion, that there is an abstract and detachable "it" upon which research can be directed, probably lies behind the defectiveness of much emotion research. . . . But in the case of the emotions, what is there is the ordering, selecting and interpreting work upon which our acts of management of fragments of life depend. (1986a, 4)

But it is widely understood that a crude referential theory of language is not adequate, and that naive realism is false. Furthermore, even a cursory review of the history of the sciences of emotion reveals that there have often been debates about what kinds of things emotions are, and even whether they exist (e.g., Skinner in *Science and Human Behavior:* "The 'emotions' are excellent examples of the fictional causes to which we commonly attribute behavior"). And it is wholly obscure what Lutz means when she says that at worst we treat the emotion words as the things, presumably the emotions, themselves. Surely no naturalist does this.[25]
    And, contrary to Harré's warning against the "illusion" that there is "something *there*" in an emotion, it is safe to say that *there is something there.* Harré grants that emotion terms are used foremost when there is "bodily agitation," surely a non-linguistic state, and one which is quite there. This ambivalence is repeated when Harré admits that: "There can be little doubt that, even if there are some universal emotions, the bulk of mankind live within systems of thought and feeling that bear little but

superficial resemblances to one another" (1986a, 12). Much about this sentence is objectionable. It is not clear how there can be *universal* emotions, or even any emotions that occur in two different cultures, while at the same time the individuals in these different cultures have only superficial resemblances to one another. Are the striking similarities between *rus* and panic just a miraculous coincidence? But what is most notable about this claim is that Harré is willing to admit there is nothing inconsistent about the observations both that different cultures have different affect terms, and that some of the emotions (that we identify with our emotion terms) are universal. But of course a naturalist would want to start research right here, at what appears universal (or, at least, pancultural)!

The social constructionists are caught in an awkward position. If all they mean to point out is that there are some states which we may call "emotions," or which are analogous to things we call emotions, but which seem to be culturally specific, and that the roles of these and other "emotions" vary with different cultures, then the social constructionist position is important but it is merely consistent with emotions being socially constructed, and is equally consistent with a naturalist view like the affect program theory. The naturalist who believes that some emotions are pancultural and that a theory of them will have to account for their biological substrates will be happy to grant that culture plays significant roles, and eager to learn from the findings of social constructionists. The important point is that the naturalist generally begins by looking for what is common, in the hope of uncovering deep structures, ideally natural kinds; thus, Harré's admission that there may be universal emotions is where the naturalist will start work. If it turns out that our emotion terms refer to some things which are not natural kinds, nor otherwise stable kinds, this is no disaster; one will amend the science of emotion to take this into account. And if the social constructionist position is a more substantial one—that there are no natural kinds or stable and biologically based kinds of emotions, nor any pancultural identity criteria for them—then the social constructionists are contradicting themselves, or at least are making claims with no clear meaning, when they freely make claims about different emotions in other cultures which supposedly reveal that there is no easy analogue in our own.

Finally, it is worth nothing that strong social constructionism that draws upon cross-cultural study is victim to the very "essentialism" it claims to oppose. For the very idea that there is "emotion" in all these different cultures is one highly open to doubt. Our best scientific evidence points toward, on the one hand, there being a host of pancultural capabilities which in our culture are called "emotions"—fear, anger, disgust, sadness, joy, and others—but, on the other hand, there is unlikely to be any interesting theory that finds significant shared features of all of these capabilities and the many such other states that we group under the term "emotion." Thus, our best understanding is that "emotion" is a useful term for a family resemblance of things; and that our best theories of emotions will be just that:

different theories of different affects. Yet, these social constructionists who seek cross-cultural evidence always talk about looking for instances of "emotion." And perhaps this is to be expected, since after all, to be looking for fear, or anger, in all these different cultures would be to admit the possibility that these are pancultural. Thus, instead, the social constructionist is looking for "emotion," presumably because this is seen as an appropriately general category to allow for their relativist stance.

Strong social constructionism based upon cross-cultural observations is therefore not a coherent position.

The Problem of Scientific Evidence

I began by suggesting that social constructionism, because it is immune to the criticisms raised in chapter 3 to irrealism, might itself be part of a coherent form of irrealism. I have just shown that strong social constructionism that draws upon cross-cultural study can be shown to be incoherent on conceptual grounds. But we should also remember that all of the evidence for significant biological determination of some emotional capabilities—the pancultural facial expressions, emotions in other species, the neuropsychological evidence that emotions are potentially independent of cognition, the neuroanatomical evidence that separates some emotion and cognitive structures, and so on—is incompatible with strong social constructionism.

Thus, the strong social constructionists are in an uncomfortable position as regards not only the status and import of cross-cultural evidence, but also as regards the neuroscientific and biological evidence. How are they to explain the many precognitive aspects of affect that we saw in chapters 1 and 2 if they claim all emotions are socially constructed? If smiling is just a socially learned behavior that is part of our socially constructed emotion of joy, why is there an independent neural pathway for facial control that allows for spontaneous smiling in the hemipelegiac? Of course, it could be that this separate track is also socially trained to a significant degree, but then why do Irenäus Eibl-Eiblesfeldt's blind, deaf, and brain-damaged subjects spontaneously smile and laugh when playing, or cry and shout when placed in unfamiliar situations? And unless we are wrong to believe that nonhuman animals can show emotions like fear and anger, then it would seem that there is something to fear and anger which is not socially constructed in the relevant sense, since it is shared by organisms that are not only outside our culture, but outside all culture: they do not in the relevant sense have a culture.

Averill has taken up the challenge presented by some of this scientific evidence, and tried to respond to it. He considers four kinds of evidence, concerning biological foundations, physiological correlates, localization in the central nervous system, and cognitive role. Averill's target in reviewing these bodies of evidence is "the association of emotional with physiological processes on the basic of extrinsic symbolic relationships" (1974, 151). For Averill, extrinsic symbolic relationships are those relationships which (in this context) are not supported by the scientific evidence (hence they are "extrinsic"). They are instead just prejudices, carried along uncritically.

Averill's objection to the view that there are biological foundations to emotions is to claim that humans are the most emotional of animals. I do not know what this means, but let us grant the claim. It does not establish that our emotional capabilities are therefore not biologically based products of the evolutionary past of humans. It is a parody of evolutionary theory to suppose it means that no species can have unique capabilities, or have capabilities exercised to some greater degree. Furthermore, for those emotions that he grants we do share with nonhuman animals, Averill conflates having different cognitive contents with the existence of taxonomic distinctions of affects: "no animal has as many [fears] as man, not only of concrete, earthly dangers, but also of a whole pantheon of spirits and imaginary evils as well" (1974, 175). But surely this only establishes that we can have different objects of fear, not that we have many different kinds of fearlike affects. We can explain many of the added features of basic emotions that we share with nonhuman animals by properly accounting for the cognitive contribution to the emotion.

Averill's arguments against the importance of physiological correlates of emotions also fail. First, he argues that in research on emotions, there has been a focus on affects, such as fear and anger, that are correlated with "vigorous muscular exertion." Thus, we should not be surprised that these lead to physiological changes. But note that this response has force only if we assume that emotions are somehow normally disconnected from action. For example, on the affect program theory, with the added supposition that some emotions carry action programs as part of their syndrome, for these emotions it is part of what they are that they are tightly connected to "vigorous muscular exertion." That is the very point of affect program theory in this regard. Furthermore, Averill argues that many nonemotional cognitive states lead to physiological changes, and so emotions are not special in this regard. But, even if it were true that some nonaffective cognitions exhibit some, or even all, of the physiological changes of the kind in dispute here, it would establish only that emotions are not alone in having physiological correlates, a result that neither supports social constructionism nor refutes a naturalist theory like the affect program theory.

Third, Averill denies that we can identify emotion systems in the brain, and so achieve a neuroanatomical separation between emotions and cognitions. But his argument is to suppose that lesion studies, in which we infer systematic roles based on deficits that arise from brain damage, cannot distinguish necessary from sufficient structures. He suggests that the neuroscientist acts like a person who removes a resistor from a radio, finds the volume decreases, and supposes that the resistor is an amplifier. This does not describe contemporary neuroscience. Researchers carry out extensive studies, not only of lesioned brains, but of normal brains, using MRIs, CAT scans, and electrical probes; of the biochemistry of brains, using a multitude of techniques; and of the effects of direct electrical stimulation of various parts of the brain. Most important, hypotheses about a systematic role are made as part of a theory, and must answer as such, so that in contemporary neuroscience a very large body of evidence is pieced together with the goal of coherent and interrelated theories. Averill argues that "the workings of any of [the brain's] parts can only be understood in relationship to other parts" (1974, 178). If this just means that the brain is a system with interrelated parts, then all properly done systems-level neuroscience takes this into account since any theory is going to be related to other theories of brain function in related structures (e.g., if I argue that fear is generated in the thalamus, I must explain the results about the role of the amygdala in fear and so respond to theories about amygdala function, and so on). If it means that no brain system can have a function that can be described alone, then it is false; we can describe a brain system independently when we specify the role independently (that is, we can discuss the role of amygdala in some clearly defined aspect of fear conditioning because we may be specifying the responses that this nucleus has to certain inputs; we don't need to also explain in this context how the organism is using that fear to act, and so explain motion control and so on). Thus, neuroscience, and specifically neuropsychology, is nothing like the approach that Averill critiques.

Fourth, Averill's claims that emotions essentially have cognitive contents construes cognitivism so weakly that it can be shared by nonhuman animals. For example, he endorses the view that some emotions are object directed. But this is shared by other species of animals also: a cat is afraid of a dog, or angry at another cat. Furthermore, he claims that emotions necessarily have an appraisal element, and therefore are essentially cognitive. The notion of appraisal is not clear here; but, more important, I will describe in a coda to chapter 8 how the affect program theory is actually able to *explain* what some kinds of appraisal are, whereas cognitive theories of emotion merely take appraisal as a mysterious primitive. And in this regard, nonhuman animals also appraise with their emotions: a frightened cat has appraised a stimulus as dangerous. Finally, Averill argues that reason and affect cannot be separated; but the dependence of reason upon affect is wholly consistent with a naturalist theory of emotion and the affect program theory.

We can see from these responses that social constructionism is often based on the intuition that humans are qualitatively different from other animals because of their culture and increased cognitive abilities—especially the ability to use language. But unless one rejects evolution, this can only mean that we have *additional* capabilities to other kinds of animals. It does not remove humans from the evolutionary chain of life. Some emotions could be basic, and any abilities special to humans could allow for additional mental states that we group together with the basic emotions to form variations that are not pancultural or, in turn, that we use to create emotionlike syndromes which are culturally specific (more on these possibilities below). And this is what we should expect given the neuropsychological evidence. Recall that much evidence is consistent with the view that there is a hierarchy of systems, and as a result there are instances of basic emotions that are distinguishable based on the degree to which they participate in "higher" cognitive functions. Cognitive instances of basic emotions allow for a biological capability to have complex and variable eliciting conditions. Averill and the other social constructionists betray a kind of inversion of the prejudice they attack. Averill argues that we have a long history of associating emotions with "animality"; but what he accepts is the idea that somehow animality is "lower" (in an evaluative sense of the term), and that nonhuman animals are subject to "biological imperatives." This is the true extrinsic symbolism in play, and it is just another version of the cognitive autonomy fallacy (see chapter 13).

Ultimately, strong social constructionism construes naturalism too simplistically. The naturalist is not in the position of seeking some simplistic mechanism that comes fully packaged at birth—because the naturalist knows, from the empirical evidence, that affects are just far too complex for this. Rather, the naturalist seeks the grammar of affects, including of basic emotions. These underlying structures of individual affects are expected to be capable of yielding immense varieties of experiences and behaviors. To reject naturalism about emotions with the erroneous claim that it treats them as simplistic universals is tantamount to rejecting the view that the capability for language and some language structures are inheritable by observing that there are different languages.

Irrealism, One Last Time

Averill holds that social constructionism is the view that "there is no invariant core to emotional behavior which remains untouched by sociocultural influences. The latter view (that there is an invariant core) is essentially *a reification of emotion into a biological given*" (1980b: 57). As we saw with most social constructionist pronouncements, this can be read in at least two ways. Suppose we identify the neural circuits that underlie fear conditioning and more complex fear behaviors. If Averill's position is that these neural structures are not a "biological core" of fear because there is nothing of interest to say about fear that is not wholly determined by society, then any naturalist who has reviewed the scientific evidence must reject this position. But if we interpret Averill's claim to be that this "biological core" is not unaltered by learning, or that it does not under all circumstances act in a way independent of cognitive capabilities which have been trained in a socially specific way, and which normally will result in socially significant behavior, then not only can the naturalist embrace this position, but she can offer neuropsychological evidence in support of it. This view is not only consistent with the naturalist program—it is actually revealed by the scientific evidence.

Does the acceptance that some affects, including the basic emotions, are consistent with these features offer the possibility of an irrealist answer to the problems raised in chapter 3? Recall that we observed that various kinds of emotional behaviors which are predicted by the affect program theory are incompatible with the interpretationist view of mind. These were behaviors in which the action program of the affect program continued beyond the satisfaction of the desires ascribed to the individual. Might not the postfunctional behavior be just a socially prescribed behavior, as understood in a weakened social constructionist theory, and not one motivated by rational consideration of beliefs and desires?

This is not a compelling approach. By definition, the social constructionist who admits scientific evidence should have to admit, or answer to, the vast and compelling evidence of the kind reviewed in chapters 1 and 2 for pancultural emotions or emotional features. But the scientific evidence, we have seen, strongly suggests that some of the affects are complex syndromes that include action programs. An irrealism meant to escape the problems revealed in chapter 3 via a weaker version of social constructionism requires then a weaker reading of the scientific evidence, one which denies that pancultural elements are sources of postfunctional behavior. This may be consistent (although I doubt it), but it is patently the less compelling explanation. It fails to explain any of the very many other things that the affect program theory explains, such as recognizable emotional behaviors in nonhuman animals, the abnormal elicitation of emotions, and the kinds of cases I will discuss in the next chapter. I predict that affect program theory, consistent with the motivation of postfunctional actions, will continue to win on the evidence.

What Can Be Learned from the Claims of Social Constructionism?

Given that basic emotions and emotionlike behaviors can be shaped by learning, and therefore by culture, we can ask what research or ideas in the social constructionist program can be part of a scientific study of emotion. As I have already observed, the affect program theory is consistent with many of the claims of the social constructionists; I will therefore take some time to see how this can be. But there are also a number of other behaviors or states that we call "emotions"—how might these cohere with the claims of social constructionism?

Social Constructionism and the Affect Program Theory

There are two obvious ways in which the affect program theory can accommodate many of claims of social constructionists: by recognizing that both the input and the output or expression of basic emotions are shaped by learning and therefore by culture. In particular, the affect program theory must allow that cognitive contents can cause affect programs to activate, and that these contents can influence and even control the output of the programs. There may also be a number of other ways in which the theory can accommodate some social constructionist claims; for example, learning may shape the very nature of the affect program. Thus, in those cases where cognitive contents like beliefs are the primary elicitors of emotions, it will of course follow that the kinds of things that people fear will be influenced by their culture. There is evidence that there are some universal antecedents to emotions (Ekman and Friesen 1975; Boucher and Brandt 1981). And, we should expect that if the basic emotions are pancultural capabilities, their will be some functional universals to those emotions, and thus to their eliciting conditions. However, without trying to limn the definite outlines of such universals antecedents, it is enough here to grant that the same kind of affect program could be caused by different representations or beliefs (which, if there are universal antecedents, would be diverse instances of general universal elicitors—e.g., dangerous things). Note also that this is not just for the cognitive emotions: it is possible that the eliciting conditions of basic emotions are shaped by learning and hence by culture even in their subcognitive occurrences. With this in mind, we should not be surprised, when we look at cross-cultural evidence, that the concrete details vary. We saw that the Ifaluk feared the ghosts of dead relatives. This is not a common fear in the United States. However, people in the United States often fear random violent crime. Note that such differences are not necessarily even a rational differentiation of environments. Few of us believe in ghosts, but people's fear of crime in the United States is disproportionately greater than is reasonable for the amount of crime that occurs. It should be possible to offer indefinitely many such examples. All of them are to be expected by any reasonable naturalism. The affect program theory can accommodate this by the observation that cognitive contents can cause the program to activate.

Furthermore, the way in which emotional behaviors get expressed in social beings like ourselves are shaped by learning and therefore highly determined by culture. If someone is a member of a culture that disdains fear, the expression of fear might normally be much more muted than in a culture where fear is seen as a good thing. And if in one culture the easy anger of youth is expected to lead—indeed, one is a failure if it does not lead—to murder and decapitation, then we should expect murder to be much more common as an expression of anger in youths there than in a culture that discourages such. And much more subtle and complex differences are seen in very similar cultures. An Italian couple sitting at a romantic dinner will touch each other many more times than will an English couple in the same situation. The affect program theory accommodates the observation that we have the cognitive abilities to direct, suppress, and control the expression of our emotions.

Finally, it can be that other forms of learning significantly alter affect programs. For example, learning may augment in various ways the nature of a basic emotion: frequent expression might make the emotion more and more frequent and powerful, whereas continual suppression might atrophy its force. This just an example of an empirical possibility, open to further research; we need only observe here that there is nothing of simplistic, brute nativism (e.g., we all inherit affect programs, we all use them the same way, they all follow the same input-output pattern, and so on) in the affect program theory.

Griffiths on Social Constructionism and Cognitive Emotions

Paul Griffiths (1997) has provided a discussion of social constructionism that is both clear and insightful. For Griffiths, "The affect program system creates brief, highly stereotyped emotional reactions" (100). He is therefore also concerned to offer some account of "higher cognitive emotions" (which he takes to include guilt, envy, and jealousy). I do not agree that the distinguishing feature of basic emotions is that they are either brief or highly stereotyped; I believe that the behaviors to which they lead are ultimately best categorized not by their duration or invariability but by their functional role and by the identification of underlying neural circuitry. Nonetheless, there are many things that we call "emotions" which may not fall under the affect program theory account. There is some difficulty that inevitably arises now concerning taxonomy: what makes these other things "emotions"? But as long as we avoid (as does Griffiths) overgeneralizing features from these other states to the basic emotions, we can here set aside such issues.

Griffiths offers a revised, more sophisticated form of evolutionary psychology that is augmented with some attention to developmental systems theory. He rejects, for example, the claim, common to evolutionary psychology, that the human mind is monomorphic (that is, that it has many universal, inherited features of the relevant kind). Traditional evolutionary psychology puts too much stress upon the genetic inheritance of humans to explain their minds. Griffiths reminds us, "The nuclear genetic material, the zygotic machinery, and the social environment are all 'inherited.' They are all passed on from the last generation to the next and interact to reconstruct the life cycle" (129). Hence, Griffiths offers a "heterogenous construction" approach to the "higher cognitive emotions," an approach which "is meant to convey the idea that the psychological phenotype is constructed through the interaction of traditional 'biological' factors, traditional 'cultural' factors, and factors that are hard to classify in terms of that dichotomy" (132). In such a framework, there can be "emotions" (perhaps generally characterized as "irruptive patterns of motivation") the constitution, and hence existence, of which specific features of a culture play a necessary role in.

Griffiths distinguishes various forms of social constructionism, one of which is the social-role model. An "emotion" can play a social role in two ways: either it can be an action that the agent will actually disclaim (such as we saw above in Averill's consideration of the case of being a wild pig), or it could be what Griffiths calls a reinforcement version of a social role. In the latter, social roles are learned so well, and perhaps at such an early age, that they appear to function like an affect program. That is, they are social roles that have become so ingrained that they are for members of the relevant culture "automatic"—one might say, "natural."

This is an important concept, and it offers a clear statement of the possibility of instances of states that are quite like those proposed by strong social constructionism: behaviors which we can identify as "emotions," or at least as being emotionlike, because of a strong analogy with basic emotions. They are, in particular, typified by kinds of behavior—behavior which might allow for, say, postfunctional actions (and therefore, as we saw in chapter 3, indicate a motivation not to satisfy a desire but rather toward a particular kind of action). But they are distinct in that the underlying capability is entirely learned. As a result, we should expect such social roles to be culturally specific, and we should expect the neural machinery underlying them to be (to some degree) distinct from that underlying affect programs. The existence of such states would be wholly consistent with the affect program theory.

Conclusion: A Grammar of Affects

I return again to the metaphor of a "grammar of affects." The affect program theory offers us a rich way to understand some of the things that we call "emotions." Griffiths's heterogenous construction approach may offer a powerful way to understand some others. From the perspective of a naturalist, we can endorse an ecumenical approach: studies of neural science and other biological sciences should be thought of as searching for the fundamental capabilities that underlie all our affective capabilities. Ideally, we may be able to discover what is pancultural, and what is not; and also what is possible, and what not. An advanced science of affects would uncover the common structures and capabilities that provide the grammar of affects, and of course, we should expect the possible varieties of affects that can be constructed out of these elements to be, as in any grammar, infinite.

5

The Intentionality of the Basic Emotions

The goal of this chapter is to describe the structure of the intentionality of
the basic emotions. I will show that some of the basic emotions can be at
least two different kinds of intentional states, either concretum directed
states or propositional attitudes. This heterogenous intentionality should
be approached not, to take a typical example, as a species of the intentionality of language (or whatever underlies our ability to entertain propositional attitudes), but rather as arising from the needs of actions. In the next
chapter I will show how this heterogenous view of intentionality offers
fruitful ways to think about some concerns that arise with one kind of intentionality for inexistent objects.

I am not going to offer a theory of intentionality in this chapter, nor of the
nature of propositional attitudes; either task would be beyond the scope of
this book. Rather, I will outline the structure of the intentionality of the
basic emotions in a way that has significant implications for future research
concerning intentionality. I will assume that representations of various
complexity exist in our minds and are available for mental processes to use,
and I will explain some aspects of emotional intentionality with reference
to these.

Paying the Cognitivist Bill

This chapter and the next three chapters also have an additional purpose.
In offering an alternative to cognitivist theories of the basic emotions, I
should explain those features of the relevant emotions that cognitivism did
manage to explain. For all their faults, reductive and doxastic cognitivism,
and those theories that made use of them, provide explanations of three
important features of emotions:

1. If emotions are just beliefs or other cognitive states, then the intentionality of emotions is, if not explained, then at least shown to be
   no additional mystery. Beliefs are undeniably intentional; reducing
   emotions to beliefs and some other states could show that emotional

---

INTENTIONALITY

By *intentionality*, philosophers mean the way in which some mental states refer to, or are *about*, things which may be external to the state. Thus, if I believe that the sun is 93 million miles away, my belief is about the sun, at least inasmuch as it refers to the sun. This term "intentionality" is easily befuddling, since it seems be a form of "intention," as in volition. But the philosopher's notion of intentionality includes but is not limited to these kinds of intentions. Beliefs, fears, even perceptions are intentional. The philosopher Franz Brentano reintroduced this medieval term when he argued that intentionality is the irreducible mark of the mental; it was also Brentano who observed that one of the most important features of intentionality is that we can have the relation with nonexistent objects. One can believe in Santa Claus, or fear a robber who turns out to be the cat. Much of the work in the philosophy of mind, practiced with Brentano's maxim assumed, aims to explain intentionality; and theories of mind which aim to unify with some other sciences are usually seeking an explanation of intentionality that is either in terms of, or in some sense unified with, such sciences. (At first glance, someone unfamiliar with the problem might think that intentionality can be easily explained by internal states of the organism being causally linked to external states. However, intentional states have a normative aspect that makes any such direct explanation insufficient; see the discussion of teleofunctions in chapter 10.)

---

    intentionality just arises from the intentionality of the relevant belief.

2. Many philosophers believe that emotions can be rational, and if emotions just were a kind of judgment or belief-desire combination, then they could be rational just in the sense that these mental states can be rational.

3. Some philosophers believe that reason should motivate us, should excite passion and commitment; if emotions are granted to be motivational, but also just are judgments or beliefs and desires, then there is no separation between reason and passion.

    The affect program theory should offer an account of these features of emotions, or deny that they are needed. Fortunately, the former can readily be done, and more effectively than the cognitivist theories can. In this chapter, I will provide an overview of how the affect program theory can be used to help understand the intentionality of the basic emotions in a way that is superior to the cognitivist approach. In chapter 7, I will offer a theory of the rationality of the basic emotions, one that also makes important use of the hiearchical view of mind; and in chapter 8, I will apply this understanding practical action.

The Form of the Intentionality of the Basic Emotions

If the way we talk about emotions can be trusted, then emotions would seem to be straightforwardly intentional. One can be afraid of a dog, angry at another person, disgusted by a state of affairs as it is described in a newspaper. In each of these cases, the emotion seems to be, at least in part, "about" something external to the agent. Assuming, then, that instances of basic emotions can properly be described as intentional states, including sometimes propositional attitudes, to understand this we must first analyze this intentionality and discover its structure. A common way to proceed in such an enterprise is to observe discourse about the relevant states and assume that it is correctly reflecting the intentional structure of those states. This is a bold assumption, and if we are naturalists about emotions we must recognize that it is quite possibly false; still, it could be a good place to start, and in some instances it may well be true and so succeed in explaining the efficacy of some of our talk about these emotions. And yet, surprisingly, if we allow ourselves to consider a range of commonsense instances of talk about emotion, we will fail to find any unifying structure for the intentionality of emotions of the kind that a doxastic or reductive cognitive theory would predict.

Before I proceed, it is necessary to clarify some terminology. The term *object* in this discussion could be ambiguous, referring both to whatever thing an intentional state is directed at, or to a (potentially) concrete thing in the world. Here I will use *object* in the former sense; hence, it is a kind of logical term, and refers to whatever thing to which the intentional state is directed. I will use *concretum* to refer to a concrete object (e.g., a snake); a concretum can be either actual or imagined (that is, if someone fears the snake in the grass when there is no such snake, then the object of the fear is still a concretum). Objects therefore include not only concreta, but also events or states of affairs (that is, the referents of propositions), either real or possible or imagined.

The problem for understanding the structure of the intentionality of the basic emotions is that these affects can be talked about in ways that have them either taking a proposition or as taking a concretum term as their referential concept; that is, we can have sentences of the form *subject-term emotion-verb X*, in which the X place is filled with either a proposition or a concretum term. We readily say things like "Eric fears that the rattlesnake is in the house," but also that "Eric fears the rattlesnake." A proposition and a term are two very different grammatical kinds, and a state of affairs or event and a concretum two very different kinds of objects to which an emotion might be directed. Only in the most superficial way does the grammatical relation of subject-term emotion-verb X reveal similar mental structures in these cases.

The obvious alternative to the grammar of concretum directedness in sentences about, or expressing, basic emotions, and which appear to take concreta as their intentional objects, is to rephrase such sentences so that they take the referents of propositions as their objects. It is an implicit assumption of cognitivism about emotions that such a rephrasing actually captures the correct structure of the intentionality of the relevant emotion. We could say that "Eric is afraid of the rattlesnake" is just a way of expressing that Eric is in a fearful state, and that this instance of fear could be more revealingly described by saying "Eric is afraid that the rattlesnake will bite him" or a similar propositional attitude construction. But taking such an approach here would be quite obviously open to the criticism that it seems we are bending the method so that it fits the desired end. That is, we begin by taking language as our guide to the structure of the intentional states, but then we revise when this guide does not yield us a neat theory. This might be justifiable, however, if we had other criteria besides just our talk about emotions. Most philosophers who advocate such an approach are probably motivated to find a parsimonious theory of the logical form of emotional or other affective intentionality, and one which will fit with accounts of other features of mind. Our question, then, should be: Can all instances of basic emotions be understood as propositional attitudes? I shall argue that they cannot: some basic emotions can occur in forms where their intentionality is only sufficiently described as concretum directed.

Affects that Are Concretum Directed

We can start with some commonsense reasons for why some instances of some basic emotions and some other affects are concretum directed intentional states, as opposed to propositional attitudes. If we are at all naturalists about the basic emotions, and see them as more than just the language that is used to express them, then we can readily think of problematic cases. Suppose that Tony is mad at Eric, not for any one particular act, but for a whole long list of acts, some of which Tony may have even forgotten, others of which Tony can recall only if he takes a few minutes to actively think about it. How should we now rephrase the sentence, "Tony is angry at Eric"? The sentence will presumably be of the form "Tony is angry that P" where P contains the term "Eric" in the right kind of usage and where "P" is presumably a conjunction of all of the things that Eric did to make Tony angry: "Eric ruined his garden, and Eric scratched his car, and . . ." But it seems likely that this list could be indeterminate in that not all of these things may be available in Tony's memory for him to recall. Surely the emotion, on the propositional attitude view, must be a mental and physical state of Tony—that is, not any idealized state in which every slight, even those forgotten, are listed—so we cannot identify the emotion with this indeterminate list. We can imagine revisions that will save the analysis: we could suppose, for example, that anger is a propositional attitude and that only one proposition of the right kind is needed; then adding or deleting conjuncts would do nothing more. For a reductive or a doxastic cognitivist this would be an odd view: the very beliefs that constitute the emotion or at least are necessary causes of the emotion could be replaceable by a bunch of others, or could be added to or deleted from, and so on. In such a case, the role of the beliefs is so weak that it starts to become not some identifiable thing that constitutes or causes the anger, but some vague collection with perhaps some extremely general shared properties (slights, inappropriate behavior toward the agent, etc.). Even if we jettison reductive or doxastic cognitivism, and adopt the view that all we need is one or more such propositions, we have the obvious problem that the only thing that is shared by all these propositions—the only thing that is common to all the possible intentional contents in such a list—is the concretum Eric. So why assume that any old proposition will do, as opposed to the concretum term "Eric"? Thus, if this case is possible, it shows that the best explanation in such a case is that the basic emotion is directed at a concretum (Eric), not at some events or states of affairs.

This problem is also acute for some other emotions which I have not considered here, but which probably are basic. Love, for example, would seem to be primarily a concretum-directed state. I can say, "Tim loves that Kristy is tall," but we also say, "Tim loves Kristy." If intuitions about this emotion are to carry any weight, my own would find no plausibility in parsing "Tim loves Kristy" as a hidden propositional attitude. What would it be? That Kristy exists? That she has properties P_1 through P_n? It would seem that a more realistic alternative is to recognize that some instances of anger, love, and emotions with similar kinds of structures are not best explained as propositional attitudes. Similarly, there are also potentially basic emotions that simply do not plausibly translate into propositional attitudes in any instances. Jaak Panksepp argues that play is a basic emotion. Taking language as a guide, we might say that rat A is playing with rat B. But I can imagine no well-formed English sentence of the form "rat A plays that P."[26] Presumably this is in recognition of the fact that play is an activity, and is not a propositional attitude. If this is correct, and if play is a basic emotion, then there are basic emotions that appear never to be propositional attitudes.

Furthermore, much scientific evidence regarding some instances of basic emotions and other affects is both inconsistent with a propositional-attitude approach, and clearly is consistent with a concretum-directed approach. Consider first other affects. We saw in the mere exposure effect that people can form preferences for stimuli that they were exposed to for such short durations they have no reportable memory of the stimulus. Here affects are wholly independent of the kind of abilities that are typically taken to be necessary for the formation of a propositional attitude, which presumably at least requires the ability to form a sentence or at least a kind of mental state that can be true or false. Another example is fear conditioning. Fear conditioning is the simplest kind of fear reaction, but we have every reason to believe that it is part of the more complex kinds of fear that we can have as cognitive agents. What is of interest to us here is that fear conditioning can have as its object or objects mere stimuli (where the recognition of *mere stimuli* is understood not to require a representation in the organism that recognizes invariance, nor that recognizes the existence of the stimuli when it is not sensed; thus, representations of mere stimuli can be even weaker than those for concreta). For conditioning on mere stimuli or on concreta, there is no need for a propositional analysis, and to try to read one in would be far too much of a stretch. Besides, the conditioned response can happen far too quickly for any complex or "higher" cognitive capabilities to be involved. Fear is perhaps special among the basic emotions in that it has this very basic form, in simple fear conditioning, which is quite clearly demonstrable under laboratory conditions. Thus, I do not claim to generalize from fear conditioning to the other basic emotions and then conclude that they have forms which are directed at mere stimuli; but it does show us that this basic emotion can be directed, in its simplest form, at mere stimuli, thus requiring a much weaker instance of representation than a propositional attitude.

With the basic emotions in other, presumably more complex, occurrences, other considerations include some of the criticisms of cognitivism rallied in chapter 2; these are also equivalently criticisms of the view that the intentionality of the basic emotions is best explained by way of construing them as propositional attitudes. First, there is the issue of direct stimulation of subcortical systems leading to emotions; and, essentially related to this, neuroanatomical evidence revealing that some basic emotions seem to be enabled by subcortical structures or at least by structures that can operate potentially independently of structures enabling language. If one believes that the abilities necessary for being able to have propositional attitudes are primarily located in neocortical structures for linguistic abilities, then these results show that basic emotions need not be propositional attitudes. Another issue is homology: unless we assume that non-human animals that have basic emotions also have beliefs and other propositional attitudes, then that we share these affective abilities, but not the relevant cognitive abilities, with other organisms shows that the affective abilities are not essentially cognitive and so not essentially propositional attitudes. And, unless we begin developing the abilities that enable propositional attitudes at a very early age, which seems wholly unlikely, then we develop affective abilities before the relevant cognitive abilities.

Furthermore, attributing propositional attitudes to an emotion is often superfluous for explaining the relevant behavior. If a rat flees a cat (and perhaps also displays other fearful behaviors in so doing), we can describe the rat with propositional attitudes: the rat believed that the cat was going to kill it, the rat desired that it not be killed, etc. But we can also posit that the rat fears the cat, and flees it: the only representational states it needs are those sufficient to recognize the cat, and track it in order to flee it (and, of course, those necessary for normal flight and other required motor functions). This latter account of the rat's mental state is preferable in its parsimony. After all the rat's fear need only be directed at the cat. Nothing else is needed to explain the flight. Also, it is interesting to note that rats do not need to learn to fear a cat (a rat never exposed to a cat can be afraid merely at smelling cat urine); so it would seem that this is a stimulus- or concretum-elicited state, unless one is willing to posit innate propositional attitudes (which seem to me problematic for lack of parsimony, and also because such states would fail to act as many propositional-attitude based theories require their propositional attitudes to be—e.g., revisable on evidence).

Finally, and perhaps most important, there are going to be instances of basic emotions—even of basic emotions which can appear in sentences as propositional attitudes—which we can describe as concretum directed intentional states and for which no gloss into a propositional attitude is going to be able to capture the same content. The obvious example here is phobic fears. In chapter 1, I reviewed some evidence that some of us inherit a fear of, or a predisposition to fear, certain stimuli such as snakes or spiders (just as rats appear to inherit their fear of cats). If this is correct, and perhaps even if it is not, then it could be that Eric is afraid of the snake even if Eric *knows* that the snake is not venomous, that it will not bite him, and so on. That is, there may be fear of a concretum for which there is no appropriate kind of believed sentence. And, it seems to me appropriate here to make an appeal to phenomenology (although I grant that in this context it is an untrustworthy guide): fear of a snake *per se* really is fear of the snake, and not reducible to fear that the snake may be venomous, that it may bite me, and so forth.

Given that some instances of basic emotions are irreducibly concretum-directed intentional states, does this mean that we should explain all of the basic emotions as such, and therefore translate propositional attitude constructions using basic emotions over into concretum-directed accounts? I do not believe so.

The Basic Emotions as Propositional Attitudes

As I have already observed, we also use sentences that describe basic emotions as being propositional attitudes. Examples could include:

Tony is angry that the Republicans gained control of the House.

Adam is afraid that he will flunk the exam.

Karen is sad that Steve died.

Tim is joyful at the birth of his daughter.[27]

What is of interest about all of these sentences is that, although there can be concretum terms that are constituents of the relevant propositions, I can see no way in which we could reliably translate these sentences into equivalent-seeming instances of concretum-directed intentional states. The reason is that, assuming that these sentences are reliably revealing the appropriate structure of the intentional state, these emotions are directed at events or states of affairs (I will assume that states of affairs are synchronic slices of events). Events or states of affairs are the referents of propositions, just as concreta are the referents of concretum terms.

Thus, if Tony is angry that the Republicans won the House, he may indeed be angry at the Republicans representatives, at campaign contributors, at voters, and others. But this does not capture what the anger is about—someone can be angry at the Republican representatives and all these others and also not be angry that the Republicans won the House. The actual object of the basic emotion is the event of their victory. Similarly, if Adam fears that he will flunk the exam, he may also fear the exam. This is a bit unclear: "exam" would appear to refer to the event of taking the exam, and not the actual paper concretum—and if this is correct, then there is no concretum term in the proposition that he will flunk the exam. But even skipping over this, we have again that someone could fear an exam and not fear flunking it; and if we accept this, then there is something therefore additional to the propositional attitude besides just the concretum term. And both joy and sadness, if they are basic emotions or otherwise even just affects of a scientifically legitimate form, appear to be concerned with events alone. There seems to be no sense, just as there is nothing well formed in the English of the expressions, in the idea of "Karen is sad x" or "Tim is joyful y" where x and y are concretum terms. Thus, some of the basic emotions, and perhaps other affects, can be irreducibly propositional attitudes—including some of the same basic emotions, and other affects, that can be concretum-directed intentional states.

Heterogenous Intentionality and the Hierarchical View of Mind

Given that at least two structures or forms of intentionality are possible for some affects, including some basic emotions, does this mean that two kinds of affects are involved, one for each case? If we were to answer all our questions about mind starting with an examination of intentional structure, we would answer affirmatively to this question. But we can instead make sense of the notion that one kind of affect appears in both cases, a kind susceptible to varying degrees of representational complexity. Two considerations direct us toward this approach.

First, it is reasonable to conclude that for some of the basic emotions, the concretum-directed intentional form is the more fundamental form. I have shown that fear and anger, for example, can occur in a form that is a concretum-directed intentional state, and they can occur as propositional attitudes. But I have argued, on grounds of homology, that other organisms can have anger and fear, but lack the abilities needed for having propositional attitudes. The occurrence of the emotion as a propositional attitude would therefore be an additional capability that we have as a result of our special cognitive skills. This position is consistent with the view that the basic emotions reveal a hierarchical structure in which the necessary and sufficient capabilities that constitute these affects are subcognitive, perhaps largely subcortical, structures that have homologs in closely related species; and that the capability to entertain propositional attitudes, can, but need not, play a role in the affect. (A related potential hypothesis, worthy of some exploration, is whether affects that appear to only take events or states of affairs as their objects—as sadness or joy may only do—are therefore not had by relatively simpler organisms which can be reasonably said not to be capable of representing events or states of affairs.)

The second consideration is that a compelling account is possible of how some basic emotions and other affects can be both concretum-directed and propositional attitudes. This is an account based upon the important role that action plays in the basic emotions.

Basic Emotions as Actions

The affect program theory already predicts that basic emotions must be intentional in one special way: they are sources of actions. Some basic emotions, and perhaps other affects, are in part constituted by and evolved from stereotypical actions: in the syndrome of some basic emotions is an action program. And if any basic emotion lacks such an action program, it can at least be said that in the syndrome of that emotion there is a change in motivation of some kind, tantamount to an essential relation to action. This suggests a fruitful way to understand the intentionality of the basic emotions, a single unifying analysis that captures not only their directedness toward concreta, but ultimately also to events and states of affairs. The form of the intentionality of the basic emotions is foremost a representational state sufficient to guide the action of the basic emotion; the basic emotions, and perhaps some other affects, are *action-directing* intentional states.

Being an action-directing intentional state means that the representational nature of the basic emotion needs to be sufficient to allow for the function of the relevant associated action. Of course, all mental states can be action directing; but we can apply Ockham's razor and assume that the kind of representation utilized by the affect is minimal or nearly minimal to guide the target kind of action.[28] Using this approach, we can see how, and why, some kinds of affects can be both concretum-directed intentional states and also propositional attitudes. Each kind of intentional structure would be useful for serving some kinds of actions.

Why Action-Directing Intentional States Can Be Concretum Directed

If Eric fears the snake, and acts upon the action program to flee the snake, the action program must be properly related to the snake in order for the action to be possible. Specifically, in order for the flight to be successful, the snake must be located, identified, and properly tracked. It will not be a case of flight from a snake if one runs toward it, or runs in circles around it, or runs away from another object. To be flight from that snake, Eric must move away from the snake, because of his locating and "tracking" the snake. He will also have to "understand" that the snake persists even if it is out of sight, such as if it slithers under the couch. Similarly, suppose that Tim's anger at a rabid dog leads him to attack it. An attack on the rabid dog must be actually at the rabid dog, which requires him to recognize and track it. Going into the house to get his gun requires him to "understand" that the dog still exists there when he turns away.

Thus, consistent with the hierarchical view of mind, some action programs can operate successfully merely drawing upon a representation of the target concretum or concreta. I take it to be a reasonable assumption that such a representation need not be a propositional attitude; that is, prima facie, this representational nature is characterized in a way sufficiently weak to distinguish it from the kinds of representations that are propositional attitudes. But I can make some comments in this regard to help establish this point. There are two aspects to such an intentional state. There must be a representational context or subsystem for controlling the relevant action in relation to the concretum or concreta, and some kind of representation of the concretum.

The former representations need not be of a kind that utilizes propositional attitudes. As noted before, I do not want to have to commit here to a theory of propositional attitudes, but we can observe that for most theories of such attitudes, they must be articulate (composed of representations), and they must be the kind of thing which is true or false and can play a role in inference. Representations in a system that controls action need not be articulate, and therefore they need not even be symbolic, since by definition a symbol is a discrete entity that plays a role in a combinatorial (that is, syntactic) system. Much of the work in motor control research in artificial intelligence (for review see Jordan and Rosenbaum 1989), for example, is or can be instantiated in connectionist networks that have continuous internal states. These magnitudes may represent the relevant states of the organism (such as the position of an arm, the degrees of freedom of that arm, etc.), or they may represent a goal state. But to serve to control action, such states do not need to be digitized or to be utilized by a symbolic system. Nor do they need to play a role in a system in which they are taken to be true or false claims about the relevant states involved. This is not to deny that such representations may be taken as elements in an articulated symbolic system (I believe that they can be), or that they may not play a role in the constitution of a propositional attitude, but rather to deny that their appropriate function requires the necessary features to be the kind of representations that constitute propositional attitudes.

For basic emotional actions to be guided by concreta that they target, there must also be a representation of the concretum that is the object. For simple affects, such as very simplistic fear conditioning, action will not need the posit of a concretum, and a mere stimulus will suffice to get the desired result. However, for most relational actions that typify basic emotions, such as attacking or fleeing, the representation will have to be of sufficient power to be a representation of a concretum. Such a representation must satisfy two criteria. First, it needs to be capable of recognizing a concretum invariantly—that is, from different perspectives, from partial observations, and so on—and this distinguishes it from a state sufficient only to recognize a mere stimulus. Second, it must allow the organism to act in such a way that it exploits the continued existence of the concretum when it is out of sensory range. Even if the representation that allows an organism to exploit the permanence of a concretum is of a sufficiently complex nature that it can be understood to be a symbol, we do not need to suppose that it requires or relies upon the ability to entertain propositional attitudes.[29] That is, a representation of a concretum might be taken up in a representational system as a constituent of a propositional attitude. But, in itself, it need not be the kind of thing that can be true or false or that itself can guide inferences based on truth value. This is consistent with the fact that nonhuman organisms that lack language, and appear to have very limited cognitive abilities of the kind that we presume go with propositional attitudes (such as the ability to draw inferences, and the abilities constituting standard notions of rationality), can clearly have such representations, since they can exploit that the concretum persists when out of sensory range. A wolf chasing prey may not stop when the prey is out of view because it runs behind some bushes; a deer fleeing a predator may not stop when the predator is momentarily behind a tree. Thus, the ability to have such representations does not require the abilities to entertain propositional attitudes. The fundamental intentionality of the concretum directed basic emotions is not propositional, and perhaps not even symbolic.

In sum, then, some of the basic emotions are, at their more basic level of complexity, concretum-directed intentional states. Representations of sufficient complexity to track objects are more sophisticated than mere reactions to stimuli primarily in that the object of the representation is recognized invariantly, and is taken to exist even when not observed.

The Utility of Action-Directing Intentional States that Are Propositional Attitudes

Basic emotions, and some other affects which might be concretum-directed intentional states, can also be described as propositional attitudes. I have observed that this can be irreducible: an event or state of affairs, and not just any concreta in that event or state of affairs, may be the object of the affect. It is useful to clarify the utility of such a state because we can thereby clarify how propositional attitudes can add something new to the system. This is not an argument that emotions are sometimes propositional attitudes; but it is necessary for, and makes more plausible, any hypotheses that they do so function or that evolutionary pressures selected for this ability.

The important consideration is that if we grant some likely claims about the appropriate function of some affects, we can readily see how they could better serve that function were they able to extend their range of objects to include events and states of affairs. Let us grant, for example, that fear serves to motivate an organism to avoid potential threats. If a rat is afraid of and flees a cat, this requires only that the fear be a concretum-directed intentional state. However, there are other threats that an organism may face, including events and states of affairs. If Adam very much values his academic career and believes that he may flunk an exam crucial to it, the event of the exam is a kind of threat to him. The ability to have events as intentional objects therefore can allow a useful generalization of this basic emotion; useful because it continues to fulfill its function, but now with a new kind of object and so in relation to a larger class of potential threats. Similar considerations can be drawn out for anger and other basic emotions. It may be useful to be angry at a rival for one's mate since one is motivated to attack and thereby discourage the rival. Let us grant that such emotional behavior serves to better or at least preserve the status of the organism. But it may be equally beneficial to be angry about an event, such as the exercise of a rule that one considers unjust. In such a case, one may be motivated to protest the situation. Here again, this could be a powerful extension of a useful behavior, generalizing it to a whole new order of cases, and so extending the utility of the basic emotion. I can state this as a hypothesis: The capability of being a propositional attitude makes a basic emotion more useful to the organism by allowing the application of the relevant emotional action to a new class of relevant kinds of objects.[30] (A natural corollary hypothesis is that this ability was selected for because of this utility.)

Some Final Considerations

An interesting issue arises concerning the degree to which a basic emotion might have both concreta and events as objects. It seems that such a thing is indeed possible and that, therefore, we ought to be able to show such differentiation in experiments. Consider again two sentences, which we can take to be attributions of Eric's mental state:

1. Eric is afraid of the snake.
2. Eric is afraid that the snake will bite him.

A description of an emotion as a propositional attitude is most obviously correct when the relevant entertained proposition is posed as a cause of the emotion. Thus, if the belief that the rattlesnake might give him a venomous bite can be taken to be the genuine cause of Eric's emotion, we quite clearly have a case of an emotion as a propositional attitude. The belief would most obviously be the primary or complete cause if, for example, Eric has no fear of snakes, and thus he had no fear of rattlesnakes until he was told that they can deliver a life-threatening venomous bite. In such a case, (2) is a straight-forward and correct description of the situation. It could be, however, that Eric has a terrible fear of snakes—perhaps even in a seemingly innate way—and his fear of the rattlesnake is much greater because he believes that the rattlesnake might deliver a venomous bit to him. In such a case, the propo-sition that the rattlesnake might give (Eric) a venomous bite is unnecessary for (1) to be true of him; (2) would be true, but the proposition would be only a partial cause. In the case of a proposition being a genuine cause, either complete or partial, it is legitimate to describe the emotion as a prop-ositional attitude.

These considerations remind us that there can be a dissociation between cognitive and subcognitive elicitors for a basic emotion. For example, one might fail to fear something that one "knows" that one should (having a cognitive reason to believe the thing is dangerous, but no subcognitive fear, or maybe even a subcognitive attraction); or one might fear something that one "knows" one shouldn't fear. Recognizing this possibility for the basic emotions can explain much (e.g., some important instances of akratic be-havior).

Helen Nissenbaum has criticized the view that emotions are object di-rected (including what we are calling here "concretum directed"). She notes that a host of different phrases can be used to describe emotions and other affective states, such as:

1. Frank loves Susan.
2. Meryl loathes her boss.
3. Paul regrets having refused to invest in Apple Computers.
4. David is dreading seeing his ex-wife.
5. Hannah is angry that she was not invited to the party.
6. Selwyn was delighted with the kitten.
7. Clive was distressed over the financial losses of his business.
8. John fears a nuclear war.
9. Stephen is ashamed of the way he treated the beggar. (1985, 3)

This is a very diverse list of attitudes and kinds of objects, and yet no one sentence here seems unusual. Nissenbaum claims that a group of very dif-ferent kinds of phenomena are being revealed in these sentences, and also that very different kinds of things are assumed to be "object directedness" by the theories that take this as an essential feature of emotion. Her conclu-sion is that the notion of being object directed is too muddled to be worth retaining. Nissenbaum can be read as arguing that there is no one notion of object directedness, and so her conclusions are consistent with the obser-vation that basic emotions can be both concretum directed and proposi-tional attitudes. But it is also useful to note that the theory of the intention-ality of the basic emotions outlined here escapes the astute criticisms that she raises.

Nissenbaum rejects that any theory of the object directedness of emotions covers all of the relevant kinds of emotion instances; she makes this argument largely by a consideration of cases, criticizing previous theories about object directedness in emotions. However, three features of this argument make it inapplicable to the idea of action-directing states. First, Nissenbaum begins with a commonsense notion of "emotion," and so her list of sentences of standard emotions includes things that I am not here claiming are basic emotions (e.g., regret, shame). Thus, her conclusions, given in answer to a theory of the intentionality of all of these states, need not necessarily apply to basic emotions alone. Given that I have argued that there is unlikely to be a scientifically legitimate notion of emotion per se, I consider it unlikely we will ever have a theory of the intentionality of emotion per se. Second, she holds that different notions of object directedness have been used in the literature on emotion, including a relation to an object, standard notions of intentionality, satisfying the way we talk about emotions, or just using object directedness as a way to explain emotional behavior. This is a diverse list of things, and she argues that "any theory that would attempt to cover the full intuitive notion [of object directedness] and therefore incorporate all four conditions would be incoherent" (1985, 12). But this is not so. Understanding the basic emotion as (in part) an action program satisfies to some degree all of these notions. The emotion is related to the object since the object is the target of the action (be it concretum or event); this requires that the guiding referential concept be an intentional state; it satisfies many (but not all) of the ways we talk about emotions; and it explains much about the behavior (Tim's anger is directed at the dog and this explains why Tim shoots the dog). Third, Nissenbaum reveals that many previous theories of object directedness are inadequate. These theories often include very different notions of object directedness—such as cause, necessary relatum, an abstract intentional object, and so on—and as a result they often suffer from fatal confusions. But in arguing by a consideration of cases, she has not established that these theories exhaust all the possible kinds of theories; and, in fact, they do not. Past theories of object directedness[31] have failed largely because of vague and conflicting notions of object directedness that attempt to cover too many kinds of intentional states. But by limiting our scope to basic emotions, and to what is required for the relational actions of these, we escape the confusions that such mixtures of notions can cause.

Conclusion: Implications for the Study of Intentionality

I have given an analysis of the form of the intentionality of the basic emotions which accounts for the different ways we describe them in common sentences. Some of these emotions, and other affects, can be described as taking both concreta and events or states of affairs as their objects. Some reflection upon the described cases suggests that some of them are irreducible to the others. The hierarchical view of mind solves this problem: some kinds of affects have a heterogenous intentionality. The representational demands of controlling relational actions defines the necessary representational requirements for the basic emotions. They are fundamentally concretum-directed states, and in many instances are only such states. However, the ability to entertain propositional attitudes extends the functionality of the relevant basic emotions, allowing relational actions to events or states of affairs. In such cases, affects can be irreducibly propositional attitudes. (With a developed theory of intentionality, one might be able to draw even more careful delimitations of the heterogenous intentionality of the basic emotions. Thus, to contrast concretum-directed intentional states with propositional attitudes may be to draw attention to two points in a hierarchy of other representational kinds. For my purposes here, it is sufficient to have made just this distinction, but we can remain open to the possibility of others.)

The heterogenous intentionality of the basic emotions and other affects reveals that a theory of intentionality must allow for both linguistic and nonlinguistic (i.e., subcognitive) intentionality. That is, something like a representational theory of intentionality will be necessary; and theories that do not allow for nonlinguistic intentionality are inadequate. Thus, views like the one that Richard Rorty attributes to Wilfrid Sellars, and which Rorty endorses, are untenable: "As Sellars sees it, if you can explain how the social practices we call 'using language' came into existence, you have already explained all that needs to be explained about the relation between mind and world" (Rorty 1997, 7–8). If I understand this correctly, all intentionality is taken to be parasitic upon the intentionality of language. This view is so alien to all of the best work being done in the sciences of mind that it is nothing less than absurd. Any attempt to defend such a view by arguing that what is subcognitive just doesn't measure up to being mental (usually on grounds that the mental is concerned with inference or normatively constrained beliefs, or some other arbitrary special human skill) would be defeated not just because it would present a parody of the complexity of the subcognitive, but also because the subcognitive and the cognitive influence each other in important ways that can have measurable symptoms and which are amenable to a functional (and, in some cases, type-reductive) description. A theory of intentionality must explain this, in part by allowing for the heterogenous intentionality of some emotions.

6

Emoting for Fictions

In the last chapter I introduced a theory of the structure of the intentionality of basic emotions. I argued that some of them are fundamentally concretum-directed states, but that they can also be propositional attitudes. In this chapter, I will consider issues at the intersection of aesthetics and the philosophy of mind, questions concerned with our ability to emote for events and concreta that are depicted in fictions (I will use the term "fiction" to refer to any work which is understood to refer to unreal events; hence, I include stage dramas, novels, and films). I hope to accomplish three tasks. First, this is a problem that will help flesh out some of the details of heterogenous intentionality. Second, the heterogenous intentionality of basic emotions can help explain two outstanding problems at this intersection, which I call *the problem of reports,* and *the problem of narrative demand.* Third, our ability to emote for fictions is inconsistent with cognitivism about emotions, and so reviewing these issues provides another powerful argument against cognitivism and related views of mind.

There are other things to be observed in our exploration of this issue. A naturalist view of emotions like the affect program theory suffers from the prejudice that it will fail to adequately account for what matters in our emotional lives. How could a theory of emotions that claims that the relevant emotions are pancultural, inheritable, and fundamentally biological phenomena, shared by other kinds of animals, do justice to our experience of emotions, or their important role in a moral life, or to the aesthetic aspects of life? I showed in chapter 3 that one influential irrealist theory of mind, interpretationism, fails to explain quite unremarkable emotional behavior. In this chapter, I can show that reductive or doxastic cognitivism fail to adequately explain—often fails to even allow for the possibility of—something so human as our ability to emote for fictions.

Many of the issues that I raise in this chapter shall ultimately be decided by empirical research. However, there is much that can be clarified by a philosophical analysis, given what we already know. Also, some very plausible hypotheses can be made to explain some aspects of emoting for fictions, and these hypotheses are suggestively consistent with some of the other views developed in this book. Thus, in this chapter I stray a bit from what is known, to indulge in some (what I hope are useful and plausible) hypotheses concerning these abilities.

Emoting for Fictions and Cognitivism

I showed a number of objections in chapter 2 to doxastic cognitivism and to reductive cognitivism, some relying upon scientific results. But there are things commonly observed and experienced by all of us that entail very obvious objections to these theories. One of the most interesting of these is music. Music need not be about anything to generate affects; we hear a particular melody and, as if entrained to the dynamic of the flow, our affective state can change. There is no plausible way for a reductive or doxastic cognitive theory to cohere with this possibility: no beliefs are required, it is unclear in what sense any complex cognitions, such as other propositional attitudes, could be required. If music can generate emotions, then these kinds of cognitive theories are simply false.[32] This alone is a compelling mystery that is, more often than not, ignored by cognitivists. But in this chapter I will be concerned with another anomaly: that we emote for the concreta or the events portrayed in fictions. If a basic emotion were to require, or were in part even constituted by, a particular kind of belief, then how can it be that we frequently have that emotion for situations in which we explicitly understand that the relevant proposition is false? Typically, for doxastic cognitivism and related kinds of reductive cognitivism, for someone to be angry, she must believe that someone has been wronged; to feel sad, she must believe that someone has suffered some loss; to feel fear, she must believe that something of value is in danger. The problem for emoting for fictions, therefore, is that we have (what some will say only appear to be) emotions for fictional characters and situations. If Karen is angry that King Lear's daughters are cruel to him, and Karen is sad for the king, then on the reductive or doxastic cognitivist theory of emotions she must believe that King Lear's daughters are being cruel to the king and that the king is suffering as a result. But Karen knows that *King Lear* is just a play, that she is sitting in the theater, that John Gielgud is an actor and not a king, that he does not suffer (at least not in any direct, morally culpable way) the harms being portrayed. Presumably she also does not believe that King Lear was an actual person. So what exactly is happening when she frowns, and turns red, or even when tears come to her eyes? As Bijoy Boruah has put it: "Why is it that the sadness, which is defined in real-life contexts by reference to an appropriate belief about the sad object, recurs in a context that excludes the rational possibility of forming the appropriate belief?" (1988, 83). On pain of contradiction, some presupposition must be rejected—either the claim that Karen is having an emotion, or the claim that Karen does not believe that King Lear exists, or the assumption that the appropriate kind of belief is necessary for the emotion.

Attempts to Save Cognitivism

A host of solutions to this puzzle have been proposed. The majority of these solutions struggle to retain a cognitive theory of emotion intact. Here are five of the leading offerings:

1. *We are irrational.* Colin Radford, whose 1975 paper "How Can We Be Moved by the Fate of Anna Karenina?" may be the origin of the contemporary debate, poses the emoting for fictions problem in the following way: Suppose a man tells us a harrowing story about his sister, and we are harrowed. But then, after completing the story and allowing it to have its effect, the man tells us that he made the whole thing up. Radford suggests that we would be relieved, and not harrowed (although we might have other emotions in addition to relief, like embarrassment or anger that we were deceived). He suggests the same is true for all these kinds of cases: if we believed P and had an appropriate kind of emotion for and because of P; then upon learning P was false we would normally stop having the emotion. These cases, Radford believes, are like our emoting for fictions in that we would feel the same kind of emotions were the fiction true and we were witnessing it or heard a report of it, but with the odd additional fact that we know the fictional situation is false, and the emotion does not end because of this. (In fact, the situations are perhaps not analogous: I return to this point below.) We might suppose that two narratives were told, both of them identical, but that in the one case we are led to believe that the narrative is a true account—let us call this kind of narrative a *report*—and therefore has an implicit claim to being true, and in the other we are told the narrative is a fiction. In the case of reports, Radford claims, we would find the emotion we experience defused when the relevant beliefs were defeated. (I will call the claim that we emote more strongly for believed than for disbelieved contents, and the consequent issue of explaining this, *the problem of reports.* I discuss it at more length below.) In the case of fictions, however, we ostensibly do not believe the content from the beginning. But if we fix the relevant background desires in the two cases,[33] it would seem that the cases could have the same contents and be thus relevantly the same. Why do we then have the emotion in the case of the fiction? Why does the disbelief not rule out, or at least impair, the emotions in the case of fictions as it supposedly does in the case of a report?

Radford implicitly argues for at least doxastic cognitivism by generalizing from examples of reports, where it may seem plausible that the defeat of the relevant belief would defuse the emotion. However, he could just as easily have rejected doxastic cognitivism by generalizing from the cases of emoting for fictions. Given that he takes the report case as primary, then he must explain what is different in the fiction case. Radford's solution is that we simply are inconsistent when emoting for fictions; he solves the puzzle of emoting for fiction by holding that we do believe in the relevant content of the fiction, and since by supposition we disbelieve it, then we are inconsistent. For example, Karen is inconsistent because she both believes that King Lear does not suffer (because she believes he does not exist) and believes that King Lear does suffer (evidenced by her emotional reaction).

But it is not clear how this "inconsistency and . . . incoherence" (1975, 78) plays itself out in Karen or any other emoter for a fiction except in that they emote for the fiction. Karen might be an impeccably rational person in all other matters, a logician by trade, continent and calm. In what sense is she prone to inconsistency and incoherence except in this case of the emoting for fictions? Inconsistency is posited only for the purpose of saving an implicit cognitivist theory of emotions. As Radford himself reminds us when drawing out the differences between emoting for fictions and for believed reports, we do not charge up onto the stage to beat (the actor playing) Goneril or warn (the actor playing) Gloucester. Thus, according to him, we are inconsistent, and act as if we believe Lear suffers in as much as we have the emotion, but we show no signs of this inconsistency aside from the emotion. We don't make false claims, we don't behave otherwise as if Lear exists, and so on.

2. *The "emotion" for the fiction is not a genuine emotion.* Kendall Walton has described vividly the puzzle of emoting for fictions:

> Charles is watching a horror movie about a terrible green slime. He cringes in his seat as the slime oozes slowly but relentlessly over the earth destroying everything in its path. Soon a greasy head emerges from the undulating mass, and two beady eyes roll around, finally fixing on the camera. The slime, picking up speed, oozes on a new course straight toward the viewers. Charles emits a shriek and clutches desperately at his chair. Afterwards, still shaken, Charles confesses that he was "terrified" of the slime. *Was* he? (1978, 5)

Walton complicates the usual puzzle by supposing that Charles fears for himself. This is a very different situation from having care for King Lear or fearing for Gloucester. It is not impossible, or even improbable, that Charles might so fear for himself (although the description is a bit unrealistic in its histrionics). However, so as to keep our focus on the puzzle, I shall reconstrue the case for now to be that Charles fears for the protagonist of the film; it shall otherwise be relevantly the same.

By supposition Charles never believes the slime is real. He also has such physiological features of fear that—setting aside any physiological changes distinguishing believing that P and not believing that P—it seems that Charles's physiological state is going to be indistinguishable (along all the relevant measures) from the kind of state he would be in if he feared *and* believed in the slime. But Walton insists that Charles's affective state is not actually fear, but rather is "quasi fear." Quasi fear is distinguished from real fear because in the cases of quasi fear the subject is only make believing that the relevant situation is actual. Walton has a theory of make-believe behavior, but for our purposes here the relevant distinction is merely that Charles by supposition does not believe the relevant propositions that Walton supposes are required for his fear (that the slime exists, that the protagonist is in danger, etc.). But since the physiology of the state of fear and quasi fear are relevantly similar, it seems that we have here two affective states, of identical kinds except that, for the one state, belief can be ascribed to the subject, and, in the other, the relevant proposition is entertained but not believed. Of course, Charles does not flee the theater, so his behavior is not indicative of the most extreme kinds of fear. But Charles might also fear great heights, rightly know that they can kill him should he fall, and still walk along a precipice because he does not want to appear a coward. In such a case, Charles certainly is feeling real fear, even though he does not flee the precipice. Walton has not established that emotions for fictions are not like suppressed emotions or emotions which otherwise result in no action. The only difference that he uses to justify calling the one emotion a quasi emotion is the lack of belief in the content.

What is at issue for Walton seems to be taxonomy, rather than some substantive point: a way of dividing emotions into two classes, distinguished only by their relation to their contents (or, more accurately, the agent's other relations to the content). Cognitivism would be saved because it would turn out to apply only to those emotions that have believed content, and not those "quasi" emotions which do not—in other words, doxastic cognitivism would be not a theory of emotion but a way of classifying emotions. But Walton denies that this is what he is doing. "The issue is not just one of fidelity to a deeply ingrained pretheoretical conception of fear," he argues. "The perspicuity of our understanding of human nature is at stake" (1990, 202). So that if we are to assimilate different instances of affective states that are fearlike together, including states of fearing for fiction, and being afraid of a genuine danger, and so on, we will "emphasize superficial similarities at the expense of fundamental differences" (202). However, it is hard to see how we can call the differences in belief fundamental, and label "superficial" the many physiological and behavioral features that he seems to allow by presupposition are relevantly identical. The question is begged in favor of doxastic cognitivism.

Thus, Walton's claim that our emoting for fictions is mere quasi emoting is at best a taxonomic move. But there is little reason to accept this standard of two different categories of emotion. Our normal discourse does not use this distinction. What is special about emotions—what separates cognitive emotions from other propositional attitudes, for example—seems to be present in both the case of emoting for a report and emoting for a fiction; after all, Walton calls them both "emotions." More important, Walton's move does not solve the real puzzle: even if we accepted his terminology, it still remains true that we have these affective states, the "quasi emotions," for fictional contents, and we might very well be puzzled by that and wonder how it is possible.

3. *We emote that these kinds of things actually happen.* Michael Weston, writing in reply to Colin Radford, has given a subtle account of emoting for fiction, accepting that these are genuine emotions, and rejecting that we are irrational when we so emote (1975). Weston argues that what actually happens when we emote for fiction is that we both emote for the content of the fiction inasmuch as we recognize that such things do or can happen in our own actual world, and that this recognition requires that, or is successful to the degree that, the plot of the fiction develops the interconnections which give to the relevant fictional situation its plausibility and meaning.

Weston is one of the few in this debate who has drawn attention to the very important issue that fictions for which we emote have narrative structure. For example, we feel no pity if told the following story: "King Lear was a king who suffered terribly from two ungrateful and wicked daughters." The focus upon what is false in fiction can convey the sense, however, that it is for, or because of, key propositions like this that we seem to emote. I will return to this insight below, where I will call the issue of explaining this *the problem of narrative demand:* that the degree of our affective reaction to a fiction is dependent upon some narrative skill.

However, although there is surely some connection between our emoting for the fiction and our understanding that some of these situations can occur in the real world, this solution is itself inadequate. For, as Robert Yanal has observed (1994, 56), I might get frightened at a vampire film, or be angry at the dragon denizen of a fantastic world in a novel, knowing very well that there are no things like vampires or dragons. Weston might well respond that something like what happens when the vampire or dragon attacks happens under other situations—such as in murder and forest fires. But this would have two flaws. It seems that it is in part the unique, essential features of these creatures that I emote for, and not bloodletting or fire in the abstract (Yanal 1994, 58). Furthermore, weakened enough in this way, the theory would start to be far too vague to be viable: pressed to the extreme by using a long list of fantastic, nonexistent objects—like vampires or dragons—we would ultimately have the object of fear being the fearful, the object of anger being the infuriating, and so on.

Finally, there are situations for which we emote which simply *cannot* occur.

4. *We emote for a possible world or for counterfactual situations.* Some scholars have suggested that the way to understand fictional discourse is as discourse about possible worlds. One might presume, therefore, that the case of emoting for fiction is quite simple: the puzzle is solved by qualifying the supposition that we don't believe in the relevant content in the fiction. Instead, we do believe it, we just believe it is true of another possible world, not our own.

This is the most easily refuted of solutions to the emoting for fictions problem. There are many fictions which describe impossible situations. Examples include Italo Calvino's "Tutto in un punto" ("All in a point")

(Calvino 1993), which dramatizes the crowded conditions at the beginning of the universe, when all living beings exist in one point. The geometries described (e.g., people getting into each-other's way) are logically impossible. Certainly we can have emotional reactions for these or other impossible, or impossibly situated, characters; and it follows that in such a case we cannot be emoting for a possible world.

5. *Reject cognitivism about emotions.* The four proposals above attempt to save doxastic or reductive cognitivism; they appear to be motivated by the assumption that cognitivism is true. But another solution to the problem is to reject cognitivism's belief condition and therefore to reject doxastic cognitivism and the relevant kinds of reductive cognitivism. Several philosophers have suggested this approach, including Roger Scruton (1974), Peter Lamarque (1981), and Robert Yanal (1994). Here I will consider the two more recent views.

Yanal proposes what he calls "realism," which is characterized by rejecting the proposition that "we feel emotions towards characters and situations only when we believe them to be real and not fictional" (1994, 69). The puzzle for Yanal then becomes something more subtle: what distinguishes our emotions for fictions from our emotions for reports and actual observed or experienced situations? Yanal suggests that our knowledge that the fiction is a fiction does it: these emotions are incapable of consummation or proper expression. We cannot treat the fictional character, or react to the fictional event, in the way we can treat or react to actual ones. Thus:

> Walton thinks pity, anger, or love towards fictions less than real, mere quasi feelings. But I think that what we have is real pity that must be kept to oneself, real anger that is forever ineffectual, real love that is never to be returned. There is a sort of pathos that often permeates emotion towards fiction, a kind of pensive nostalgia, bordering sometimes on the melancholy, sometimes on the bittersweet—exactly the sort of pathos one expects to find with passions incapable of consummation. (74)

This insight might still leave us wanting for a more elaborate account of what kind of thing the fictional object of the emotions is. Lamarque has gone some steps in this direction by suggesting that fictional propositions are like Fregean thoughts: "Fictional characters enter our world in the mundane guise of descriptions . . . and become the objects of our emotional responses as mental representations or, as I shall call them, thought-contents characterized by those descriptions" (1981, 293). Lamarque then distinguishes between emoting *by,* which applies to the real object of the emotion, and emoting *of,* which applies to the intentional content of the emotion. Being frightened by a tiger requires that the tiger exist; but being frightened of a tiger, Lamarque claims, does not require that the tiger exist. And, in the case of fictions, the intentional content becomes the real object,

---

GOTTLOB FREGE

Gottlob Frege (1848–1925) was a mathematician and philosopher. In addition to inventing much of modern logic, Frege offered careful analyses of concepts, reference, and meaning. His distinction between sense and reference—in more contemporary terms, between meaning and reference—is an important staple of any consideration of reference. By "thoughts," Frege means something like our notion of a proposition: a thought is the meaning of a complete sentence.

---

and we are frightened by the mere thought that is evoked by the fiction. Thus, he holds—as Frege did—that reference in fiction is indirect reference: it is reference to sense.

I believe that Lamarque's approach is essentially correct in that it holds that the content of the propositions of fiction, and not the usual referents, is that for which we emote in these cases. However, a general endorsement of a Fregean position will leave a number of outstanding problems. First, if we take it that fiction actually is indirect reference, then there is a formal problem with the not uncommon kind of fiction where stories are told within stories. Second, merely observing that we emote for the fictional content does not explain why the features of good storytelling are requisite for emotions to occur.

A Naturalist Explanation

We have seen that rather pedestrian examples of emotions provide strong counterexamples to doxastic cognitivism and to some forms of reductive cognitivism: we can emote for a fictional situation when we fail to have the beliefs that most forms of cognitivism entail are necessary. Claims to get around this are not credible, and reveal more an eagerness to save an erroneous theory than any plausible insight into emotion. Can the affect program theory do better?

The first thing to note is that the affect program theory does better by default because it simply does not allow for the formulation of the problem in the first place. The affect program does not require that the agent believe a proposition for it to cause an emotion. Instead, we have granted only that basic emotions can be propositional attitudes, and (what may be an equivalent statement) that they can be caused by beliefs or other propositional attitudes. Furthermore, since basic emotions have a heterogenous intentionality, they can also have as their object concreta, which need not be actual; again, emoting for fictional concreta is not a problem, since we have not assumed the concreta must be actual.

But it would be helpful to actually flesh out these claims, since it seems intuitive that we should emote for beliefs and actual objects first and fore-

most. Thus, in what follows, I will use the notion of the heterogenous intentionality of the basic emotions and of the hierarchical theory of mind to
explain in part why we can have affects for fictional events and concreta.
The case of emoting for fictions provides a way to explore more clearly the
nature of the intentionality of the basic emotions.

A Neo-Fregean Account of Emotional Content

Peter Lamarque offered the fruitful suggestion that we see emotions for
fictions as emotions for fictional contents. Paradigm cases where Frege's
indirect reference occurs are in opaque contexts. If Karen believes that
Malcolm X is a Moslem, it does not follow that Karen believes that Malcolm
Little is a Moslem, since she may not know that Malcolm X is Malcolm
Little. For Frege, a proper name that appears in such a context cannot have
its usual referent; instead, its referent is its sense. This fits nicely with the
fact that we treat, for example, "King Lear" as a name, but one without an
individual King as its reference. However, this doctrine quickly leads us
into trouble. For, if Tim believes that Karen believes that Malcolm X is a
Moslem, then it seems by simple recursion of the opaque contexts that what
"Malcolm X" refers to in this thought is the sense of its sense. Whereas there
is an intuitive plausibility, largely arising from the great utility of distinguishing between sense and reference, in taking the reference of a proper
name to be its sense when it occurs in such contexts, it is obscure what a
sense of a sense is, or what a sense of a sense of a sense is, and so on. Michael
Dummett has suggested that this problem of compiled senses of senses
threatens to refute the very approach:

> Since we cannot say what the simply indirect sense of an expression
> is, we cannot even say what its *referent* is when it occurs in double
> *oratio obliqua;* it would seem to follow that we cannot even know how
> to judge the truth-value of a sentence involving double *oratio obliqua.*
> This constitutes a reductio ad absurdum of the whole theory. (1981,
> 267).

If fictions operated as indirect reference in a Fregean framework, then we
would have this same problem. Chaucer's *Canterbury Tales* is a sequence
of stories told by narrators who are all characters in one overarching story.
If fictional discourse is indirect discourse of the same kind as other opaque
contexts, then it follows that each story within the story conveys senses of
senses. Again, it is not at all clear what such a thing is, and there does not
seem to be any relevant difference in our reactions to a fiction as a result of
whether it is within another fiction or not.

A logical framework and accompanying cognitive theory that will escape
this problem has been developed by Nino Cocchiarella (1995). Cocchiarella
suggests that the best way to model fiction is to treat fictional discourse as
happening within a fiction operator: (In the story S . . .). Of course, that a

narrative is a fiction is usually given by convention, so we do not have to preface the fiction with any such phrase; the operator is implicit. But one thing this operator captures in a logical representation of fictional discourse is that we do not have sense of senses piling up, but rather whatever happens within the operator, regardless of how many levels of stories within stories there are, is all sense (to use Frege's term) of the same order.[34] The principal import of the fiction operator is not to draw our attention to the fact that we will focus upon the story's sense alone, but rather to indicate that we understand that what happens within a story is to be taken as having *deactivated reference.* We understand that in the story *The Hound of the Baskervilles,* the term "Sherlock Holmes" does not actively refer to anyone in the actual world. However, the term does still have a sense—it is a referential concept that the reader understands. Fiction is therefore a relation of contents that lack active reference, and readers can care about and have emotional reactions to those contents.

Our reactions to fictions, inasmuch as they are reactions to propositional contents, are not therefore reactions about possible worlds, nor about the actual world, but about a human construction of intensional contents. And as a result, another advantage of Cocchiarella's approach is that we can meaningfully say or think about impossible things in the fiction. This does not cause logical confusion because we understand that the reference to such objects lacks active reference. Allowing for this is necessary for any realistic theory of human cognition, since fictions incorporating impossible objects exist, are understood by us, and therefore are meaningful.

What is it for a referential concept to be deactivated? Presumably in adults it is understood that the terms are meant to have a sense like their activated counterparts, and that the terms can play the same kind of roles in sentences as can actively referring terms, but they have no referent. Of course, someone may lack an explicit concept of reference or activated reference and yet still understand the distinction between a fiction and a report. What separates the two kinds of narratives is at least an understanding that the things referred to by deactivated referring concepts cannot be encountered in the world, that they cannot effect changes in the actual world, and that we can do nothing to make changes in or for the referent of the deactivated referring concept. Thus, we could read "deactivation" as indicating that these objects are not active in our world and that we cannot act upon them. We understand that though we might be able to help the crime victim we hear about on television, or we might be a victim of the same criminal, we cannot help von Helsing in his struggle with Dracula, nor can we ourselves affect or be affected by Dracula.

The Fiction Operator and the Ability to Recognize the Unwarranted

I argued in the last chapter that some basic emotions can have both concreta and events or states of affairs as their objects. We can now see how this facilitates the ability to have emotions for imaginary objects and situations. According to the neo-Fregean approach, we emote for the contents of the relevant referential concepts, or of the proposition, that is the intentional object of the emotion. It may seem paradoxical that we would take these inactive referents as the objects of emotions; but this would be so only if we had to, in some sense, alter the normal function of the relevant affect in order to get it to take the imaginary concretum or event as its object. That is, as the problem of our emoting for fictions is normally presented, one might have the impression that belief is a fundamental or primordial cognitive state, and that we naturally only emote for the believed contents and have to learn to emote for fictions—a kind of corrupting irrationality learned as a form of entertainment. This is particularly compelling if we assume a highly cognitive view of mind, and see autonomy and the normal function of the mind as arising from having the correct kinds of beliefs and using these to guide action.

The truth, however, is to flip this picture on its head. We can refer to both development, and homology, to establish this. Children of a very young age do not yet understand the deactivation of reference in a fiction.[35] It is because of this that, until a child has learned to understand the difference between fictional and actual content, a parent is well advised to protect the child from frightening fictions lest both child and parent find sleep impossible. Observing this fact, we might just say that the child believes all content. This makes some sense, but without the notion of deactivated reference, or merely entertained thoughts, the notion of belief is not clearly defined. A better explanation is that the child has the ability to entertain propositional contents, and treats them all as of the same value, and that from our perspective this treatment is quite like the kind of commitment we reserve for belief. The child must in turn learn to separate out some thoughts as warranted beliefs, others as fictions; that is, to have the ability to apply the fiction operator is essentially related to the ability to apply notions of warrant to propositions. To have beliefs and acknowledge them as warranted is a learned and special skill; and, just so, to entertain content for content's sake, while being aware that it is merely entertained because it is unwarranted, is a learned and special skill. We understand that that is what we are doing when emoting for a fiction. This is consistent with the plausible posit that nonhuman animals which both share with us homologs of basic emotions,[36] but lack the cognitive skills necessary for distinguishing warranted from unwarranted contents, are incapable of merely entertaining propositional contents. That is, there are no dog dramas and there can be none, because we cannot train a dog to separate mere pretending from actual activity (at least, not for enough activities).

Thus, our experience with development, and the special case of emoting for fictions, suggest the following hypothesis: The ability to distinguish belief and the related ideas of activated reference and satisfaction (that is, whether a proposition is true or false) are the more advanced cognitive skills, and merely entertaining content is the more fundamental and devel-

opmentally prior capability. Distinguishing between active and deactivated reference, and warranted beliefs and mere thoughts, is something that
must be learned or at least that must develop. One must have the idea of
false propositions, and then of imaginary propositions, to be able to formulate a notion of deactivated reference in the first place.

At the level of the subcognitive emotional reaction, warrant and the fiction operator probably play no role. If one has a subcognitive fear of (the
actress playing) Goneril or a subcognitive anger at (the actor playing) the
conspirator, the affective reaction, although perhaps weaker for various
reasons (e.g., because we suppress it), is not fundamentally different than
would be the same reaction for an active referent. The point is that the idea
of warrant simply may not apply at that level. However, with our ability to
distinguish warranted from unwarranted beliefs or imagined propositions
should arise the ability to understand deactivated reference. Does this ability change our emotional reactions to such contents?

The Problem of Reports

We can now see why Radford is wrong to suggest that false reports and
fictions are analogous. It is an empirical question whether, and to what
degree, our emotions are more intense when they have as content a proposition that we believe, as opposed to one that we do not. I do not claim to
know one way or the other. It may seem plausible that we emote more
strongly for believed contents; to be told a harrowing story about a friend is
quite a different thing from being told such a story about a fictional character just introduced to the reader (say, on page 1 of a novel). But the difference here may entirely depend upon the greater associations that one has
in the former case. It may well be that we care a great deal more, and emote
much more intensely, for well-developed characters in a beloved novel
than for some person known only in name, about whom we hear on the
evening news. This is a question that cries out for empirical research.

However, let us suppose that there is some difference in the intensity of
our emotions for believed versus disbelieved contents. We normally understand from the beginning of a story that we are dealing with a story and
hence the propositions we will hear are in the scope of the fiction operator
and the referring concepts are deactivated. If there is any doubt, we may
find ourselves in a strange emotional state, wondering whether the narrative is a report or a fiction, and—like people passing a man lying in the
street—unsure of whether we should get involved. This does not explain,
however, why we might react differently to a report that turns out to be false
than we do to a fiction that we understand is a fiction from the beginning.

If we do show a differential response to believed and disbelieved contents, it is reasonable to suppose that this is a product of our learned ability
to separate out warranted from unwarranted cognitive contents. Thus, we
may indeed be suppressing, in some sense, our emotional reactions in those
cases where the content does not warrant belief. In the hierarchical model

of mind, this would entail something like our learning to suppress the connection between cognitive contents and the affect as part of learning to distinguish warranted from unwarranted contents, and active from inactive references. If there is a differential reaction to believed versus disbelieved contents, then, we can hypothesize that we emote more for a report than a fiction, or at least differently for a report than for a fiction, because we have learned to (or perhaps developed the ability to) suppress the emotion-eliciting nature of disbelieved contents. Emoting for fictions is not then an irrational aberration or a heroic feat of disbelief; but it may involve a relaxation of the suppression of the emotional import of the relevant contents. To turn the phrase: enjoying a fiction is not a willing suspension of disbelief, but rather a willing suspension of affective suppression. Thus, perhaps a withdrawn report will not evoke emotions like a fiction will because we reassert the suppression of these imports; and, given the social impropriety of lying, we should expect this reasserted suppression to be vigorous, since the liar in Radford's story (who told a false report about his sister) would have essentially insulted or at least mocked the listener. There is a vulnerability revealed that one would want to quickly eliminate; one way to do that would be to suppress the emotional reactions that one had, in part in sympathy, for this person.

The Problem of Narrative Demand

These tools, and the heterogenous intentionality of the basic emotions, allow an explanation of the problem of narrative demand: although we do not need to believe the propositions of a fiction, nor believe that the concreta in it are actual, we do require that the fiction be developed in the correct way. To repeat my previous example: we emote for the characters of Shakespeare's *King Lear* and not for characters in a proposition like "King Lear suffered at the hands of his ungrateful daughters" or "Gloucester had his eyes stamped out by evil conspirators." Evoking emotions requires that some narrative demands be satisfied: that a good story be told and told well. Understanding this requires special attention to the heterogenous nature of emotional intentionality. Inasmuch as art can appeal directly to the subcognitive emotions, the basic emotions can be elicited more directly, although the ability to exploit these subcognitive elicitations itself creates a kind of narrative demand. Inasmuch as art appeals to the cognitive elicitation of basic emotions, it must appeal either to subcognitive elicitation indirectly through cognitive elements, or it can portray prototypical events or states of affairs that typically cause the emotion (given that conditions are appropriate).

In focusing upon written fictions, such as novels, we might easily pass over several other features of how works of art can generate emotions in us. One way, perhaps best exemplified in film, is through stimuli that do not appear to need to generate any relevant kind of conscious cognitive content in order to be effective. There appear to be several distinct ways that this may occur. First, stimuli may either directly prime the affect, or be excitatory of the relevant affect. Thus, a frightening film can take advantage of dark scenes, sudden loud noises and motions, and unsettling sounds and music. All of these things appear to either prime or elicit fear reactions in a way quite independent of whether the viewer entertains the relevant kinds of propositions; that is, it does not appear that the viewer need conclude, "a dark place is frightening," "a loud noise is frightening," and so on. If this is priming, then the subject is being put in a state in which he is more disposed to have the relevant emotion; if it is directly excitatory, then the subject is actually having the emotion as a result of these stimuli. Both are possible; future empirical research may settle the issue. In either case, the artists are knowingly undercutting our cognitive filters (and we encourage them to do so), to evoke basic emotions and other affects in direct ways that are difficult or impossible for us to control.[37] Second, the appropriate object of our emotion—such as a frightening person—can be presented directly, and in a way that fixates our fear upon the object without actually appealing to any propositional constructions. The antagonist may be a man who sneers menacingly at all times, and is very strong. In such cases, we are given a concretum for the emotion without actually any direct appeal being made to an inferential chain concluding with, for example, the proposition that this concretum is a threat. We can think of this as a way in which the artist can exploit the subcognitive aspect of concretum-directed intentionality.

For written fictions, these kind of avenues are not available: everything must pass through cognition, being taken in as sentences, or at least as language. But the successful novelist understands that there is nothing frightening in saying the protagonist is in danger. Rather, the novelist has other tools at her disposal. One is to build ambience in a way somewhat similar to the way the filmmaker does, but which clearly relies upon cognitive capabilities. A novelist can build a frightening ambience, for example, through careful details. How this fosters emotions demands further study. However, one speculation is tempting: perhaps the novelist evokes cognitive contents (like those which the filmmaker actually shows) which, even if not directly ostensibly frightening (that is, the reader may not believe that a dark night is frightening), are associated with frightening contents. That is, the subcognitive kind of priming of the relevant emotions that can occur in films can also be indirectly stimulated by cognitive contents that refer to the same (kinds of) stimuli. We can hypothesize that these emotive contents are exploited by stimulating a semantic network of connections which can allow for increased stimulation of the contents associated with the relevant emotion, and ultimately for the elicitation of that emotion.[38]

More important, in all these artworks, the artist has at her disposal the re-creation of the very kinds of situations which if actual would evoke emotions; what psychologists sometimes call prototypical situations. Thus, for example, a prototypical scene that may evoke anger would be if someone whom we value is mistreated. The novelist carefully elicits these values by both getting us to sympathize with the protagonists, and thus to value them and their motives, and by then placing those protagonists in carefully constructed prototypical scenes. In the fiction, then, the characters are treated to situations that are quite like reports, with the exception that the reference is not active. Supposing that active reference is unnecessary will give us the useful result that an account of the cognitive elicitation of emotions in both situations can be essentially the same.

The one difference, of course, is that we need the additional posit that the basic emotions can be had in sympathy. This is something which appears to me an extremely plausible hypothesis, since it is, as far as I can see, entailed by the fact that we do emote for the protagonists of fictions. Also, this hypothesis has some very important corollary explanatory power. For example, it suggests another possible explanation of the role of cognitive emotions: that increased representational complexity serving basic emotions may not only have the benefit of allowing an extension of the utility of those emotions (as suggested in the last chapter), but also may have evolved with our ability to understand other minds and to organize social bonds with them. Thus, some instances of basic emotions with cognitive content may function foremost through a sympathetic modeling of the concerns and values of others, and thus evoke sympathetic emotions in us. Also, understanding sympathetic emotions can be of fundamental importance to understanding important aspects of moral motivation (I will return to this possibility in chapter 8).

Conclusion: Weak Content Cognitivism

In chapter 2, I introduced the term *weak cognitivism* as a label for the view that basic emotions can be, and perhaps often are, propositional attitudes. What these insights reveal is that weak cognitivism should be weakened even further. It is not just that the basic emotions are sometimes elicited by beliefs or are propositional attitudes that share their content with beliefs. More important, the basic emotions are sometimes elicited through the entertaining of cognitive contents, or are propositional attitudes that have as their content merely entertained propositions. And, consistent with the heterogenous intentionality of the basic emotions, sometimes we emote directly for concreta that may or may not exist. A proper theory of the relation of the basic emotions to cognition should thus be a form of *weak content cognitivism:* the view that basic emotions often have or are caused by propositional content, but that content need not be believed.

My exploration of emoting for fictions required several hypotheses about the mind. First, I have argued that the best explanation of emoting for fictions is that we emote for contents just like the kind of contents that would cause emotions in a report, except that we understand that the reference is deactivated. Second, the differences between a withdrawn report and a fiction were explained by reference both to social standards of how such stories should be taken, and to our ability to suppress our emotional reaction to contents. Third, that we emote for fictions, and that fictions must be well told, might both be explained by the three ways fictions exploit our emotive capabilities: sometimes they utilize the possibilities for subcognitive elicitation of affect by the presentation of the kind of concreta and stimuli that can prime, excite, or be the objects of the relevant affect; other times they utilize a kind of semantic excitation that allows an indirect stimulation of subcognitive and cognitive elicitation via cognitive contents; and most often fictions re-create prototypically emotional situations. To use the terminology of neurosciences, weak content cognitivism allows for a ready kind of stimulus substitution. That is, certain stimuli (such as the contents of a fiction) activate brain circuitry, and thereby produce emotions that might normally, or at least under other conditions, be activated by other stimuli (for example, by beliefs). There is no place for these possibilities in a cognitivist theory of emotion, but they are all consistent with the affect program theory.

7

The Rationality of the Basic Emotions

In this chapter, I outline how the basic emotions can be rational. As observed in chapter 5, clarifying this is part of paying the debt of having rejected cognitivism about the basic emotions, since one of the advantages of cognitivism may be considered the direct way in which it can plausibly explain how some emotions, and therefore the relevant motivational states, can satisfy standards of rationality (because these standards can be applied to beliefs and desires). In this chapter, I show how the affect program theory is consistent with a more refined analysis of the ways in which the basic emotions can be rational, and in the next chapter I will show how this approach is superior to cognitivism in resolving the problem of internalism concerning practical action.

Rationality is not a well-defined concept. In general, an agent is deemed rational inasmuch as she can be said to satisfy sufficient rules of reasoning. A proper naturalist account of the basic emotions should guide an understanding of the capabilities and limitations of the basic emotions, which in turn clearly constrains the standards by which they can be judged. But in attempting to clarify how the basic emotions may satisfy criteria of rationality, we are confronted with an immediate problem: because there is no general agreement of what such criteria are, it is easy to use criteria that cannot apply to basic emotions, or on the other hand to use criteria that the basic emotions easily satisfy. In this chapter, I will argue that the basic emotions can be, in a robust sense, rational, both in their cognitive form and even in their subcognitive form. Ideally, I could attempt to establish this by settling upon some criteria which are, or resemble, those that have been offered in other widely accepted accounts of rationality. This approach, however, is barred when our concern is the basic emotions in their subcognitive instances. This is because the vast majority of the standards for rationality on offer apply solely to propositional attitudes. Thus, I will attempt to find plausible analogues to these standards, which will apply to basic emotions in their subcognitive form. In this way, I hope to show that these standards are robust and nonarbitrary.

Common Notions of Rationality

One guiding conception common to all claims to define rationality is that the rational agent uses certain kinds of capabilities to help it achieve its goals. An additional constraint may be that the agent's goals need to be appropriate (Nathanson 1985; Rescher 1988, 92ff). That said, many of our philosophical notions of rationality are of the former kind, and are quite closely linked to notions of inference and other logical skills. Typically, an agent is deemed to be rational inasmuch as it draws the right kind of inferences from the beliefs it holds, in order to satisfy those desires it holds. These are fundamental criteria of B-D rationality, and also underlie many conceptions of cognitivism. Christopher Cherniak (1986, 7) calls an idealized and equivalent form of this the *ideal general rationality condition:*

> If *A* has a particular belief-desire set, *A* would undertake *all* and only actions that are apparently appropriate.

Thus, the ideally rational agent is fully consistent in its beliefs, and, after inferring via its beliefs the consequences of possible actions, it takes those actions that satisfy as much as possible its desires.

Criteria like these have the advantage that the standards applicable to an ideally rational agent (in this sense) can be modeled clearly with first-order logic. Cherniak rightly observes that, even though such criteria are understood to be ideals—indeed, they are usually stated in such a way as to be impossible to achieve—they are so strong that all natural agents fall far short, and as a result such standards incline us to favor irrealist accounts of mind, such as interpretationism. Cherniak offers the alternative that an agent need only be minimally rational; agents can be minimally rational, and hence are rational, if they satisfy the minimal general rationality condition:

> If A has a particular belief-desire set, A would undertake some, but not necessarily all, of those actions that are apparently appropriate. (9)

We might call this minimal B-D rationality. The basic idea of what constitutes rationality remains the same: the agent reasons through beliefs via proper logical inferences, in order ultimately to satisfy its desires. This talk about agents having belief sets and desire sets is very misleading, and probably leads inevitably into errors (see chapter 8). Hence these notions too, at best, must be taken as idealizations.

Other criteria for rationality abound. Jonathan Cohen (1992) observes nine kinds of standards of rationality that have been typically given:

1. conforming to the laws of deductive reasoning;
2. making correct mathematical calculations;
3. correctly utilizing the meanings of words in reasoning;

4. properly forming theories from inductive cases;
5. making correct assessments of mathematical probability;
6. making inferences licensed by an accepted factual generalization;
7. performing actions that further the purposes or interests of the agent;
8. choosing the appropriate kinds of ends;
9. making appropriate inferences to foster communication.

These criteria, like those concerned with B-D rationality, seem to be drawn from compelling commonsense norms concerning inference and others kinds of prototypical human reasoning. The notion of rationality derived thus is prejudiced in favor of those skills that are special to human cognition. As a way to define or understand rationality, this can lead to a trivialization of the notion into a list of skills that humans uniquely have.

However, one sophisticated work in this regard is Jonathan Bennett's *Rationality*. Bennett's explicit aim is take the human—and hence our cognitive capabilities—as definitive of rationality: "I use 'rationality' to mean 'whatever it is that humans possess which marks them off, in respect of intellectual capacity, sharply and importantly from all other known species" (1989, 5). But he attempts a conceptual analysis that works from the simple to the complex, to discover the necessary conditions for rationality. He does this by beginning with the idea of a very simplified language—the "language" of honey bees—and tries to build a conceptual analysis of rationality by asking what we need to add to such an ability to have rationality. Bennett's conclusion is that "the expression of dated and universal judgments is both necessary and sufficient for rationality" (94). The guiding thread of Bennett's conceptual analysis is the idea that the rational agent can learn from his experience, arriving at general claims (even theories) about the world that can guide action to help achieve the agent's goals. A compelling feature of Bennett's analysis is that instead of assuming that rationality is embodied in inferences, he takes it to be exemplified in the formation of theories about the world that are both practical and revisable by experience. Although he ultimately argues that language is necessary for rationality, the basic insight is that rationality is exhibited in forming generalizations from experience, revising them as needed, and being guided by them. He offers, thus, a standard theory of rationality, but he aims to explain aspects of good reasoning beyond inference. This is also consistent with the clarification of the notion of belief that I introduced in the last chapter, and which we might add to the idea of B-D rationality: the rational agent must understand some criteria of warrant well enough to distinguish beliefs from merely entertained propositions. Bennett's notion gets at having conscious standards of warrant for beliefs, and so can be taken to offer an essential part of a reflective cognitive rationality.

The idea that one's goals must answer to certain norms in order for behavior to be rational is an important consideration, for indeed it seems that such norms are part of our implicit standards of rationality. Nicholas

Rescher points out that this requires us to distinguish between one notion of preferences (which economists typically assume as primitives in their account of rationality) and preferable goals (goals that one ought to prefer—that is, goals that satisfy some norms of appropriate goals). Thus, goals must have a justification:

> The pursuit of what we want is rational only in so far as we have *sound* reasons for deeming this to be want-deserving. The question whether what we prefer is preferable, in the sense of *deserving* this preference, is always relevant. Ends can and (in the context of rationality) *must* be evaluated. (1988, 99)

Here, having the appropriate goals is being able to give reasons for them. However, Rescher does allow that a person's best interests include preferences that arise from biology: "health, normal functioning of body and mind, adequate resources, human companionship and affection, and so on" (100). Some of these may correspond to, or overlap with, primary reinforcers: states for which an organism will work, without requiring that the organism learn any positive associations with that state (see Rolls 1999). Primary reinforcers act upon inherited biological capabilities of an organism; thus, we can think of an organism as having some built-in goals. Other goals can be inferred or reasonably attributed on the basis of primary reinforcers, or some platitudes about biological function (e.g., organisms seek to continue their survival). It is these kinds of inherent goals that I will make use of in the next section.

One striking thing about all these approaches is that, with the exception perhaps of this allowance by Rescher of some universal interests, they leave no room for capabilities that an organism may have, other than those exhibited by some form of B-D rationality, that can be rightly valued according to their performance upon some norms such as those advancing success for an action. Another instance of the cognitive autonomy fallacy is implicit here, given that rationality is often seen as a factor in autonomy, and yet the standards of rationality mix both ideas of success in achieving goals with the requirement that one have uniquely cognitive skills. But many organisms, *including humans*, do a multitude of things to achieve their goals (in a very basic sense of "goal") that do not fit these standards of rationality because: (1) these goals are appropriate in some sense independently of cognitive justification (although they can have cognitive justification also); (2) the abilities used are revisable, correctable, and controllable; and (3) these abilities are subcognitive. Indeed, these subcognitive abilities are the primary source of autonomy for organisms, but are not properly described as fulfilling B-D rationality. Most philosophers have traditionally made little of these skills and have assumed that what is not guided by an engine of inference and fueled by beliefs and desires is just so much stimulus and response, insignificant to a theory of mind. The profundity of this error is perhaps best understood by AI researchers, who well know that although many of the skills taken to exemplify the excellence of cognition (playing chess, solving proofs) are quite easy to reproduce, what appears to most to be simple (motor control and its integration with perception, exhibited even in something so common as the flight of a bee from one flower to another, or two spiders dancing with each other in a ritual dispute over territory) is well beyond our current capabilities to engineer. Since I discuss these issues in the final two chapters of the book, I will set them aside here, and need only observe that we can identify norms that must be satisfied to ensure that these other skills succeed in guiding the actions of an organism to achieve its goals, and therefore ultimately enable such organisms to be autonomous. I turn next to an outline of some of these norms.

The Subcognitive Rationality of the Basic Emotions

To varying degrees, nonhuman organisms have autonomy in a broad but robust sense: they are able to negotiate their environments, compensating for changes as they seek to achieve their goals, the most basic of which is the satisfaction of their biological needs. I will develop this notion of biological function at more length in chapter 10; meanwhile, it will be useful to describe some of the general norms that organisms can satisfy in such behavior. *Rationality* is a term traditionally reserved for what I have here called "B-D rationality;" but I want to use, with some stretching of the term, a related notion of rationality that offers a clear sense both of how emotions can be successful and appropriate and can help to constitute the ability for autonomy, and also how they can enable some of the kinds of behavior that we would consider typical of B-D rationality. I will use the term "subcognitive emotional rationality norms" for the standards that we can apply, without reference to cognition, to the basic emotions. Satisfying these standards will demonstrate a kind of rationality specific to the basic emotions in their subcognitive instances; let us call this "subcognitive emotional rationality."

Guided by the idea that norms of rational behavior include the operation of faculties which lead to success in the pursuit of goals, being able to revise the operation of the faculties, and perhaps also having the correct kinds of goals, we can identify a number of senses in which the basic emotions, without reference to cognitive skills, can demonstrate abilities that satisfy such norms. These include at least four norms that we can apply to these emotions in the individual organism.

(1) *Subcognitive instances of basic emotions are intentional states that can succeed in having and tracking the correct object.* If an organism is angry at a rival, or afraid of a potential predator, or disgusted by the smell of some particular potential food, the organism must be angry at, afraid of, and disgusted by the appropriate object in order for the emotion to be successful. For example, if the role of anger is to motivate an attack of a potentially

defeasible threat (and regardless of how successful such an account is as a general description of the function of anger, we can identify individual classes of eliciting objects about which we should be able to find broad agreement on the most plausible function of the corresponding emotion; an obvious kind of case would be one where an organism is angry at a sexual rival that attempts to copulate with its mate, and consequently attacks that rival), then the anger must identify and "track" the appropriate object. It is a complete failure of the function if the organism is made angry by a rival, and ends up attacking a bystander, for example. Similarly, to flee a fearful object one must recognize and track the very object that inspires fear. And to avoid a disgusting—presumably toxic—substance, an organism that is disgusted must rightly recognize and avoid ingesting the object of its disgust. And so on.

These capabilities are nontrivial. For example, nonhuman animals have been altered to show deficits in these skills. The decorticate cat experiments referred to in chapter 2 also produced the observation that cats so prepared could be enraged by particular stimuli, but then end up misdirecting their angry behavior.[39] Thus, there is a norm of success that applies to having and tracking the appropriate object, and which, to varying degrees, the organism can satisfy.

(2) *Some subcognitive instances of basic emotions can be shaped by learning in an appropriate way.* Fear conditioning demonstrates that an organism, including even a relatively simple organism, can learn to associate a novel stimulus with the occurrence of a noxious stimulus. Furthermore, in organisms with more complex nervous systems, more complex differentiations can be made through such learning, such as distinguishing tones that signal a shock from tones that do not. Similar kinds of learning have been shown for disgust; and it is reasonable to assume that anger and other basic emotions are susceptible to such learning. Thus, the eliciting conditions of some, perhaps all, of the basic emotions can be shaped by learning; organisms learn which objects merit particular emotional responses, and over time they may learn to refine their differentiations. This is a skill which is clearly necessary if one is to be able to use these emotions in a successful way.

(3) *Some basic emotions are, in various senses, revisable in their subcognitive instances.* Fear conditioning can be extinguished by learning. That is, if we pair a noxious stimulus with a novel and unconditioned one, and form a fear-conditioned association, then later a large number of exposures to the previously unconditioned stimulus can sometimes result in the disappearance of the conditioned behavior. Thus, a rat that is taught that a particular tone precedes a shock will jump when it hears that tone; but if that tone is played again and again without a shock, it may "extinguish" this reaction, so that eventually the rat will not jump when the tone is played.[40] It is likely that similar kinds of revision are available to the learn-

ing that characterizes some of the other basic emotions. At the very least, an organism that treats another as a rival might, after repeated exposure in which the latter no longer is a rival, stop reacting in anger. And so on.

Such abilities allow for a fundamental flexibility in basic emotions: they can be learned but also "revised," which greatly enhances the usefulness of learning for navigating the environment by allowing for continual enhancement of appropriateness of emotional reactions. Such affects can be said to be satisfying a norm of revisability to the degree that they are appropriately revised.

(4) *Some basic emotions demonstrate generalization in their subcognitive instances.* Different subcognitive instances of basic emotions reveal different degrees of generalization in the learning that shapes the sources of their elicitation. A monkey can learn to fear a particular other monkey, say a more dominant male, but also learn to fear tigers in general. An organism that is disgusted by some water at some particular place may learn to be disgusted by warm water, or water that smells a particular way, or so on. These generalizations need not be based upon a distinction between particular and general reference; but could arise from attention to differing degrees of relevant variables, both within one and several modes (e.g., taking one feature, versus many features, of a smell as relevant; or taking a smell, versus taking both a smell and visual features, as relevant). Thus, they can be concerned solely with concreta, and be based upon properties had by those concreta, and so are not necessarily cognitive. I am unable to offer an empirical account of under what conditions such generalizations occur, but we only need note that some instances of such generalization do occur and can serve to make the basic emotions more useful in some cases. There is thus a subcognitive emotional rationality norm or set of norms that can be applied to assess how appropriate such generalizations are.

These four criteria help us see how some basic emotions can be subject to some robust norms, and as such can be said to succeed to differing degrees, and ultimately to be in some successes "rational." This subcognitive emotional rationality requires nowhere a reference to the kind of capabilities that constitute propositional attitudes or other capabilities typically considered cognitive, such as language or conceptual categorization of a kind that is available for report. Thus, inference and other logical notions (such as consistency) need not apply for these norms to be appropriate. These criteria are all also given in terms of the individual organism and its own perceptions and reactions. There may also be, for those organisms that live in social groups, socially generated criteria that are brought to bear upon the relevant basic emotions. At least three such criteria would seem to be plausible, and so we can hypothesize that they also apply:

(5) *Social appropriateness of the subcognitive emotional reaction.* Animals that live in groups with hierarchies of social dominance must, to nav-

igate such a hierarchy, have the appropriate social reactions. They should be angry when rivals challenge their own rank, and fearful of those that dominate them and that they cannot best. Failure to have the appropriate reactions in these cases can result in social failure: being fearful of individuals that otherwise would not be dominant will lead to a precipitous drop in rank; having no fear of those that are clearly more dominant might lead to great bodily harm. There can also be other kinds of social interactions that depend upon or reinforce appropriate basic emotions. Thus, a social grouping can bring norms to bear on the kinds of emotions that the organism should have in particular social situations.

(6) *Appropriateness of the expression of a subcognitive instance of a basic emotion.* Organisms that live in groups, or even that just require interaction with others of their kind at some times, may also be confronted with a number of situations in which how they express their emotions can shape their success in social endeavors. Jaak Panksepp gives a fascinating description that might be an example. He hypothesizes that play is a basic emotion that serves important functions in development. But exercise of play is constrained by apparently social requirements:

> Play dominance clearly emerges if two rats are allowed to play together repeatedly. After several play episodes, one rat typically tends to become the "winner," in that it ends up on top more often during pins. On the average, the split is that the winner winds up on top about 70% of the time, while the "loser" achieves less success, but the continuation of play appears to require reciprocity and the stronger partner's willingness to handicap itself. If one animal becomes a "bully" and aspires to end up on top all the time, playful activity gradually diminishes and the less successful animal begins to ignore the winner. (1998, 284)

Thus, if the exercise of play is a necessary part of development, a rat would best be served by, as Panksepp puts it, "handicapping" itself if it is in a position otherwise always to win. Another example may be controlling the expression of anger in dominance fights; many organisms clearly do not attack social rivals with the ferocity they reserve for prey.

   Any situation where social successes require the control of the degree, or even the form, of the expression of a basic emotion can be seen as providing norms for the successful exercise of the relevant emotions.

(7) *Some basic emotions in their subcognitive occurrences can maintain useful social norms.* An organism that exists in a social group may receive necessary benefits from that social group. But maintaining that social group in its appropriate form is something that the individual members must do. Basic emotions may play important roles in such maintenance. I have already observed that anger and fear can work to sustain dominance hierar-

chies. Social emotions, such as love or the withdrawal symptoms that can result from social isolation, both of which may be basic emotions, clearly serve essential functions in maintaining group cohesion. And play, which Panksepp argues is a basic emotion, clearly may serve important social purposes. Thus, if the necessary flourishing of an organism depends upon social structures maintained by the exercise of basic emotions, then the exercise of such emotions will be appropriate in the relevant sense, including in subcognitive instances.

These last three social norms are more speculative, and await more research (or at least, a future and careful review of existing research). But we can understand an organism to exercise subcognitive emotional rationality to the degree that it succeeds in satisfying some of these seven criteria.

The Rationality of the Cognitive Basic Emotions

Basic emotions can be tightly wrapped into our cognitive abilities. This allows them to be beholden to norms that refer not only to the subcognitive capabilities that enable the basic emotions, but also to their cognitive role. The first thing to note is that criteria analogous to the subcognitive emotional rationality norms will apply to the basic emotions as cognitive states but these analogous norms can also make reference to the kinds of capabilities that constitute B-D rationality. However, one issue now comes to the fore. It is quite plausible, and I have assumed, that the basic emotions can play useful roles in their exercise in nonhuman organisms. But there has been of course some controversy over whether the basic emotions and similar kinds of affects play a useful role in humans. This question then provides a criterion which alone might be taken to constitute whether or not the basic emotions are rational in human beings. I will turn to it first before reviewing the relevant standards of emotional rationality.

Is It Ever Appropriate to Have a Basic Emotion?

Basic emotions could be said to be appropriate in some cases because we can readily identify situations in which their occurrence can be useful to an organism. If an organism has as a goal dominance over another, one way to achieve that goal (perhaps the only way, given its capabilities) is to become angry at the rival and therefore be motivated to attack. If an organism is threatened by another organism and it is endangered, one way to achieve the goal of continued survival is to be afraid of the other organism and to flee it. And so on.

However, it could be argued that in humans this type of motivation is not appropriate because it is never better than an alternative. Such an alternative is the one offered by B-D rationality: that we never get angry or afraid or disgusted, or whatever the relevant basic emotion, but rather that, given our desires and our beliefs, we pursue those behaviors that can lead us to satisfy those desires. This might be better, prima facie, since it should not lead to postfunctional behaviors such as we saw in chapter 3, or akratic behaviors arising from basic emotions, or merely expressive behaviors (which, at the very least, might be said to waste energy). It might be argued that although the basic emotions can be appropriate in nonhuman organisms that lack B-D rationality, humans would be better off to always act according to B-D rationality, and not according to basic emotions.

There are two fundamental problems with this argument. The first is that it presumes, as is typical of much philosophy of mind, that desires are actual kinds of states, and that they are sufficient to motivate all appropriate behaviors. The second is that it applies impossible standards to real organisms and their behaviors.

The notion of "desire" is largely a formal one. There is no scientific evidence that there is a kind of mental state that fulfills the role that "desire" does in typical descriptions that use the term. For example, as I observed in chapter 3, it is almost certainly the case that in some instances where it is appropriate to ascribe a desire, we are in fact describing a motivational aspect of a basic emotion or other affect. Thus, if Eric is afraid of the snake, the affect program theory entails that he is motivated to flee; but someone might also say that Eric desires to flee. This ascription of desire explains nothing. Furthermore, even if there were a mental state that roughly corresponds to desire—a state that, if it does not satisfy all the usual uses of "desire," satisfies some, and it is not obviously some other kind of affect— we have no reason to believe that such a state would be sufficient to motivate all the appropriate kinds of behavior. That is, we have no reason to believe that this kind of state will actually get an agent to flee from a snake, or strike back at an injustice, or turn away from something noxious. Philosophers tend to be extremely naive about these things, positing all kinds of necessary connections between beliefs and relevant motivations, or claiming that certain motivations must exist. Thus, many philosophers have claimed that the kind of well-documented dissociations that I discuss in chapters 1, 2, 8, and 11 are impossible. The point is that it is not a necessary truth, nor is there any evidence, that any universal motivational state like desire exists and can do all the work that B-D rationality requires; evidence that we have seen and will review again counsels quite the opposite. This is not to deny that an organism that has a general motivational state and acts only according to instances of that state is impossible; clearly such an organism is, in some weak sense, possible. The point is that no evidence indicates that any terrestrial organism is such a thing, nor even that any terrestrial organism has a general motivational state of this kind.

Furthermore, our standards of rationality should be standards that can be satisfied, at least to some degree. We should not accept that (1) there might be no such state as desire which can motivate in all the appropriate situations and ways, but that (2) only such a motivation can lead to rational action. We might hold ideal standards, of course, but they must allow us to evaluate actual behaviors (thus, ideal standards for inference allow us to rank some different examples of inference as better or worse, perhaps just on the basis of how many mistakes are made, or how basic the mistakes are, etc.). Otherwise, these ideals are not standards. After all, our goal is presumably to single out some behaviors as better than others, regardless of whether optimal solutions exist or are ever used. If we want to distinguish more reasonable possible behavior from less reasonable possible behavior, we obviously must use norms that can be applied, not ones that require capabilities absent in the organism.

Hence, we cannot conclude that basic emotions are inappropriate because a better alternative exists; we have no evidence that a better alternative does exist in any of the relevant organisms (e.g., mammals) for the relevant cases. I will assume, therefore, barring further evidence, that for each basic emotion there are some situations in which it can be appropriate and for which there is no other motivation that could serve that role or be more appropriate.

These considerations touch upon the groundbreaking work that Ronald de Sousa has done on the rationality of emotions. De Sousa argues that emotions can be rational in that they take up the slack where a belief-desire account of action fails because the salience judgments that such an account requires threaten to be unbounded:

> We need to know when not to retrieve some irrelevant information from the vast store of which we are possessed. But how do we know it is irrelevant unless we have already retrieved it? I proffer a very general biological hypothesis: Emotions spare us the paralysis potentially induced by this predicament by controlling the salience of features of perception and reasoning. (1987, 172)

I understand de Sousa's argument to offer another reason to doubt that B-D psychology and B-D rationality offer a plausible, or even possible, account of the actual performance of organisms.

Basic Emotions and the Maintenance of Social Norms

An additional issue is relevant here. As we saw for the norms for subcognitive emotional rationality, there is another sense in which it may be appropriate to have basic emotions, regardless even of whether some general form of desire exists: when basic emotions maintain a norm. Cognitive instances of the basic emotions can also serve such a function, as in more complex and "abstract" social arrangements that depend upon cognitive abilities. These are most evident in cases in which the kinds of motivations that arise from basic emotions can play important roles in maintaining social norms. In this way, certain kinds of emotional actions can seem to be irrational if they are meant to benefit the agent, but are rational if either they are expected by other agents, or if their goal is taken to be the upholding of certain institutions. This can explain, for example, why some instances of postfunctional actions (as seen in chapter 3) are actually very useful. In *Passions within Reasons,* Robert Frank discusses a number of such cases. Here is one example:

> Jones has a $200 leather briefcase that Smith covets. If Smith steals it, Jones must decide whether to press charges. If Jones does, he will have to go to court. He will get his briefcase back and Smith will spend 60 days in jail, but the day in court will cost Jones $300 in lost earnings. Since this is more than the briefcase is worth, it would clearly not be in his material interest to press charges. . . . Thus, if Smith knows Jones is a purely rational, self-interested person, he is free to steal the briefcase with impunity. Jones may threaten to press charges, but his threat would be empty. (1988, x)

So Smith shall steal the briefcase, and Jones shall do nothing. But what if Smith knew that Jones would be very angry about such an affront? Jones may have a reputation, or just make it clear via his "body language" and other expressive features, that he is quite capable of moral outrage. In that case, Jones will have communicated that he is a person who will become angry, and as a result be strongly motivated to retribute—in this case, press charges—regardless of the cost. In terms of postfunctional actions, we can explain this by saying that anger is a motivation to a kind of action (which has retribution as an instance, in this example), and is not simply a desire to be listed along with others that must now serve an idealized calculation of maximal desire satisfaction. And thus, knowing that Jones is prone to anger for such an affront, Smith would be wise not steal the briefcase, and the disposition to anger benefits Jones!

Another possibility arises if Smith does steal the briefcase. Jones himself derives no benefit—court costs exceed the value of the briefcase—but his anger will support a social system that Jones values, and from which Jones himself, and others that Jones cares about, benefits. This kind of result is consistent with some of the findings of experimental economics. Roth (1995a, b) explored the responses of players of "ultimatum games." Two players go through a number of rounds in which they must divide up $10. One player controls the money, and the other can only veto the distribution that player makes; when a distribution is vetoed, no one gets anything. What is of interest is that a rationalist economic theory predicts that the controller of the purse will tend toward always keeping $9 and distributing the minimal $1 to the other player, who will accept because $1 is better than nothing. But, unsurprisingly, people don't actually follow this pattern, especially if they are allowed face-to-face communication. Most of the offers by the controller tend to be much closer to $5 than the simple economic model would predict, and people are also willing to veto other kinds of offers (Roth 1980a, 297). One interpretation of the willingness to veto can be that people get angry. This is not so unwise as it sounds; as Frank noted, an expectation of anger could be what brings a more equitable distribution. But it is possible that anger could, under certain conditions, serve to maintain social standards—such as equitable distributions of money—even if the angry agent does not in that particular situation experience a gain. If someone gets angry at perceived injustice, he may work to maintain standards of justice from which he and others he values, on balance, benefit.[41] And thus, such a system of justly angry responses could help maintain a social standard that serves everyone. The affect program theory explains nicely how such a thing will work: if anger is not like a desire that motivates some goal (such as, maximize my wealth) but rather a motivation to a course of action (punish this unjust individual) it can serve as an enforcing motivation even when such actions are not immediately or individually beneficial.

Given that it can be appropriate, and hence rational, for a human to have a basic emotion, I can now try to discern some of the standards that might help us see when such an emotion in a cognitive form is, and to what degree it is, rational.

The Norms of Cognitive Emotional Rationality

The standards for subcognitive emotional rationality have analogues in cognitive emotional rationality that apply when the relevant emotions are augmented by the special abilities that enable B-D rationality. Although I reject the idea that there is a generic motivation state corresponding to the philosopher's desire, I do accept that something like B-D rationality can be illustrated with a general notion of motivations that recognizes that motivations are diverse. To help clarify this point, I will use the term *cognitive rationality* for B-D rationality understood as satisfying, to varying degrees, the minimal general rationality criterion: maintaining some consistency of beliefs; and as having and applying conscious criteria of warrant to one's beliefs; all without a commitment to a generic motivational state corresponding to desire.

The first four of the cognitive rationality standards that can apply to basic emotions derive their amenability to a normative evaluation to the fact that they (by definition) are caused by or otherwise are a propositional attitude, and that a proposition or propositional attitude itself is amenable to normative evaluation. However, this evaluation is relevant to the role of the emotion itself.

(1) *Cognitive basic emotions can include propositional contents that succeed in representing the correct object of the emotion.* If a basic emotion, or other affect, is to perform some function in relation to an event or state of affairs, two things must occur. First, it must properly categorize that event or state of affairs. A threatening event must be recognized as the danger it

is, an infuriating state of affairs must be seen to be such, and so on. Second, the recognition of the event or state of affairs as emotionally salient must cause the emotion to occur. This is nontrivial: we have already seen, and will review again in the next chapter, examples of individuals for which this second condition fails. Thus, we can evaluate emotions to the degree that we can recognize the emotionally salient as such, and can be motivated by that recognition.

(2) *All cognitive instances of basic emotions can be shaped by learning in an appropriate way.* A basic emotion that is cognitive, and hence a propositional attitude, can be caused by a belief or beliefs. Just as such beliefs are beholden to standards of warrant, whether the emotion is appropriate will be indirectly beholden to such standards. Thus, a certain social situation may cause no anger; but if one later learns that she is being treated less well than others in that situation, for example, she may come to believe the situation is an unfair one, and now become angry. Imagine, for example, that someone is being paid for a service, but later learns that the service is very much more valuable that she thought, and that others performing it are being paid much more than she is. Similar kinds of abilities must be possible for the other basic emotions: I may learn that something is a danger (and so rightly frightening), or contains a parasite (and so rightly is disgusting), and so on. When basic emotions are appropriate (e.g., useful) responses to these situations, rightly understood, then their ability to be guided by such learning means that they are beholden to standards of the proper exercise of this capability.

(3) *All cognitive instances of basic emotions are revisable.* Beliefs that cause a basic emotion can later be found to be erroneous. Just as many beliefs can be revised, and some of these beliefs can be eliciting conditions, so the reaction to a kind of situation that leads to the basic emotion is revisable. This allows for the correction of inappropriate emotions, and so also is a capability the proper exercise of which should be a standard for a rational cognitive basic emotion.

(4) *All cognitive instances of basic emotions demonstrate generalization in their learning ability.* Whereas the sense in which basic emotions without cognitive content can "generalize" may not require any ability to abstract away from particulars to kinds, the ability to have cognitive basic emotions can include such an ability. Being treated cruelly in one instance can teach one that all situations of the relevant kind are infuriating. Being able to make such generalizations allows the ability to have the basic emotion appropriately for novel particular situations. (Note that abilities (1)–(4) correspond to a version, for the basic emotions, of Bennett's criteria for rationality [1986])

(5) *Appropriateness of the occurrence of the cognitive basic emotion.* Each society has some standards about when it is appropriate to have a basic emotion; thus, in the example in which a woman learns that she is underpaid for both the value of her service and relative to others, I was appealing to our standard that such a situation merits anger. The proper acculturation of such standards is necessary to being an effective social agent.

Emotional judgments are also rational in the sense that they will play a role in a system of socially explicit rational organization. This means that both the values expressed in an emotional judgment, and its intensity, can be deemed by others in the society as appropriate and thus be reinforced, or as inappropriate and thus be sanctioned.[42] Emotions are often expressed in a way open to observation. Others can then judge the reaction, and apply social sanctions to inappropriate reactions to pressure the person to revise his evaluation. Children will mock a child who is terrified of small insects, teaching him that they do not approve of his fear and encouraging him to revise, or at least suppress, it. A man who is afraid to fly and wants a job that may require travel will try to hide his fear, suppress it, control it, and if possible overcome it. And so on.

(6) *Appropriateness of the expression of the emotion.* But even if one learns the general kinds of situations that merit certain kinds of basic emotional responses, the expression of the emotion (the "output") must be constrained in particular ways. One constraint is on the intensity of the emotion felt. Even if some beliefs that cause an emotional judgment are true and appropriate, the person having the emotion or another person may judge that it is inappropriate in its force. The agent may not even be able to overcome the force of the emotion, and so may have to experience it regardless of this judgment, but she can attempt to suppress it, which means at least to not act or to not act fully on the motor program. Another set of constraints will apply to the kind of action to which a basic emotion leads. Thus, no matter how angry a person becomes, our laws never sanction killing because of anger (although, notably, they do reduce punishment for it). Very extreme anger is inappropriate, and expressions of it—such as attacking the object of the anger—are often wholly prohibited. Social reinforcement of appropriate kinds of emotions, their intensity, and their proper expression are all provided. These different ways in which emotional judgments can be criticized ensure that they play the correct kind of role that a rational order requires; and our cognitive abilities allow us to redirect the motivational force of basic emotions into more appropriate (and hence more rational) endeavors.

(7) *Some emotions can maintain useful social norms.* Finally, as described above, it may also be appropriate to have an emotion that supports or maintains a social norm.

Conclusion

That the basic emotions, and other affects, can both be criticized and directed in a rational order, and can play a role in that rational order, is not to claim that emotions are always rational, nor that they are wholly controllable. These affects can be rational insofar as they can contribute, to a significant degree, to rational action (such as motivating behaviors that help us achieve goals) and also in that they are to a significant degree amenable to alteration in order to satisfy certain standards. The flexibility of these affects, however, does not have to be total. We still may find that some irrational fears just cannot be overcome, or that some events infuriate us even when we judge that they should not.

8

Internalism and the Basic Emotions

Having outlined two senses in which the basic emotions can be rational, one fundamental to the basic emotions, the other requiring them to be cognitive, I can now illustrate how some of our best philosophical and scientific understanding of basic emotions and other affects can help us approach one of the central problems in philosophical psychology: the debate about internalism and externalism regarding judgment and motivation. There are actually a number of somewhat different debates that have been given this label (see Cohon 1993, 266–267). I shall understand internalism to be the view that belief in a practical proposition (such as a proposition that properly expressed in an English sentence will contain an "ought" or "should") is accompanied by a relevant kind of motivation. Thus, if an agent believes that "one should turn left at this light" or "one should tell the truth," then on the internalist view the agent is motivated to turn left at the light or to tell the truth. The relevant problems to be solved here are to discern if this is actually true and, if it is, to outline what this relationship of "accompaniment" is (for example, are practical judgments *necessarily* accompanied by a motivation?). Alternative ways of formulating this debate include asking what conditions have to obtain for it to be appropriate to say that someone has a reason to act, and whether these conditions include the relevant kinds of motivations; or asking whether internalism is really a matter of ascribing or interpreting the agent as rational (i.e., does being rational require that practical judgments include the relevant motivations?). My concern here is the more interesting and fundamental issue, where motivations are understood to be real, measurable features of the individual in question.

I formulate this as a problem concerning practical judgments, but the primary interest in these issues has been with ethical judgments. I shall understand ethical judgments to be kinds of practical judgments. On at least one view of ethical judgments, the origin of which we can trace to Kant, such judgments are not a species of practical judgments; rather, ethical judgments are very special (even unnatural) judgments for which internalism must be true. But (in addition to perhaps not cohering with a naturalist account) this only muddies the waters, since our concern remains whether judgments that one ought to do something are accompanied by an actual motivation to do that thing. Thus, the most perspicuous starting assumption is that ethical judgments are a species of practical judgment. I will muster some arguments for this assumption, but more important, it is my hope that the richness of the naturalist view reveals in comparison the sterility of the alternative.

Internalism for ethical judgments can be similarly formulated; as Thomas Nagel puts it:

> [On the ethical internalist] view the motivation must be so tied to the
> . . . meaning of ethical statements that when in a particular case some-
> one is (or perhaps merely believes that he is) morally required to do
> something, it follows that he has a motivation for doing it. (1970, 7)

The alternative to this is externalism. W. D. Falk, whose work in this area is one of the sources of the contemporary debate, explains externalism clearly:

> For we imply that morality needs a sanction whenever we say that
> merely on account of the fact that we ought to do some act we have not
> yet any incentive sufficient for doing it; and that, whether we shall have
> the latter or not, will depend on conditions distinct from and addi-
> tional to the former. (1986, 27)

The debate about internalism and externalism in ethics and in practical reason is often a debate about which of these alternatives is correct. Thus, these two positions are usually taken to be mutually exclusive possibilities. Of course, for any particular instance of an agent believing in a practical proposition, the options may be mutually exclusive: if we are able to clarify the kind of motivation we are talking about, then perhaps either she is, or is not, motivated in the relevant way. But internalism and externalism are meant to be more general theories, and hence, if they are to be exclusive, at least one of them must be a universal claim over the relevant cases. I shall call the claim that internalism is universally true of the relevant cases *simple internalism*.

Internalism in ethics is inextricably linked with questions about cognitivism in ethics; here is one of the many places in which the term "cognitive" is used in a different (but related) sense than that of "cognitivism concerning emotion." In its basic form, ethical cognitivism is the view that moral judgments are beliefs, or at least can be beliefs; at issue is whether moral judgments are the kind of thing that can be true or false (they may fail to be that kind of thing, but at least on cognitivism they are meant to be that kind of thing). Another view, which may not be called "cognitivism" by some, but which strikes closer to our concerns here, would be to suppose that moral judgments are at least mental states that can play the kinds of roles that beliefs or other propositions can play in B-D or cognitive rationality. To avoid confusion, in this chapter I shall use the awkward but necessary phrases *ethical cognitivism* and *cognitivism in ethics* to refer to "cognitivism" and its cognates as they are used by ethicists; and *cognitivism about emotion* to refer to the theory discussed in chapter 2 and elsewhere in this book (that basic emotions are or require propositional attitudes). Keeping this distinction is important because, on some noncognitive views in ethics, where moral claims are understood not to be statements of belief, they are instead often seen as expressions of affective states (where affects are often understood in an impoverished way). On such views, internalism follows quite naturally from the idea that affective states are motivations. Given my own doubts about the role of cognitive abilities in emotions and in autonomy, I suspect that this dichotomy between ethical cognitivism and noncognitivism is just too crude a tool to clarify the nature of mind as it is relevant to practical action. In this chapter, it will be sufficient to start instead with the question of whether the agent is actually motivated to act in the relevant way or not, given that they do believe some relevant practical claim. I will then stake out a middle ground between the two extremes of a simplistic ethical noncognitivism and ethical cognitivism.

It is lamentable that, given the very extensive debate that has been dedicated to these issues, there has been little or no attention to what our best scientific and theoretical findings about motivation and the mind can offer to tell us about them. In this chapter, I review some results in neuropsychology that provide clear counterexamples against simple internalism. Some of these results we have already seen (in chapter 2), but they deserve reiteration for their implications in this context. Next, I consider how this conclusion relates to some of the contemporary debate concerning internalism, and show how a disregard of psychology has resulted in a number of erroneous but widespread notions. Then, rather than taking the failure of simple cognitivist internalism as a victory for ethical noncognitivism or for a universal statement of externalism, I show that, given what was discovered about the rationality of emotions in chapter 7, one form of cognitivist internalism could be true of a significant class of practical judgments as they relate to these basic emotions. Finally, in a coda to the chapter, I have some remarks concerning the nature of appraisal.

Counterexamples to Simple Internalism

Traditionally, the most compelling arguments against internalism and for externalism have been appeals to the commonsense notion that there are amoral people (who believe something is morally right but are indifferent to it) and evil people (who believe something is morally right and do not do it and may even do something contrary) (see Stocker 1979, Brink 1989). We can add to this the more general notion of the apractical person, who believes something ought to be done (not necessarily for moral reasons) but is indifferent to it; the amoral person is a special case of the apractical person. The internalist has answers to these proposed counterexamples.[43] She can deny that there really are apractical people, including amoral people, or bad people; this is a common move (see Dancy 1993, 4–6). One way to do this is to argue that we sometimes use normative talk to identify the values not of ourselves but of others. Thus, anyone who professes to know she should do φ but who claims indifference to φ or claims to desire to do the opposite of φ can be understood as someone who sees φ as an ethical claim of others to which she is indifferent or even opposed. Hence, when she says that she should do φ, she really means that others believe that she should do φ. This is one answer, perhaps not a very satisfactory one, but it at least keeps the debate alive. Jonathan Dancy (1993) and Alfred Mele (1995, 1996) have argued for another kind of counterexample to internalism: an individual can lack motivation because of a mood like depression. I agree, and my conclusions below are consistent with this; however, I expect that an internalist might argue that the depressed person does not lack motivation to do what she believes is the right thing, but rather her depression suppresses motivations, or otherwise is somehow an inhibitor of existing motivations. This is at least plausible, and, lacking sufficient understanding of how depression affects motivation, I would not know how to respond to it. I want then to pass over Mele's and Dancy's example, and consider the problem of the apractical person in a different way.

To show that an amoral or apractical person can exist, we need an example of someone who can sincerely pronounce that she ought to do φ, but then she is not motivated to do φ and does not do φ. There are examples of just such people that can be taken from contemporary neuropsychology and neurophysiology, perhaps the most striking of which are found in those individuals with damage to their orbitofrontal cortex. Edmund Rolls et al. (1994) studied such patients who showed a very striking kind of perseveration. These patients had various kinds of ventral frontal lobe damage, and they demonstrated various kinds of inappropriate social and emotional behavior (inappropriate sexual advances, boasting, tactless comments, overfriendliness, etc.). Some of them also reported significant changes in their emotional experiences since the events that caused their brain damage. The task that Rolls et al. utilized was a simple one: subjects had to choose to touch or not touch a screen that showed one of two pictures for 7 seconds at a time. At first, subjects were given points for touching one picture, and debited points for touching the other picture. They were also told to attempt to gather as many points as possible. They were given no instructions regarding which picture to touch, and had to learn this. After a period in which one picture gave them points for touching, and another penalized them for touching the screen, all the subjects learned the task. In the follow-up, subjects were given either an extinction task (in which touching the screen always was incorrect) or a reversal task (when suddenly the point earning scheme reversed). Normal subjects, including subjects with brain damage elsewhere, quickly learn the extinction or reversal task. But the ventral patients were much less successful. They were quite able to verbally recognize that the task had changed, but continued with their behavior:

> On the first reversal trial patients generally made some objection or comment that clearly showed their awareness that the contingencies had changed (for example, "they've switched!", or "it's changed over"), and the same was true when extinction began. Some patients seemed to try to instruct themselves to respond in a way that would yield points, but without success. Case 8, for example, in extinction, announced at trial 24 that she would not touch any more stimuli. She restrained herself for a few trials, but then touched the next seven stimuli in succession, whereupon the test was ended. Similarly, case 2 bewailed the fact that he always touched the [formerly positive stimulus] "wrongly," but continued to do so for a total of a further seven trials before the test was ended. Case 4 often said "No!" to himself, but then touched the stimulus, and commented, "I knew I was wrong." On one occasion he was asked whether it would be correct to touch a stimulus. He correctly answered "No," hesitated, and then did so. (1521)

This failure to act accordingly also showed no relation to the IQ of the patients who were tested for IQ (this included seven of the ten ventral frontal lobe damage subjects). All of these had average IQs, within one standard deviation of the mean. They also scored well on a battery of other cognitive neuropsychological tests (1523).

If we can assume that the behaviors in these cases reflect the motivations of the individuals, we have here very striking examples of apractical individuals. They have normal cognitive skills, and they can literally state the correct course of action, but then not take it and even perform its contrary. The claim that this reveals their motivations—and that therefore they are not motivated by their practical judgments—is of course not directly established here. But the alternative—that there is another, stronger motivation acting—is highly implausible. We can also support this conclusion (that they are acting as they are motivated to act, and they are not significantly motivated to act according to their practical judgments) by a similar study already mentioned in chapter 2: the case of EVR studied by Antonio Damasio and his colleagues.

To recap: EVR is an individual of above-average intelligence who had the misfortune to get a brain tumor in his frontal lobes, just above the eyes. To remove the tumor, he underwent a bilateral excision of the orbital and lower mesial cortices. After this surgery, EVR exhibited what Damasio calls "acquired" sociopathy. Although he had been a successful businessman, family man, and was considered a role model to his siblings, following his surgery, EVR made a series of disastrous judgments, went bankrupt, and was ultimately unable to care for himself. He showed signs of sociopathy, including the inability to maintain enduring attachment to a sexual partner.

He appeared to be unable to properly weigh long-term options. But, strikingly, EVR scores normally on the usual battery of psychological tests and has an above-average IQ.

Damasio and his fellow researchers were able to uncover a series of measurable deficits in EVR. I already noted that EVR and patients with similar lesions were studied in an experiment in which they were shown pictures meant to elicit an emotional response, while their electrodermal skin conductance responses were monitored, and that EVR and similarly frontal lobe damaged patients showed a very significant deficit in autonomic responses (Damasio, Tranel, and Damasio, 1990). More relevant to the issue here is another set of experiments, in which special gambling tasks were developed to test EVR and others like him (Bechara et al. 1994; for review see Damasio 1994, 212ff). One task required him to choose from among several decks of cards; each card would result in winning money, but could also result in losing some. Some decks provided occasional large wins, but over time resulted in a net loss from large payouts; other decks resulted in steady but slow gains with only occasional small payouts. What was discovered is that normals soon discern the slow and steady wins of the better decks and prefer to choose from them; and, consistent with the notion that an affective reaction is helping in their decision-making process, it was found that normals, while learning the differences between the decks through trials, have autonomic reactions, and therefore presumably affective reactions, that slowly increase as they prepare to take a card from one of the costly decks. But EVR and similar patients show reactions to a large win, but fail to show any reaction in anticipation of drawing from a deck (although EVR told the researchers that he was a fiscally conservative individual!; Damasio 1994, 214). Their behavior confirms the hypothesis that they are disconnecting: EVR and similar patients tend to stick with the deck that provides big wins but steady overall losses. They get some motivational charge out of the winning, but their motivational apparatus is sufficiently impaired that the future consequences leave them indifferent.

These gambling task experiments also reveal a different kind of deficit. But what is relevant to my argument here is that the galvanic skin response measure shows a failure for appropriate autonomic responses. Assuming that these reflect the arousal caused by affects, then this corroborates the view that these ventral frontal lobe damaged subjects are impaired because of a lack of appropriate affect, and not as a result of opposing affects (that is, other motivations).

To my knowledge, EVR and other subjects in these studies have not been tested with explicitly moral judgments. However, it is reasonable to hypothesize that this impairment in practical judgment extends to moral judgments. EVR should be just as indifferent to some of his moral judgments as he is to the gambling task or the disturbing pictures. And his behavior seems to indicate that this is so; his failure to live up to his familial obligations must surely have included a number of failures to act on correct moral judgments. If this is right, EVR and others like him present a clear instance of a failure of internalism not only in practical reasoning but also in ethics. These subjects can intellectually recognize that they ought to act in a certain way, without having the relevant motivational reaction at all. It can truly be said of some of them what the simple internalist view would entail is a contradictory sentence: he ought to ϕ (by his own standards and even his own pronouncement), but he is not motivated to ϕ. Thus, simple internalism is false.

Ethical Examples, and the Hierarchical View of Mind

For those concerned that the evidence of these subjects does not explicitly touch upon moral judgments, it would be useful to refer here to scientific evidence that is consistent with the conclusions drawn from these cases of frontal lobe damage, and which is also undoubtedly of some direct relevance to ethics. One such body of studies includes research on the fear-conditioning impairments of criminal psychopaths. The psychopath is someone whose life is distinguished by aimlessness, impulsive behavior without regard to consequences, and a lack of long-term goals, of truthfulness, and of empathy (Patrick, Cuthbert, and Lang 1994). One theory that has been used to explain these features of psychopaths has been that, as psychologists phrase it, semantic and emotional processes are dissociated; to put this in terminology more akin to that of philosophers, the cognitive capabilities of the psychopaths are not properly integrated with their affective capabilities (Cleckley 1941). Thus, the electrodermal response of psychopaths who are anticipating a shock are smaller and occur later in the warning interval that do those of normals (Hare 1965). Psychopaths will also consistently choose delayed punishment over immediate punishment (Hare 1966), and the suppression of behavior that punishment causes reduces more rapidly as the risk of punishment decreases (Siegel 1978). One more recent study (Patrick, Cuthbert, and Lang 1994) measured the reactions of psychopaths to simply repeating either normal or fearful sentences. Their autonomic reactions were measured using skin conductance response, and they were also asked to report on their feelings of fearfulness. Although varying degrees of psychopathy are indistinguishable in terms of their reported fearfulness, their autonomic reactions are significantly different: the worse the psychopathy, as measured by standard tests, the less reaction they showed, in comparison to normals, when repeating fearful sentences. These results are consistent with two hypotheses about psychopathic behavior. First, it can be that their lack of the ability to properly care about the future causes them to be indifferent to punishment and to the consequences of their own actions. Second, the violence of some psychopaths may arise because of an affective deficit that results in a failure in empathy. On this view, they fail to have proper empathy because they are unable to generate and have many normal emotional reactions.[44] Both hypotheses are likely true. These results concerning psychopaths are consistent with the results we saw for subjects with ventral frontal lobe damage. If we accept that the psychopaths have affective deficits, we have an explanation of their behavior inconsistent with simple internalism: these psychopaths are dangerous criminals not because of a lack of knowledge or intelligence, but because of a lack of affects. Indeed, these results show that psychopaths may even learn to pretend that they have normal affective reactions.

The traditional internalist should be tempted to respond that EVR and criminal psychopaths are not appropriate counterexamples because they are abnormal. Without a more sophisticated notion of motivations, this objection amounts to the claim that these exceptions to simple internalism are irrelevant because they are exceptions to simple internalism. However, the view I develop here can explain the sense in which these people are exceptions, but also should allow for us to actually predict their existence. That is because these results, and those of frontal lobe damage cases, are consistent with the hierarchical view of mind. As we have seen, our best scientific understanding of the basic emotions is that the necessary and sufficient conditions for their existence are to be had in subcognitive functions that can operate independently of certain cognitive abilities. And other affective capabilities can similarly be independent of cognition. The hierarchical view of mind entails that there is some modularity to the affective and cognitive systems, and therefore we should not be surprised by instances where there are affects without the relevant kinds of cognitive content, or some of those cognitive contents without the appropriate corresponding affect.

But Is This Addressing Internalism?

I have discussed a clear counterexample to simple internalism; other evidence concerning deficits in affects is consistent with this; and the hierarchical view of mind tells us why this is. But the traditional debate concerning internalism has been often formulated in a way that aims to show a conceptual link between practical judgments and the appropriate kinds of motivations. It could be argued that I have failed to show anything about the internalism issue because it is not an empirical problem at all. There are two issues here that are particularly prominent: one is the widespread attempt to do psychology a priori, and another is that metaphysical arguments are sometimes made regarding internalism. I will address each in turn.

A priori Moral Psychology

There are a number of reasons, none of them good, that lead some to treat moral psychology as an a priori endeavor. One of the foremost is the presumption of a simplistic notion of motivation. I have criticized the posit of desire as a generic motivational state on the grounds that we have no reason to believe in such a state. But such a posit also makes a priori moral psychology, not to mention irrealist approaches to mind, seem appropriate because the notion of desire is really nothing more than an extremely broad formal relation between actions and beliefs. That is, since we have no evidence that there is an all-purpose generic universal motivational state (and plenty of evidence to the contrary), the term really serves as little more than a formal notion used to explain actions. This is a fault of the simplicity of the concept, and of ignorance concerning motivational psychology; but it is often touted as evidence either that there are no real motivational states, or that these motivations are not the kind of thing that science can explain.

Thomas Nagel makes a distinction between motivated and unmotivated desires. The latter include things like hunger; the former are those desires which we arrive at after deliberation. However, it is unclear whether motivated desires are actual (for example, physically measurable and distinct) states; Nagel suggests that they are merely a formal ascription, and that physical motivational states are unnecessary:

> Therefore it may be admitted as trivial that, for example, considerations about my future welfare or about the interest of others cannot motivate me to act without a desire being present at the time of action. That I have the appropriate desire simply *follows* from the fact that these considerations motivate me; if the likelihood that an act will promote my future happiness motivates me to perform it now, then it is appropriate to ascribe to me a desire for my own future happiness. But nothing follows about the role of the desire as a condition contributing to the motivational efficacy of those considerations. It is a necessary condition of their efficacy to be sure, but only a logically necessary condition. It is not necessary either as a contributing influence, or as a causal condition. (1970, 29–30)

John McDowell endorses this view:

> Suppose, for instance, that we explain a person's performance of a certain action by crediting him with awareness of some fact that makes it likely (in his view) that acting in that way will be conducive to his interest. Adverting to his view of the facts may suffice, on its own, to show us the favourable light in which his action appeared to him. No doubt we credit him with an appropriate desire, perhaps for his own future happiness. But the commitment to ascribe such a desire is simply consequential on our taking him to act as he does for the reason we cite; the desire does not function as an independent extra component in a full specification of his reason, hitherto omitted by an understandable ellipsis of the obvious, but strictly necessary in order to show how it is that the reason can motivate him. Properly understood, his belief does that on its own. (1998, 79)

This conclusion is plausible only when we ignore the scientific evidence, consider only B-D consistent actions, and hold a merely formal notion of desire. Worse, if we assume that desire is the sole motivational "state" of relevance to the debate, a view like this is entailed for B-D consistent actions. The proper response to these ascriptivist claims (in addition to the overwhelming scientific evidence that there are identifiable affects, and that some of these affects can operate independently of cognition) is that the naturalistic approach is far richer than the ascriptive one; the ascriptive one is, after all, vacuous when used to explain motivation. Working with this merely formal notion of desire ensures that something like a priori moral psychology appears appropriate because one not only avoids actually dealing with the real motivational states, but posits motivational states that can only be understood and explained a priori. We end up with claims about moral psychology sounding like claims about meaning: about what these terms mean, or what it is to be rational, or under what conditions we might say that someone had a reason. These are all interesting questions, but they obscure that the issue is indeed one of moral psychology, and not of linguistics or game theory or idealized notions of rationality.

A related example can be found in some influential papers by Bernard Williams (1981, 1995), in which he considers an issue closely related to the internalism issue. He applies the internalism/externalism distinction to reasons; an internal reason is a reason that either is in or is a product of reasoning from, one's "motivational set." External reasons, if they were to exist, would be reasons that do not have this relation. In what I consider an indicator of how such moral psychology is deeply problematic, Williams ultimately offers a host of different accounts of his own position in trying to sort out the various issues that arise. He talks about internalism in this context as if it were an issue about what we really mean by our talk about reasons (1981, 111), arguing that there is something illogical about the very idea of external reasons: that if I have a reason to do ϕ, then I must be motivated to do ϕ, since, he claims, that is what it means to have a reason. But he also argues that reasons have to be internal because "reasons must figure in some correct explanation of [an agent's] action" (102); and that internalism is required of an agent for it to be rational (109).

These principles are independent: none of them entails or requires the others. But the fundamental problem with Williams's account is the idea of a motivation set. The agent cannot have a reason to ϕ without having some relevant motivation in his motivation set to ϕ, or without being able to get the relevant motivation into that set after some deliberative reasoning. But what is a motivation set? Ubiquitous though the idea is, it is already problematic to conceive of people as having belief sets—it suggests a brain-bound list of beliefs, when most likely the things we call "beliefs" are various kinds of mental states, many of which may just be learned capabilities which are manifested in dispositions, and as such exist in no clear collection deserving the appellation "set." Most objectionable is the connotation that, as set members, beliefs are therefore clear and discrete entities. This kind of problem is a magnitude more severe for motivations. First, it is not at all clear what it is to "deliberate from" this "set." Williams grants that different kinds of motivations exist but what he fails to recognize is that these many different motivations need not all have the same kind of potential cognitive roles. In particular, some may not be propositional attitudes, or otherwise may not be capable of playing the kind of roles that would be required for one to be able to "reason from" those motivations to some action by any standard notions of reasoning. Second, we have no reason to believe that someone's motivations are discrete and distinct entities. Thus, it can be difficult to make sense of reasoning from some motivations to another motivation that is a reason of the right kind. Third, and most importantly, we have no reason to believe that an individual's motivations are organized in a way that makes it reasonable to describe them as all part of one set. That is, there is a connotation in the very notion of a set that the motivations are somehow transparent to each other as members of that one set, so that we can deliberate from one just as easily and directly as we can from any other. But very likely some motivations are independent of and unaffected by others. For example, in EVR and in Rolls and his colleagues' subjects (1994), there is a kind of opacity between some of their motivations (such as those that lead them to say that a particular action is wrong) and others (that lead them to undertake the wrong action regardless). There need be nothing like a common pool of motivations, where each is beholden to the others under the overruling power of deliberative reason. By grouping motivations under an idealized model, and making them the kind of thing from which one "deliberates," it can seem self-evident that if EVR is motivated toward some goal he will be motivated to take all the relevant steps along the way if he is able to see those steps for what they are. Such erroneous "self-evidence" can arise because it would seem a simple one-step inference to get from one motivation to the other. But the sense of deliberating from a motivation is far too simplistic: we need to recognize that you may have a motivation that may be sufficient to give someone a "reason," but that motivation may fail to connect up with the relevant other kinds of motivations and so may fail to motivate the specific and relevant action.

Williams may indeed be, in some cases, correct: perhaps sometimes it is best to say that someone has a "reason" only when they have a motivation in the relevant sense. But a scientifically informed view of motivations will make debate over such an issue superfluous, since there is nothing like the kinds of entities that these debates are taken to explain. We will have to modify and clarify when motivations succeed, how they relate to other motivations and to beliefs, and so on, to such a degree that any universal claims about "internal reasons" are likely to be qualified into insignificance. Moral psychology must cohere with psychology and other sciences of mind, and these sciences reveal that the mind is far more complex and dynamic than a priori psychology has allowed or even imagined.

Metaphysical Moral Psychology

Another problematic approach to moral psychology, often allied to a priori moral psychology, is to argue that there are metaphysical reasons that ensure motivations a particular nature. A common version of this view is nicely summarized in Mele (1996, 745–746):

> It is, to be sure, an intriguing idea that from putative conceptual or metaphysical truths about the nature of morality (namely, that morality entails or presupposes constitutive internalism and is essentially cognitivist) and the premise that some human beings believe themselves to be morally required to do certain things, we can deduce the substantive psychological truth that among the mental states of human beings are some noncompound, truth-seeking, motivation-constituting attitudes.

But, as Mele shows, those who hold such a view "run the very real risk in so doing of committing themselves to a conception of morality that does not mesh with the psychology of real human beings—a conception that accords moral agency to no actual human beings" (1996, 745). The claim that internalism is metaphysically necessary (a kind of necessity that is almost never well defined) is a claim granting to internalism a non-natural status, even though internalism is explicitly concerned with the actual psychology of human beings as they act in the natural world. The reasoning is at best wishful thinking; at worst, armchair psychology. Claims that internalism is metaphysically necessary can therefore be rejected immediately, on the grounds that the arguments therein made are invalid.

Some approaches of this kind are more subtle. John McDowell holds that we should reject the separation of belief and desire, of cognitive representational state and purely motivational state. McDowell is correct to reject such a division, but his alternative is deeply problematic: McDowell offers to replace this simplistic dichotomy with the notion of a worldview. If I understand him correctly, a worldview is inspired by Wittgenstein's notion of a form of life, and refers to the irreducible network of beliefs and dispositions of a person in her social context. Unfortunately, this solution is easily dismissed by many clear counterexamples which show that motivation and cognition can fail to cooperate. McDowell appears to be willing to reject such observations by using an appeal to metaphysical considerations; thus, confronting the specter of the amoral person, McDowell takes the standard tack of denying that there is such a person, concluding:

> The idea of the world as motivationally inert is not an independent hard datum. It is simply the metaphysical counterpart of the thesis that states of will and cognitive states are distinct existences, which is exactly what is in question. . . . The notion of the world, or how things are, that is appropriate in this context is a metaphysical notion, not a

scientific one: world views richer than that of science are not scientific, but not on that account unscientific. (1998, 83)

The implicit accusation that those who posit the need for motivational states beg the question (by supposing that cognition and richly cognitive states alone cannot explain action) is bogus because on a robust naturalist account the motivations are not just explanatory posits linking action and belief. They are scientific posits, and one may measure their symptoms quite independently of any observable action. We do not therefore have to worry about whether worldviews are scientific entities because we can identify counterexamples without having to make use of worldviews in our explanation. Instead, we have an explanation consistent with the behavior, with a vast body of other evidence, and with a compelling general view of affects and their relationship to mind.

The simplistic division that McDowell rejects between inert cognition and dumb motivations is in error not because no distinction exists between some cognitive states and some motivational ones, but because a vast array of cognitive and motivational states is used by a mind. Some kinds of motivational states have differing degrees of representational contents (and so some are not separable under a wider notion of cognition); some have important but contingent links to different kinds of cognitive contents; and so on. Consistency with this is an important feature of the affect program theory and of the hierarchical theory of mind.

A New Cognitivist Internalism

I have shown that a cognitivist version of internalism fails for a significant class of judgments. However, although this might normally be taken as proof that externalism or noncognitivism are vindicated, this would be too hasty. I have not established that all kinds of internalism are always false; and we have good reason to doubt the simplistic view of affects with which the noncognitivist alternatives are usually associated. Just as some defenders of cognitivist internalism and related views oversimplified the case of motivation, the alternative of noncognitivism about ethics often moves with emotivism in oversimplifying the nature of many motivational states, including those of the basic emotions. In fact, there are a number of ways in which versions of an internalist cognitivism in ethics might be true of significant classes of practical (including moral) judgments and their corresponding motivations. We can see how some kinds of practical judgments can be internalist if we establish two points: first, that some emotional judgments are motivating and also merit the title cognitive (in the ethical sense of cognitive); second, that these emotional judgments are practical judgments or are otherwise properly related to the relevant kinds of practical judgments.

Harmony in the Two Rational Orders

Because some basic emotions can be propositional attitudes, these affects are both motivating and cognitive (in the ethical sense). That is, cognitive instances of basic emotions are those that are normally guided by propositional attitudes, and as a result they should be beholden to some of the kinds of standards that are given in cognitive rationality and that underlie the idea of cognitivism in ethics. This establishes our first point in a weak way. However, I have argued that the basic emotions are not necessarily propositional attitudes, and can and often do have subcognitive instances. Thus, the connection between cognitive emotions and cognitivism in ethics that this establishes is prima facie very weak. Although I reject the suggestion that any necessary connection exists between practical judgments and motivation, there is a strong connection that actually exists. I can establish this by showing that a basic emotion, even in a subcognitive occurrence, is beholden to some standards of rationality sufficient to constrain the way that the emotion relates to emotionally relevant practical judgments. The point is that although my concern here is with cognitive instances of basic emotions, even if one were to argue that a basic emotion in a cognitive instance is a combination of a conative state and a propositional attitude, this would not establish a kind of noncognitivism nor an evisceration of internalism, because the basic emotion in its subcognitive state is itself beholden to some norms of rationality and is constrained to harmonize in various ways with cognitive rational judgments. Hence, just as it was erroneous to deny that there is a distinction between some cognitive states and motivational ones, it is an error at the other extreme to suppose that motivational states are without any representational content and are not susceptible to rational organization.

How might instances of basic emotions that exhibit subcognitive emotional rationality relate to cognitive judgments of the kind that can constitute the content of a cognitive instance of a basic emotion? There can be a kind of harmony between those aspects of a basic emotion that are subcognitive and those that are cognitive. To clarify this notion, we need refer back to the two levels or kinds of rationality that I identified in chapter 7 for the basic emotions. That model points the way toward a different kind of cognitivist internalism. There are two rational orders relevant to some of the basic emotions and other affects, because there are two sets of rational criteria we can bring to bear and two potentially distinct phenomena that both can and usually do measure up to those standards. But the subcognitive emotional rational order and the cognitive rational order are not wholly independent of each other. How the two are related is sharply constrained. I will use the term *harmony* to describe when these constraints are met; the terms *consistency* and *coherence* I have reserved for their usual logical usage, and because the basic emotions in their subcognitive form are not propositional attitudes, these notions do not apply. At least two kinds of constraints can lead to this harmony: the causal influences between the two levels, and functional constraints.

The causal influence between these two levels go both ways. The top-down influence is evident when a cognitive judgment causes appropriate kinds of emotions. Thus, if I judge that I have been wronged, I may become angry; if I judge that I am in terrible danger, I may become frightened; and so on. This is a platitude, but it does remind us that, in normal conditions (where normal is understood in a teleofunctional and not statistical sense) emotionally relevant judgments cause appropriate emotions. This is a weak downward constraint. But other constraints are also possible as a result. For example, given cognitive elicitors of emotions, the kind of constraints that can hold between cognitive judgments (such as consistency) might sometimes translate into constraints on the basic emotions, even when those basic emotions are understood as potentially independent of their cognitive content. Thus, certain emotionally relevant judgments, such as that something is infuriating, can normally be inconsistent with other judgments, such as that this thing is delightful. Thus, suppose that observing that something is infuriating leads to the secondary conclusion that it is not at all delightful, and is even disgusting. If these secondary judgments can also alter the chance of a corresponding emotional reaction, reducing the chance of joy and increasing the odds of disgust, this would create another kind of constraint on affects. That is, not only could judgments cause appropriate affects, but they might cause and rule out other affects.

There are also very likely some powerful bottom-up causal influences. The most obvious such case is in emotional congruence in perception. I will review some of the evidence for the theory in chapter 11; but the basic idea is that the way we perceive the world will tend to be shaped by our affective state. A frightened person, fearing a burglar, is more likely to judge a sound in a dark room to be a person lurking there than he would be in other conditions. A sad person may be more likely to view a situation pessimistically. And so on. A weaker, but still very significant, notion is the one that Panksepp used in his criteria for defining emotional brain systems: "Emotive circuits change the sensitivities of sensory systems that are relevant for the behavioral sequences that have been aroused" (1998, 49). Thus, fear might make us very attentive to the environment in a way that accommodates flight. In as much as either of these factors operates, powerful constraints act from the occurrence of a basic emotion upon the kinds of judgments that one might make: the subcognitive basic emotion can cause changes in judgment and perception. Other kinds of relevant influences also shape our experience such as affective influences on both the formation and recall of memories (I review these also in chapter 11); if memory is influenced by an instance of a subcognitive emotion, that emotion can in turn affect the kinds of cognitive judgments one makes and thereby affect the kinds of cognitive instances of basic emotions one has.

The functional constraints are more important. They can arise because the kinds of things that inform the relevant kind of judgment should also often inform the appropriate subcognitive emotional reaction. That is, our subcognitive abilities are able to recognize some things as frightening or infuriating, for example, just as we are able to make a cognitive judgment that the same thing is frightful or infuriating. Thus, there will be many instances of basic emotions in which the object of the emotion has properties that can be taken by the cognitive and subcognitive systems both in the relevant way. This will in part happen because there will be a recognizable similarity, if not an identity, between some of the functions that ground particular kinds of practical judgments, and also the functions of subcognitive occurrences of basic emotions. My goal to survive will ground both my judgment that heights are dangerous, and (albeit, in a different sense) my subcognitive fear of heights. These constraints are not complete (e.g., not all of the things we may judge emotionally relevant will independently be elicitors of subcognitive emotions, in part because only cognitive emotions can have as objects events or states of affairs), but they will operate over a significant portion of cases.

Finally, we can also observe that we may want to bring criteria to bear on an individual's activities based upon some implicit notion of emotional harmony. In as much as the norms that apply to both subcognitive instances of emotions and emotionally relevant practical judgments, or perhaps even the evolutionary success of the organism, can influence how we learn to control those emotions, these can shape how the subcognitive emotion and the cognitive emotion or cognitive judgments harmonize. An individual is going to act rationally just to the degree that she is able to bring these into alignment. If she judges that things are frightening but finds them not to be so subcognitively, she will be slow to react if she reacts at all; if she has a subcognitive fear of something that she cognitively knows is harmless, this can impede success in various projects (e.g., fear of flying). As a result there will be social and biological pressures which, to the degree that affects are susceptible to learning, drive us toward increasing the harmony between the cognitive and subcognitive emotional orders.

Thus, the idea of harmony is relatively straightforward: when our beliefs counsel some action, our affects should ideally also motivate that action; and when we are motivated to undertake some action, ideally we should also be disposed to judge that that action is rational. There can be exceptions; it follows from the hierarchical model of mind that the independence of the different systems may result in inharmonious, including inappropriate, combinations of states. And this potential for disconnection is very likely necessary or at least useful for learning. But a normal and rational agent should not have many instances of inharmonies. These things can happen, but to the degree that they do happen the individual is going to be inclined to fail to act rationally. When the two separate too much, we should expect a situation not unlike what we see in EVR. And, to expand upon the point, if one were to have a rational set of beliefs and judgments, but have affects all askew that impel one to actions inconsistent with them (something that may be tremendously unlikely, given the constraints mentioned above), then such an individual would be in even worse shape than EVR. Conversely, if we have rational emotional reactions, but our beliefs are constantly inharmonious with them, we can expect such an agent to act in consort with his emotions most of the time, but such an individual might fail to achieve complex tasks that require a cognitive understanding.

I have argued that there are reasons—clearly in need of further study—to believe that strong constraints exist which foster a harmony between sub-cognitive emotions and emotionally relevant practical judgments. This establishes a more robust foundation for the kind of cognitivism concerning the relevant cognitive instances of basic emotions, since the link between the affect per se and the cognitive content is stronger than the mere observation that cognitive contents can be the objects and causes of basic emotions.

Emotional Judgments as Practical Judgments

Having shown that some instances of basic emotions can be cognitive in the relevant sense, and in a strong way, I next must show that these basic emotions have the right kind of relationship with practical judgments.

Suppose that Eric sees a snake before him, and judges—let us suppose even says aloud, sincerely—"That snake is terrifying." To sincerely so judge is to make both a claim about the object of the emotion, and also about the mental state of the speaker: the object is judged terrifying, but the speaker also must be frightened. Some kinds of judgments—let us hereafter call them *emotional judgments*—can concern both the world and the state of the individual making the judgment. I have already discussed (in chapter 7) how the judgment about the world can be beholden to standards of rationality (both social and individual). Here, the sense in which the judgment is also about the agent is particularly relevant.[45]

On the affect program theory, augmented with special attention to the relational action programs that help constitute the syndrome of some basic emotions (and recall that all the basic emotions at least motivate), an emotional judgment when true has a special property: it is essentially related to a motivation of a particular kind. That is, if Eric judges that something is terrifying, and this judgment is sincere and no deficit bars normal mental functions, he will be afraid, and therefore he will be motivated to flee or otherwise avoid the object of that fear. Similarly, if Eric judges that something is infuriating, he will be motivated to attack or otherwise harm or punish the object of his anger. And so on. Thus, emotional judgments are special not only because they are claims about the agent but because when true the agent is motivated in a particular way determined by the relevant basic emotion.

I need now to make a plausible hypothesis: there will be inferential or reasoning links from many practical judgments to emotional judgments, and vice versa. These links need not be weak: some will be, as inferences, a kind of essential link (although whether the link is actually followed up is of course contingent, as is whether the final emotionally relevant judgment causes the basic emotion). Consider an example of a practical judgment: You should not drive across that bridge. If we are to reason why, or ask another person why, the answer could be: because the bridge is old and uncertain, and your car may fall right through it. Knowing that this might kill you, and valuing your own life, you can conclude that this is a frightening possibility, and therefore be led by several steps from "you should not cross that bridge" to "crossing that bridge would be terrifying"—which, if a sincerely held judgment, would mean that by definition you are now motivated to avoid this event, and hence motivated not to cross the bridge. (You still might, of course; there could be motivations that out weigh your fear.) In this situation, there is an essential link between the practical judgment and the emotionally relevant judgment, and a strong natural link (in a well-functioning individual) between the emotionally relevant judgment and the basic emotion (and so the relevant motivation). Furthermore, by definition the emotional judgment is in one sense correct if the individual is so experiencing that basic emotion, so if we are certain that the emotional judgment is reached (that is, it is entailed and the agent reasons through this entailment and so makes the emotional judgment), then there is an essential link directly from the practical judgment to the relevant motivation (again, assuming the entailed emotional judgment is sincere).

Finally, one way to show that emotional judgments can yield a kind of internalist cognitivism in ethics is to show that some of these can be ethical judgments. This is common sense, and is a commonly held view in ethics (for an excellent recent example, see Blackburn 1998). To briefly illustrate the case, I will muster some examples. Judgments that something is harmful to something one values, which therefore are judgments that (for that person) satisfy the general eliciting conditions for anger, are the most obvious kind of example if the value is taken to have moral import. Thus, suppose that Tony is told: you should vote against the Republicans. If he queries for a reason, he might be told that they legislated for and will continue to legislate for weakening the Endangered Species Act. Tony might believe that such legislation is morally inappropriate, and, because it harms things he values, thereby infuriating. If this is indeed true of Tony, then reasons can be given, acceptable to him, establishing a link between this ethical claim and a judgment that the Republicans are infuriating, which therefore by definition would motivate him to retaliate in some way. Similar kinds of arguments might be made for other emotions; some believe, for example, that there is a moral dimension to disgust, in which we might judge certain inappropriate behaviors disgusting; one would therefore be motivated not to perform them. Also, if we allow that basic emotions can be had in empathy, there are many more kinds of relevant emotional judgments. One might judge that some behavior is morally wrong because she believes that it would sadden, terrify, or infuriate another person, and she may herself empathize with that individual and so feel the motivation (albeit perhaps weakly) that that individual would feel under those circumstances, thus experiencing a relevant kind of motivation.

We have thus seen how a form of ethical cognitivist internalism can be true of a significant class of practical actions.

Coda: Appraisal and Motivation

Psychologists and philosophers agree that emotions normally include or constitute some kind of appraisal or evaluative element (I will take "appraisal" and "evaluation" to be the same). There is something more to an affective state than just an observation, like observing that the grass is green. Rather, in being angry or afraid, we seem to be making an assessment of the value of a thing. I may judge that a rabid dog is going to hurt or possibly kill me, and given that I value myself, this judgment involves an evaluative element. It is this insight which appears to guide, in part, some judgmentalists, who, although wrong when they claim to have an identity theory of emotions, are often right in some of the broad outlines about how emotions can function in our own lives. Indeed, one common kind of argument that emotions must be cognitive is built on the claim that basic emotions must start with, or otherwise be in part constituted by, an appraisal of some kind, which is assumed to be cognitive. The final debt to cognitivism is to show how the affect program theory can explain appraisal.

Taken as a primitive, the idea of appraisal, like the idea of a disposition to action, is obscure. Typically, the cognitive theory of emotions can seem plausible in this regard because it can allow for cognitive judgments, which are then assumed to be powerful enough to include appraisals. This does not in any way help explain what appraisals are. However, the same parsimony earned in explaining the disposition to action (by drawing attention to the motor program or other essential motivation to an action that constitutes in part a basic emotion) can be earned in explaining some kinds of appraisals. As I understand it, the intuition underlying the notion of appraisals is that they are special kinds of judgments or mental states; they are special because unlike many other judgments, they are states that are sufficient for motivating action in some situations. We can clarify this intuition substantially. I propose that we can define "appraisal" in the following way: *an appraisal is an affect or is a representational state that is of a kind that reliably excites an affect.* The emotional judgments discussed above are examples of appraisals. One judges that something is infuriating, or terrifying, or disgusting in these cases, and as a result one is motivated to attack, or flee, or expel. This motivational aspect explains what makes an appraisal the kind of state it is (as opposed to a representational state that is not sufficient to motivate).

This definition is prima facie like most standard notions of appraisal, with the very important exception that a view like the affect program theory means that the appraisals will fall into categories depending upon the kind of affects they are or excite. That is, there will be different kinds of fundamental appraisals corresponding to different kinds of affects. Thus the ubiquitous talk about "negative" and "positive" appraisals at best describes rich cognitive states that will have complex and very indirect (and hence, perhaps unreliable or irregular) relations to affects. More fundamental appraisals are things like fearful, disgusting, terrifying, and depressing. In between, there may be kinds of states, including kinds of cognitive contents, that are to varying degrees appraisals; such things might include judgments that are closely related to (perhaps in that they directly entail) emotional judgments.

I have said that an appraisal is a representational state, because the notion does not need to be cognitive in the sense that I use the term "cognitive" in this book. We may have representations of concreta or of mere stimuli that are not propositional attitudes, but which excite an affect. Thus, there can be subcognitive appraisals.

9

Four Puzzles for Consciousness

In recent years, there has been an explosion of interest in explaining phenomenal experience. But although most of us would consider affective experiences prototypical examples of phenomenal experiences, these have largely been neglected by the philosophers (if not by the scientists) concerned. This neglect of emotions can hide long overlooked opportunities and serious problems when our goal is to understand the nature of consciousness. In this chapter, I will pose four puzzles about affective experience that any full account of consciousness will have to solve, and in the next chapter I will offer a theory that solves these puzzles.

A Very Basic Review of the Terrain

(Those familiar with the contemporary consciousness debate may wish to skip to the next section.) We can make a distinction between the functions of consciousness and phenomenal experience itself. This distinction is merely conceptual—it is not an argument or claim that these things are distinct in the world—but it does roughly correspond to the most significant division in the present consciousness debate. On one side of the division are those who believe that this conceptual distinction is so fundamental that phenomenal experience is not going to be explained by any account of the working consciousness. For these theorists, the very existence of phenomenal experience is a fundamental problem that seems to fall outside any kind of functional account of psychological processes. This is because there seems to be a difference in kind between phenomenal experience and working consciousness; phenomenal experience does not seem to be a functional notion. David Chalmers calls this "the hard problem," the problem of giving an account of the nature of phenomenal experience without just supplying an account of working consciousness (1995). To varying degrees, Ned Block (1995), David John Chalmers (1996), Frank Jackson (1982), Thomas Nagel (1979), and others accept that there is a profound difference in kind between the things explained in our functional theories and our phenomenal experience. From the perspective of these philosophers, although we have theories of how people learn, how they perceive, how they use and understand language, we have little or no insight into why it is that people feel—why the universe has anything like feeling at all. The progress of the sciences of mind have nothing to say about the existence of phenomenal experience, and so the questions about such experience become more and more compelling: why is not human life just brute mechanical processes, the way that many of us think a landslide or a planet's orbit is? Does not the scientific worldview make it perfectly possible that human life could be like this? Giving a solution to the hard problem amounts to offering some kind of account of why there should be experience at all.

Any reader who is not a philosopher may be confused by this perspective. After all, psychologists have always been concerned with consciousness, and they have made great strides in understanding it. Why claim it is a mystery impervious to science? Anyone who feels this way can be placed on the other side of the divide. The biggest alternative to the hard-problem

---

AMBIGUITIES OF "CONSCIOUSNESS"

The term *consciousness* can refer to a kind of ability to report features of one's own mental state, to being awake and aware, to the felt experience of being in the world, or to other things. The philosopher Ned Block draws a primary distinction between phenomenal consciousness and access consciousness. Phenomenal consciousness is the *what it is like* of an experience. Block writes: "[Phenomenal] consciousness is experience. . . . [Phenomenal] conscious properties include the experiential properties of sensations, feelings, and perceptions, but I would also include thoughts, desires, and emotions. . . . I take [phenomenal] conscious properties to be distinct from any cognitive, intentional, or functional property" (1995, 230). Whereas in contrast access consciousness is a functional notion: "A state is access-conscious . . . if, in virtue of one's having the state, a representation of its content is (1) . . . poised for use as a premise in reasoning, (2) poised for rational control of action, and (3) poised for rational control of speech" (231). Block has also suggested that there are several other notions of consciousness, including self-consciousness and monitoring consciousness (235). Other philosophers have introduced similar distinctions. For my purposes, each of these senses of consciousness can be placed into one of two groups: phenomenal experience, the notion of consciousness as experience; and working consciousness, being Block's notion of access consciousness and also including notions of awareness, attention, ability to report on a mental state, and so on. (In chapter 1, I required that for a mental state to be working conscious the subject must be able to report on it in some way; here I will drop that strong criterion, and assume that the intuitive, albeit vague, notions of consciousness listed above are sufficient to distinguish working consciousness from phenomenal experience.)

camp, what we might call the working-consciousness camp, is to argue that accounts of consciousness as it is studied by scientists—focused on awareness, ability to report on a mental state, being able to follow instructions, and so on—are sufficient to explain phenomenal experience. For philosophers, a wide range of views can cohere with this perspective, including identity theory (with the claim that phenomenal experiences are just brain states) and varying kinds of functionalism (with the claim that phenomenal experiences are just functional roles). Many scientists are in this camp, if only because scientists who concern themselves with consciousness may not distinguish between working consciousness and phenomenal experience. After all, scientists must begin with what appears to be causally significant—what is "working," in the sense we are using it here. Thus, typically, neural scientists or psychologists aiming to explain "consciousness" are working on an account of how some aspect of working consciousness arises and helps us solve problems; and some of these scientists may believe that such an account will be a sufficient explanation of phenomenal experience.

These alternative perspectives on consciousness are in tension because they tend to go hand in hand with very different approaches to consciousness. Those in the hard problem camp tend to continually want to shear the notion of phenomenal experience away from any straightforward kind of functional explanation. It is not clear how legitimate such a move is. On the one hand, it is indeed the case that conceptual differences can reveal differences in the world. If someone tried to explain number in terms of gravity, or weather in terms of hope, we would tell them that they were making a category mistake, that they were mixing two very different kinds of things. Perhaps these mistakes are of a kind with the mistakes that the hard problem camp philosophers claim to identify in functional accounts of phenomenal experience. On the other hand, it is difficult to know when such distinctions are legitimate. Anyone with empiricist inclinations—that is, anyone who believes that experience is the sole or at least primary determinant of knowledge—will have grave doubts that there are conceptual distinctions that do not just reflect some, perhaps unconscious, theoretical presuppositions. In this case, the conceptual difference that separates our understanding of phenomenal experience from our understanding of working consciousness may be nothing more than an expression of some prejudices. But it is equally fair to say that most in the working consciousness camp tend to deny the very thing at issue, or at least its subtleties. Most theories in this camp tend to have a "consciousness is just *x*" account that leaves us no more clear about why there is experience, or how experience fits into the natural world, than when we started. It is quite easy, after all, to proclaim that "consciousness is just a brain state." This really does not offer much for our understanding of experience.

At this stage in our understanding of consciousness, the most fruitful method of theorizing may be to tread a course between these extremes. One can start from the working consciousness camp, and take lessons about how to develop a naturalist theory of working consciousness, but should always keep an eye on the hard problem camp, and try to make progress in understanding how phenomenal experience is related to working consciousness or to physical body states. The most promising accounts of consciousness that take such a middle path include the representational theories of consciousness, explicitly endorsed by William Lycan (1987, 1996) and Michael Tye (1995a), but also implicit in the theories of Paul Churchland (1989b) and in the approaches of many scientists. It would seem that the representational theory of consciousness is the natural starting place for any thinking about consciousness. Working consciousness, for example, will need to be explained in representational terms: attending to some mental contents, explicitly manipulating them, forming memories and recalling memories; these are all the kinds of things that will require at least some minimal notion of our conscious state as using representations. But the theory also has much to offer to help us understand phenomenal experiences. A pain in my finger is about something—it carries information (assuming things are functioning normally) that some kind of damage has been done to my finger—and as such this phenomenal experience is an intentional state. As I will briefly discuss below, this approach may also solve some other problems that phenomenal experience raises. Most important, if phenomenal experiences are representations, then we have a way to explain the role that they can play in a mind.

In this chapter and the next, I will develop and defend an alternative version of this kind of theory: a teleofunctional account of consciousness, in which the conditions that allow for representation, but not representations themselves, are necessary for an account of phenomenal experience. The views I will explore are definitely not an answer to the hard problem. Rather, I am interested in an account of the relation between working consciousness, physical body states, and phenomenal experience. I will begin by seeing what our best understanding of emotions can tell us about consciousness. I pose these insights as four puzzles. The first is general, and applies to any theory of consciousness; the rest are concerned with a representational theory of consciousness.

Puzzle 1: Why Do Hollywood Zombies Shuffle and Mumble?

My first puzzle is concerned with any theory of consciousness that separates the function—if any—of consciousness from phenomenal experience. This includes generally two kinds of theories. The first is epiphenomenalism, where the phenomenal experience of consciousness does no functional or causal work. Frank Jackson (1982) is an example of an epiphenomenalist. The second kind of theory is one in which phenomenal experiences may play a functional role, but that role can, to some degree, be played by different qualia;[46] I will call this *token role theory*. For a token role theory, a red quale might be said to be playing a role in my navigation of my environment, but the quale could be switched with another quale and, as long as the quale-role correlation remains consistent, this role could still be fulfilled. Paul Churchland (1989b) holds such a view; Michael Tye (1995a) comes close to it.

A host of thought experiments have been offered as evidence, or at least as motivation to believe, that the concepts of working consciousness and phenomenal experience, with their distinct intensions, can have distinct extensions. The method is to urge that these concepts are so distinct that what we mean by each can be had without what we mean by the other. Here I will consider two such thought experiments: the inverted spectrum and the phenomenal zombie.

In the widely familiar inverted spectrum thought experiment we are asked to suppose that, say, Adam's blue were my and your and Karen's red, and vice versa, and that this relation were consistent and continuous, so that Adam's experience of the spectrum were like an inverted mirror image of Karen's, and both Adam and Karen call the same things by the same color terms, even though the phenomenal experience would usually be different. The result is that although their color terminology would function always the same way, their individual experiences would be distinct. This seems a possibility because, in this coldly abstract case, there seems to be nothing in our concept of the experience of color that presupposes any specific functional role for that specific color experience. The phenomenal experience of color seems to be just a kind of tag, and the functional role of color recognition relies only upon a consistent and regular tagging, and not upon the idea that the tags be of any particular kind.

INTENSION VERSUS EXTENSION

Intension and extension are logical notions. A concept or term's extension is the collection of all the things of which it is true. For example, the extension of "has a kidney" will include all those organisms which have a kidney (all humans, dogs, etc.). Intension is a more subtle notion, amounting to something like meaning. No clear and uncontroversial definition is available as of yet; however, it can be easily motivated by contrasting it with extensions. The extension of "has a liver" might be the exact same set of organisms that have kidneys—that is, it could just be a contingent fact that everything that has a liver also has a kidney, and vice versa. But this does not mean that "has a liver" and "has a kidney" mean the same thing. We say that their intensions are different. This is relevant here because it could be that everything that has phenomenal experience also acts in a way exactly corresponding to what we would expect if phenomenal experience played some functional role, but that the two were still different things. This is essentially the thing at issue in the first puzzle.

There are many reasons to doubt that the inverted spectrum describes a possible or even coherent situation. It could turn out that the nature of this tagging may itself require the order of the spectrum. The experiment could also have seemingly absurd consequences, such as the possibility that color experiences could disappear, or continuously change. If one is an epiphenomenalist, these changes and disappearances of phenomenal experiences would have no effect, and would go unreported. Nonetheless, I will suppose for a moment that this experiment at least shows that the prior intension—our common or pretheoretic understanding of the meaning of concept[47]—for our concepts of phenomenal color experience and of the function of color recognition together do not rule out the possibility of the inversion. If this inversion were actually possible, then this would be consistent with either a token role theory (different color qualia can serve the same function) or an epiphenomenalism (if color qualia did no work then their order would be insignificant).

The thought experiment of the phenomenal zombie (Kirk 1974) takes this kind of intuition a large step further. If we can invert the phenomenal color spectrum, why not get rid of it entirely? We are asked to imagine that there is a person physically identical to one's self but who has no phenomenal experience. The appeal here really lies not in the reference to physical identity—which is something of an appeal to ignorance since we do not know all the important aspects of our physical features and hence are unsure how they relate to phenomenal experience—but in the idea that phenomenal experience is doing no work, and that normal function could continue without it. Things like talking, moving around, typing, or playing chess are all things that machines might do, and we generally presume that these machines (at least if simple enough) are not conscious. So can't all the things one does also be done by something that is not phenomenal conscious? Could there be a kind of zombie that has no phenomenal experience but is just as competent as a person who does? Here again, if we admit for the sake of the argument that this thought experiment describes a coherent, meaningful possibility, then the thought experiment at least makes it possible that the prior intensions of our concepts of phenomenal experience and working consciousness can be so separated that what we mean by working consciousness can seemingly be had independently of what we mean by phenomenal experience. If the zombie were possible (or, more accurately: if a zombie world that is physically identical to our world were possible), then it would be evidence for epiphenomenalism—the same tasks could get done without phenomenal experience, so it would seem phenomenal experience does nothing.

Conceivability is not a strong argument for an actual distinction, especially because although the notion is meant to be a logical one, it depends upon our mental capabilities. A host of objections are relevant. We may simply be mistaken in thinking that there is a coherent possibility for zombies or inverted spectra; there could even be a contradiction in the experiments that is in principle accessible to us—one that we could easily under-

POSSIBLE WORLDS

Philosophers have a way of talking about possibility which can be a bit deceptive to those who first encounter it: they describe possibilities as possible worlds. Possible worlds are meant to be completely described situations. It is often easiest, at least for reasoning through the logic of a situation, to suppose that the situation is complete—that there is nothing absent or indeterminate about it. Since the situation is in principle complete (no one ever actually writes down a complete description, of course; only a description of the details that matter to the argument) you can think of it as an in-principle description of a whole world. Some philosophers actually do believe that these possible worlds are out there "somewhere," and so are really in some sense "existing"; but normally it is understood to be just a useful way of talking about how things could be different. It is worth pointing out all of this because there have often been unfair criticisms made by nonphilosophers who fail to understand the distinctions being drawn: it might seem that philosophers are off on wild flights of fancy when they start talking about these other, slightly different worlds. But if we are going to attempt to understand in what sense two things are dependent upon each other, we will need some notion of what it would be like if things were different. Scientists do this whenever they perform experiments, since they control for different variables and so vary the conditions. For example, if a scientist wants to learn how effective a new drug is at fighting a particular strain of the flu, she cannot just give the drug to everyone and see if they get better. Suppose they did get better; she would be unable to tell whether this was the result of the drug, or just the natural course of the flu. So, instead, she will give some people the medicine, and others a placebo. In this way, she is comparing two different situations, and so will be able to see what it is like with, and without, the drug. In the same way, there are all kinds of dependencies that we would like to test by looking at how they hold up under different conditions. However, when we are doing metaphysics—when we are asking questions even more fundamental than are usually asked by scientists— we often do not have the luxury of controlling different variables. It is perfectly coherent, for example, to wonder what the universe would have been like with much less, or much more, matter (this is a question cosmologists often ask). But we simply cannot create a universe with more, and another with less, matter (although we now often simulate these in computers). Similarly, we may wonder about the relation between phenomenal consciousness and brain states (as described by contemporary neural science). If there is some new, undiscovered principle that links the two, we could speculate that in a complete situation (a world) without this principle, there could be these brain states without there being phenomenal experience (the zombie "world").

161

stand but miss because we have not yet managed to bring the relevant material into our understanding; the required distinction between pre- and posttheoretic intension may be illegitimate; and some impossible situations seem readily conceivable, suggesting that conceivability is not well matched with "possible world" semantics. However, setting these concerns aside, I believe that the real force of these thought experiments lies in their ability to change the nature of the debate about the role of consciousness: they help make plausible certain possibilities (and they may make plausible a shifting of the burden of proof from the epiphenomenal or token role theories to the type physicalist theories—see Chalmers 1996, 96 and 104). The end result is a static balance of conflicting suppositions: the epiphenomenalist will assert that the conceivability of these thought experiments shows that phenomenal experience is prima facie not functional, and the token role theorist will assert that the inverted spectrum shows different qualia could play the same role; while the reductionist may deny that the thought experiments describe conceivable situations, or will assert that although conceivable they are somehow deceptive and prove nothing. Without further information about consciousness we are at an impasse, where each side can insist that the burden for showing why their own presuppositions are inconsistent or otherwise unwarranted belongs to the other side.

One way out of this impasse can be found by examining yet neglected aspects of consciousness. The examples that are used in the thought experiments are invariably color.[48] This choice is not innocent, because our concepts of colors just are concepts for which—persumably because of some features of the phenomenal experience of colors—a distinction between phenomenal experience and functional role is naturally made by many. For the phenomenal experience of emotions, however, no such distinction is natural. To see this, consider the plausibility of these two thought experiments with affects instead of color vision taken as the example of phenomenal experience.

The *inverted affects* thought experiment would ask us to suppose that Adam's experience of happiness were your and my experience of sorrow, and that Adam's experience of sorrow were your and my experience of happiness, but that Adam acts in each case as is appropriate (by my and your standards).[49] It is absurd to suppose that Adam—imagine him having an evening out with close friends—could go around having the phenomenal experience of intense despair, all the while smiling and laughing. Similarly, it is absurd to suppose that Adam—imagine him now at beloved friend's funeral—could have the intense phenomenal experience of happiness and all the while frown and weep, lose his appetite, and so on. (Of course, these inversions could be, in a weak sense, possible for anyone if they were a good enough actor, but in this thought experiment we are supposing that the person is doing it all the time, from conception onward; that they are sincere; that uncontrollable autonomic responses of the relevant kind are occurring; and so on.)

The inverted affects thought experiment is grossly implausible because our concept of the experience of some affects is both richly phenomenal *and* functional; and the particular phenomenal experiences—the affect qualia—are specific to their function. Here "function" need not refer to the achievement of some plan or goal, but merely some behavior, any behavior, since what is at issue is whether phenomenal experience plays some causal role; hence weeping is enough of a function of sorrow for the phenomenal experience to be doing work. Something that is sad causes in us a phenomenal experience that is inseparable from the motivation to weep, to avoid other instances of this kind of event, and so on; something joyful has an experience that is inseparable from the motivation to laugh, to seek other instances of this kind of thing, and so on.

The affective zombie is a more difficult case because instead of having experience at cross-purposes with action we have the relevant action supposedly happening without the experience. Still, there is no intuitive appeal to a zombie that lacks affective experience but still demonstrates a behavior that is normally the particular consequence of an affect. We must conceive of a zombie that shows the signs of, say, rage, and acts as if it was filled with rage—that strikes out at others with fast and furious intent, shouts vigorously, turns red and gets hot, has increased blood pressure, and so on—but which all the while *feels* nothing inside. Seen in this way, the zombie is much less plausible. It is not accidental that we have traditionally imagined zombies as shuffling, affectless brutes. Our intuition is that without affects the zombie is a kind of uninspired automaton, and that as a result it behaves as if little more than dead. And even if we can conceive of the zombie having the appearance and behavior of rage, it is not plausible that the zombie acts out of something called "functional rage," which is what normally fills the role of rage but which here excludes the heat and overwhelming experience of rage. Our phenomenal experience of an emotion is inseparable from the motivation that that emotion provides, and the experiment's seemingly enraged zombie that feels nothing requires us to imagine a behavior without its cause—to imagine an effect without an affect! We want then to ask what, if not the phenomenal experience, is motivating the behavior; we want to fill in the void created by the supposition. Just as with the inverted affects thought experiment, the "affective" zombie thought experiment asks us to split a concept that in practice we do not split, and then requires us to discard the half that we cannot do without.[50]

This is the first puzzle: the phenomenal experiences of basic emotions and other affects are not at all distinct from the physical states that co-occur with them, nor from the motivation they provide. Can we find a theory of consciousness that accounts for this—or can we explain it away?

Puzzle 2: Why Doesn't 2 Hurt?

A representational theory of consciousness is built on the thesis that qualia are representations. The theory is compelling because we can show that some of the more perplexing features of consciousness can be explained by supposing that experiences are representations. But even given the utility of this approach, is there any direct reason for why we should think that phenomenal experience is representation? One reason that we have already seen is that phenomenal experiences can be thought of as telling us something, as carrying information. A pain in the arm is "about" the damage to the arm, and not just some undirected experience. Generally, representations can be best understood as intentional states that function inside a mental system as stand-ins for some object or stimulus in the body or environment, so that some kind of relation to the thing can be managed even if the thing is absent (or even nonexistent). Since intentional states are about something else, it would seem reasonable that pains, colors, and sounds are also kinds of intentional states. They inform us about things in our environment, damage to our bodies, and so on.

But on a closer look, there is a distinctiveness here that is being glossed over. A pain in my finger might be said to represent the pinprick in my finger. Tony's experience of anger and Adam's experience of disgust may both be said to represent the changes in their bodies that these emotions are causing. Furthermore, these experiences are all very distinct. My experience of disgust is very different from my experience of anger, and both are very different from my experience of pain. At first glance, explaining these kinds of differences seems easy: the phenomenal experiences represent different things, and so of course they are different.

But there are many kinds of representations. Consider the concept of 2. This is ostensibly a referential concept—although what it refers to is controversial. Nonetheless, the concept of 2 represents something; it represents whatever is shared by two ducks, two cats, two mice, and so on. Or consider the referential concept of inflation, or of entropy, or of mass. Each of these concepts represents something quite different. But these concepts, when entertained and so when instantiated as mental states, are not distinguishable on their phenomenal experience. There is no felt difference between thinking about 2 and about inflation—at least not in the same way that there is a striking difference between feeling anger and feeling joy. Note that this distinction is even more clear when we contrast the experience of an emotion and the concept of the emotion. The referential concept of anger does not have a phenomenal experience of its own that distinguishes it from the referential concept of joy, but we surely can distinguish the phenomenal experience of anger from that of joy. There are a host of representations for which there is only the experience of thinking—not also some unique phenomenal experience.

This is the problem of representational distinctiveness:[51] the phenomenal experience of some representational mental states are indistinguishable from or very similar to each other, while the phenomenal experience of some other states (such as basic emotions and other affects) are quite distinct. But if phenomenal experience is just representation, why is there any such difference? The second puzzle is to explain this distinctiveness of experience understood as representations.

Puzzle 3: Why Doesn't 2,000 Feel a Thousand Times More Intense than 2?

Not only are some representations different in terms of how distinct their phenomenal experiences are, but many are also different in that they admit of varieties of intensity. There is a huge difference in being mildly annoyed with someone and being overcome with rage at them. Basic emotions and many other affects—anger, disgust, fear, depression, elation—admit of great differences in intensity. But many other representations do not do so. Thinking hard about 2 does not result in an increasingly intense phenomenal experience of conceiving of 2. So some phenomenal experiences vary in intensity, but some representational mental states do not.

This is particularly important because ignoring the issue of intensity makes a token role theory of phenomenal experience more plausible. If experiences are just qualitative simples (quale) then they would seem quite analogous to symbols: they would be tokened, or not, in a representational system. But intensity, being a magnitude, suggests that there is a stronger and more complex relation between the experience and the body state that underlies it.

This is the puzzle of intensity: can we explain how some phenomenal experiences, especially affects, admit of varying degrees of intensity? And can we explain why some representations do not? If the representational theory of consciousness is correct, then since some representations (such as the referential concept of 2) seem to just be either tokened or not, how are these other states, that admit of intensity, represented?

Puzzle 4: Do We Need the Representation in the Representational Theory of Phenomenal Experience?

It may seem common sense that phenomenal experiences represent. But the term "representation" is ambiguous. We can say that tree rings in a tree represent years, that pain in my finger represents damage to my finger, that "two" represents the concept 2, and that a road sign represents the curve in the road ahead. But these are very different things. The first is a static, natural correlation in the world; the second is an event in a body; the third is a term; the last is an iconic artifact. We need to clarify the sense of "representation" in which phenomenal experiences may be representations in order to make more sense of the representational theory of consciousness.

Michael Tye offers that representations occur whenever there is causal covariation under optimal conditions:

S represents that $P =_{df}$ if optimal conditions obtain, *S* is tokened in *x* if and only if *P* and because *P*. (1995a, 101)

All the heavy lifting in this definition is being done by the notion of optimal conditions, but the idea is straightforward. It is also obviously too weak. Tree rings co-vary with years, so tree rings "represent" the age in years of the tree. What then distinguishes a phenomenal experience like pain from tree rings? Much more is needed. Tye gets it by offering his PANIC theory of consciousness: the claim that phenomenal experiences are Poised Abstract Nonconceptual Intensional Contents. They are said to be poised because they "stand ready and in position to make a direct impact on the belief/desire system" (1995a, 138).

As I have shown extensively, we have no reason to believe that desire is anything other than a convenient but vague and unscientific notion, and also many affects can operate quite independently of beliefs and the kind of capabilities that would presumably constitute a "belief/desire system" (such as B-D rationality). But in making his case that phenomenal experiences are representations, Tye has linked them essentially to beliefs and desires. This makes it unclear how subcognitive affective states can have phenomenal experience. The answer might be that a state like subcognitive fear, to be conscious, must then be poised to act on the belief-desire system since one is by definition in some sense aware of it and so able to have beliefs about it. But this would be vacuous, since anything could so be poised. More important, on such a view, nonhuman animals that lack the kind of skills necessary for a belief-desire system must lack phenomenal experience. Many are willing to bite this bullet (e.g., Rolls 1999), but I consider it an absurd and indefensible consequence.

If we consider a phenomenal experience that is not so obviously able to play a role in a belief-desire system, this problem becomes more acute. Mood is such a state. Tye's account of mood is unobjectionable. He takes depression as an example of a mood, grants that moods have characteristic phenomenal experiences, and also grants that although a mood usually is elicited by cognitive conditions, it can be free-floating: one can feel depressed "without there being anything in particular about which [one] is depressed" (1995a, xv). But, he claims, moods are representational:

What exactly they represent is not easy to pin down, but the general picture I have is as follows: For each of us, there is at any given time a range of physical states constituting functional equilibrium. Which states these are might vary from time to time. But when functional equilibrium is present, we operate in a balanced, normal way without feeling any particular mood. When moods descend upon us, we are responding in a sensory way to a *departure* from the pertinent range of physical states. (129)

Thus, the phenomenal experience of a mood is somehow the representation of a whole new functional equilibrium. But in what sense can we represent our whole functional equilibrium? Tye gives the same answer that he gives for emotion and similar states: the alteration of body states that occurs when we are angry, for example, results in a phenomenal experience of anger because we are undergoing the representation of these states. "[B]odily reactions . . . are registered in sensory receptors, thereby providing the input for the mechanical construction of a complex sensory representation of the pertinent body states" (1995a, 130–131). This is plausible in the case of emotions both because there are autonomic changes to which we can refer (getting hot when angry, the heart beating more quickly when we are afraid, and so on) and dedicated neural systems that respond to such body states. But we have no reason to posit a neural system dedicated to representing the body's whole functional equilibrium, including the state of the neural system. Perhaps what Tye means is that our experience is not a particular representation but rather is the product of the differences in all the representations that happen as a result of the mood. There would be something it is like to be in the mood, but this would not lie in any particular representation; it will have to be a global change in representations. Let us suppose that this is the claim. The problem now is that the positing of representations seems to add nothing to the explanation of the mood experience that is not already had without representations; it is the global state (including of representations), not a representation of the global state, that is changing.

Besides explaining the intentional nature of phenomenal experiences, what work do representations do for the theory? Representations are events, had or used by one individual, and are intensional. Tye observes that although all and only animals with hearts have kidneys, and although sometimes there is something it is like to have a heart and also sometimes there is something it is like to have a kidney, the experience of having a heart is distinct from the experience of having a kidney. This seems to mirror an intensional context, and it suggests that we can explain this difference as being a product of the representational nature of experience. But Tye's own example of how it can be that there is something it is like to have a kidney refers to kidney pains. Thus, there is only something it is like to have a kidney when one's kidney hurts. This is certainly distinct from being aware of one's heart beating. The neural pathways that are excited in the two cases are different, the brain states that will be caused are distinct. A causal explanation suffices to explain the distinction. Tye also provides two examples that play upon complexities surrounding personal identity. He claims that there is a phenomenal experience typical of his having a back pain, but that there is a different experience associated with being

Tye. Furthermore, he claims that there is something it is like to be Fred, and also something different that it is like to be Fred when he is embarrassed: "What it is like to be the butt of Raucous Roger's jokes is acutely embarrassing. But what it is like to be Friendly Fred is not acutely embarrassing, even though Friendly Fred is the butt of Raucous Roger's jokes" (1995b, 125). In each of these cases, we are to suppose that a back pain and embarrassment are experiences on a par with being someone. But this is certainly a category mistake. There is nothing it is like to be someone if paradigm cases of what it is like to experience something are to be pains. Rather, there is only something it is like to be someone in the sense that there is a collection of phenomenal states, with a certain continuity over time, experienced by an individual. What it is like to be Tye is therefore not at all a property like the pain of a backache. What it is like to be Tye is at most a collection of properties, along with dispositions to certain moods, typical responses, typical cares and thoughts, and so on. Furthermore, a causal, and not a representational, explanation is suitable for this difference: again, there are different causal events, one a specific pain event and one a collection of events (most of which are of like complexity and duration as the pain); or one a specific instance of suffering (among other things) and the autonomic changes caused by embarrassment, and the other a collection of events that compose the phenomenal experience of Friendly Fred. To explain these, different causal stories must be told. The basic causal story alone is not going to be wholly sufficient: we need to explain why these are experiences for Tye and for Fred, and we need some account of what makes pain pain, and what makes these other phenomenal experiences what they are. But do we need representations plugged into a belief-desire system to do that?

These difficulties arise because of ambiguities in the notions of fulfilling certain normative constraints and being a representation. We can identify that something has a biological function, for example, and as such it can also ground some representations. In contrast, the notion of representation as a mental event that readily plays a role in a belief-desire system would seem to require the idea of a token that is "standing in" for something else inside a representational system (and hence the representational theory of consciousness is prima facie consistent with the token role theory). In these cases, representation is something more than just satisfying the right kind of normative constraints. All of this matters because, although we may take as a primitive fact that phenomenal experiences like anger are "about" something, we need to understand the exact nature of this about-ness.

This is the fourth puzzle: In what sense of "representation" are phenomenal states representations? Our understanding of basic emotions, and affects like moods, shows that we do not need the notion of representation as a token in a representational system that itself is part of a belief-desire system. Can we use some weaker notion, like intentionality or teleofunction?

10

A Systems-Based Teleofunctional Theory of Consciousness

Having posed four puzzles for phenomenal consciousness that are made acute by reflecting on the role and experience of the basic emotions and other affects, my goal in this chapter is to solve these puzzles. Some have suggested that consciousness is essentially affective (e.g., Cytowic 1998) but I doubt this (for example, to my own phenomenal experience, it seems plausible that there is such a thing as a color sensation that is in no direct way affective); for that reason, my goal in this chapter is to provide the outlines of a theory of the relation of phenomenal experience to body states. In other words, basic emotions and other affects point us toward neglected aspects of phenomenal consciousness, which in turn must be explained with a more general theory concerned with all phenomenal experiences.

I will proceed by taking a last look at epiphenomenalism and token role theory, and setting both aside. Instead, I suggest that a better theory of the relation of phenomenal experience to body states should describe a strong supervenience relation between the nature of those experiences and the teleofunctions of the body states that give rise to them. This requires a review of the notion of teleofunctions, and of contemporary accounts of function. I argue that a systems-based approach to teleofunctions is the best solution. I then provide both an argument for, and an application of, this approach by showing how it elegantly provides solutions to the four puzzles posed in the last chapter. Finally, I briefly discuss how this approach yields a better understanding of the notion of autonomy.

A Last Look at Epiphenomenalism and Token Role Theory

I have argued that our phenomenal experience of affects indicates that an inseparable experiential link exists between the function or role of an affect and its phenomenal qualities. This is some reason to reject epiphenomenalism and token role theory; however, it is not conclusive since phenom-

169

enology can err. But there are other reasons to reject either alternative. I take it that the standard objections to epiphenomenalism, familiar though they are, remain sufficient reasons to reject the view. First among these is the simple observation that if we make consciousness something that can play no functional role, then we seem to have placed it beyond even the possibility of scientific theory. This does not show that epiphenomenalism is wrong, but it does suggest that one should not resign to accept it unless there is no alternative. After all, when we know so little about the mind, and we are learning so much every year, we should delay indefinitely accepting any theory that, without anything like a substantive proof, counsels us to give up any hopes of having a natural account. Another reason to give up on epiphenomenalism is that there are reasons to believe that phenomenal conscious states do play (that is, are strongly related to) some role. Our experience of affects is that they are motivational. But there is also the simple matter that we can talk about our phenomenal experiences. This would suggest that they are playing some causal role—they are causing or helping to cause talk about them. This is not an airtight argument: we also talk about numbers, and yet 2 does not play a causal role in our world. However, we have some theories about the kinds of things that numbers are. They are logical constructions, which refer to whatever is shared by two cats, two dogs, two trees, and so on—for any two instances of items falling under some concept. We have no such account of phenomenal consciousness. It is a state, of some kind, in which a conscious agent can be. It is not a logical construction. For these and other reasons, I will not consider epiphenomenalism a viable approach.

These concerns do not apply to token role theory. My first puzzle was that our experience of emotions is inconsistent with both token role theory and epiphenomenalism. But, recognizing that first-person reports are not infallible, we might suppose that not only are inverted spectra possible, but that my experience of sorrow can be your experience of joy (although we both act the same at funerals or at parties). On such a view, the phenomenal experience is acting as a representation that could be replaced by any other phenomenal experience as long as the representational role is the same.[52] This approach is objectionable because it fails to explain anything. First, it does not explain experiential distinctiveness or intensity. Second, we might still want to explain why it seems that our emotional experience feels inseparable from its motivational role. After all, the nature of experience is what is in question in the consciousness debate. Although first-person reports should never be taken as reliable, it is in large part the nature of the first-person report that we are trying to explain. Third, and much more important, separating the token that represents the experience from the experience it stands for threatens to eliminate the experience. For if my experience of joy could be switched with my experience of intense sadness, and the external roles be the same, then why isn't there anything more to the experience of joy than just the information that one is smiling? This objection is more subtle than it at first sounds. The token role theorist's first answer is presumably that there are other behaviors that joy causes besides smiling, but that all of these, not just smiling, constitute joy. But then, why suppose that all of these can send a completely different message—in particular, the message that intense sadness sends—to wherever consciousness happens? That is, even from a neurocomputational perspective, why assume that the token is separable from the experience, or at least from the thing reported? There may be something of the fallacy of what Daniel Dennett calls "the Cartesian theater" (1991) at play here: the view that there is a kind of theater in the brain somewhere, and in it consciousness happens. We imagine the various activities of sadness outside the theater, sending in some arbitrary message, which in the theater is by a kind of convention understood to mean "I am sad." The problem here is that both taking representation as the explanation of the experience and separating the representation from the experience seem to defeat the very purpose of the explanation. It would seem that no reference to the experience need be made at all. All that is being accounted for is the gross behavior of the affect and that we are able to report that we are aware of it. Paul Churchland is right to criticize the view that there is some strange essential token, the quale, that is needed to explain all this (1989b, 27–28); but it would be equally strange to suppose that all of this is experience not of the functional role, but rather of some token being sent to a brain theater—a token which can be replaced by any other.

Weak and Strong Supervenience

If we could account for the seeming relation between experience and role and motivation in these cases, we would have a theory that explained more. We must begin by explaining the kind of stronger relation we need to identify. My rejection of epiphenomenalism and of token role theory present a starting point in this endeavor. Token role theory outlined a kind of dependency and co-variance relation: that qualia play a role in a person's actions, but that these qualia could be moved around. This relation is very similar to *weak supervenience*.[53] We can understand weak supervenience to mean that if some set of properties[54] S weakly supervenes on another set of properties B, then:

> In any one world, for any objects x and y, if x has the same properties of S that y has, then x has the same properties of B that y has.

More simply, weak supervenience states that in any world, if the supervenience relation holds, then anything that has the supervening properties has the base properties. So, if in some world the experience of seeing red weakly supervenes on a particular kind of neural brain state, then in this world whenever a person will have a particular experience of red that neural brain state occurs. The supervenience relation is weak because it specifies that things hold this way only in a single world, in a single complete

SUPERVENIENCE

Supervenience is a useful philosophical notion that has become a standard tool of the contemporary consciousness debate. The details can become quite complicated, but the fundamental idea is very simple. Supervenience allows us to formulate a relation of co-variance and dependence (Kim 1993d). We say that some set of properties or events supervenes upon another set of properties or events if there can be no change in the former without some change in the later. For example, the market capitalization of General Electric (the total value of all the shares of stock) supervenes on the stock market: there can be no change in the price of all of GE without there being some change in the market (I allow that identity is trivially a supervenience relation). Supervenience is thus a useful notion because often when we develop theories we aim to outline the way some things are dependent upon others, and the ways in which they change together (as a scientist might put it, we aim to discover the dependent variables in a system, and the nature of their dependency).

The notion is open to a great deal of refinement. The principal way we can sharpen the notion of supervenience is to specify the kind of possibility involved, and also the scope of this possibility. This really is just clarifying what we mean by "can" when we say that there *can* be no change in the supervening properties without some change in what they supervene upon. The kinds of possibility include things like logical possibility or physical possibility. As it is usually understood, something is logically possible if there is not a contradiction in its appropriate description. Thus, it is logically possible that Adam is five meters tall, even though neither he nor anyone else is five meters tall; but it is not logical possible that Adam has a mass of more than and less than 100 kilograms. The notion of natural or physical possibility is stronger. We would say that a situation is naturally possible if we mean that the occurrence of that situation does not contradict the laws of physics and whatever other sciences we believe properly describe the natural world. Now, it may be that in the natural history of our universe the naturally possible situation in question never occurs. But we can mean, by saying that it is (naturally) possible, that given a specific different history, with the same natural laws, the thing would have occurred. For example, if the universe had had the same natural laws but much more, or much less, mass, things might have worked out very differently.

way that things could be. In another world, that same brain state could result in a green experience.[55]

There are two issues here that need to be considered. First, token role theory can be even weaker than this, since some token role theorists entertain the possibility that your red experience here in this world is my green experience here in this world (although we both call it "red"). For my purposes, it is sufficient to criticize the stronger version of weak supervenience given above. Second, for other versions of token role theory, depending on what goes into the base properties, the relationship may be superficially stronger than weak supervenience. This is because there is something that stands as the representational token for the experience and this may be included in the things upon which the phenomenal experience supervenes. From the perspective of someone who denies weak supervenience, however, this approach will be practically the same, since the base properties will not include this token, but rather a larger set of things that constitute the functional role of the corresponding body state. That is, if the base properties of anger are taken to be the rise in blood pressure, the change in heart rate, the brain changes specific to anger, and so on, then the token that the token role theorist takes to represent anger—but which by their own supposition can be replaced by another, different token—can be excluded from the base properties because it is arbitrarily correlated and hence replaceable. The result would be, at its strongest, something like weak supervenience.

Given this characterization, my goal is to outline a relationship of strong(er) supervenience. Some properties S strongly supervene on some other properties B if:

> For any two worlds, and for any objects x and y, if x in one world has the same properties of S that y in the other world has, then x has in its world the same properties of B that y has in its world.

This is stronger because it says that the supervenience relation must hold in every world. Strong supervenience is the kind of relation that a naturalist about phenomenal experience will be seeking if she expects to link, in any way stronger than just token role, the experience to the behavior it can cause or of which it can be a part. Note that strong supervenience as defined here is consistent both with phenomenal experience being identical to some brain states, and with the view that some natural law links the two (under some notions of natural law, strong supervenience will entail that if they are not identical, then such a law links the two). Strong supervenience is also consistent with our experience of the basic emotions and other affects. If our experience of anger is inextricably linked to a (motivation to) attack, then we should expect the relation to be one of strong supervenience of the experience upon the teleofunctional role of the corresponding body states: you cannot switch these kinds of experiences around, while keeping the body states and their role the same. There can be no zombie world, and no world where the experience of depression and joy are switched, because these things are necessarily linked to the roles they play. I am assuming, in these cases, that the notion of possibility and necessity is one of natural nomic possibility: that what is consistent across these worlds are natural laws of the kind that one hopes to uncover in a natural science. Finally, I should note that I believe that the occurrence of the kinds of systematic teleofunctions that I describe below are sufficient for the occurrence of the relevant phenomenal experiences, and this is stronger than the relationship of strong supervenience (which only outlines necessary conditions); however, to solve the puzzles posed in the last chapter this standard notion of supervenience will suffice.[56]

Getting the Function of Consciousness

Our experience is consistent with the claim that at least some aspects of affective experience strongly supervene upon the role that the affect is playing: any change in these phenomenal experiences should be explained by reference to a change in the functional role of the body state from which it arises. To make sense of the notion of an affective state playing a role, we need to identify what it is for that state to have a teleofunction (hereafter, I use this term to avoid any confusion with the use of "function" in its simpler, mathematical sense). The representational theory of phenomenal consciousness nicely captures our sense that our phenomenal experience is about something (if only because it strongly supervenes upon a physical state that is intentional): my experience of a sunset is of, or about, the actual sunset; my experience of pain is of, or about, my body state. But in linking phenomenal experience to representations, the problem of specifying teleofunction remains—although it can be rephrased as a problem of representational intentionality: How is it that my representations manage to be *about* something in the teleological sense? In a more general teleofunctional account, the question becomes how some capability can have a function which is specified seemingly in reference to future possible occurrences. This problem is now a familiar one, and the goal of solving it is the goal of providing an acceptable naturalist account of a kind of teleological explanation.

To briefly review the issue: to say that the teleofunction of fear, for example, is to motivate flight from some kinds of threat, is—on the surface of the claim—to refer to future events as an explanation of a present action or capability. For, on normal usage of such teleofunctional ascriptions, this is the teleofunction of the neural circuits underlying fear even before they ever so operate. Similarly, it seems correct to say that the teleofunction of sperm is to inseminate an egg, even if the sperm is had by an individual who has no children nor ever will have children. And, even more complicated a matter is that the future event in question need not even be possible in any strong sense: the function of the sperm of the last man remains to inseminate an egg, even if this were now historically impossible. Thus, the primary problem with teleofunctional explanations or ascriptions is that very weakly possible future events are used to explain present capabilities; but our best scientific explanations refer only to past events to explain all events or states. The challenge is to provide a theory of teleofunctions which coheres with our best naturalist approaches. Two approaches have become standard: etiological historical accounts, and systems-based accounts.

Etiological Accounts of Teleology

Perhaps the most obvious sense in which teleofunctions can arise is in the design of objects (Kitcher 1993). A hammer can be manufactured with its form specifically so that it can hammer nails; and it seems therefore that hammering nails is uncontroversially its teleofunction. However, some artifacts seem to come to have their teleofunctional form through trial and error on the part of the manufacturer (Bigelow and Pargetter 1987, 185–186); and, of course, almost all biological systems are not designed. However, there may be a sense in which we can think of biological systems (and perhaps also trial-and-error inventions) as being "designed": they have been "designed" by evolution.

The most developed theories of teleofunctions have been etiological ones: approaches that attempt to explain teleofunctions by reference to a history of the thing with the function. An early and clear statement of an etiological account is found in Larry Wright, who, expanding on ideas in the work of Charles Taylor (1964), argues that "teleological explanations are causal in the very broad sense that they explain what produces or brings about the behavior in question; they offer an etiology" (1976, 25). Wright's teleological explanation of functions is of the form (81):

The function of X is Z iff:
   (i) Z is a consequence (result) of X's being there,
   (ii) X is there because it does (results in) Z.

Thus, the function of the heart is to pump blood because (i) the pumping of blood occurs because of the heart; and (ii) the heart is there because it does pump blood.

This is a useful analysis. It has come under some major criticism because it allows us to count as teleofunctions some things which seem quite obviously not to be such (Boorse 1976). But, setting these aside for a moment, the trick is to explain clause (ii): in what sense is the heart said to be there *because* it pumps blood? The foremost answer to this question in an etiological account has been to turn to evolutionary theory; variations on this approach have been developed by Peter Godfrey-Smith (1994), Paul Griffiths (1993), Philip Kitcher (1993), R. G. Millikan (1984, 1993), K. Neander (1991), and others. The basic idea is that the relevant item or ability is in the individual because it was selected for the teleofunction in the genotype, and that means we can rightly identify this as the teleofunction of the item. A bit of a story is usually necessary to flesh this out. A heart's teleofunction is to pump blood because the reason that the heart exists is because it pumps blood; if it failed to pump blood the organism would die and not reproduce. And in some sense, it will be right to say that the heart evolved because of selection pressures. But such an explanation is going to be complex and indirect: there is not going to be an organism with a heart competing with a close relative that is the same but for lacking a heart. Instead, over

time, selection pressures could select for features that ultimately constitute, in descendants in some future population, a heart. Evolution, the idea
goes, selects (and here we can read "selects" very weakly) for certain traits;
this selection pressure explains why those traits carry on; and this explains
the sense of "because" in clause (ii) (although it may be a very indirect
explanation!).

A number of problems plague this kind of etiological account. For example, it is unclear how we can account for the fact that capabilities change
their teleofunction over time; that is, what historical pressures must be
referred to in order to identify the present teleofunction of a structure, if the
teleofunction appears to be different now than at some earlier time? This
problem has given rise to the recent history theories of teleofunctions
(Godfrey-Smith 1994): one might propose that it is not the history of the
origin of the item or ability, but rather it is the most recent history of it that
matters. But I need not discuss the fine details of the various etiological
accounts to show why they are not appropriate to be used to identify the
supervenience base of phenomenal experience. They are inappropriate because they aim to explain teleofunctions in a weak sense inappropriate for
any subsequent application of the right kind of supervenience claim.

Let me begin with an example. Suppose that our theory of the teleofunction of color recognition was an etiological-historical account that refers to
selection of a trait in order to identify the teleofunction; and suppose that
phenomenal experience were to supervene on this teleofunction. Roughly,
mental state S represents color E if it is a proper function of S to correlate
with seen occurrences of kind E. This is the proper teleofunction of S if S
were ever selected for its correlating with instances of kind E (again: the
story will be more complex, since it may never come down to competition
over this particular capability; but the point will hold regardless of how we
later bootstrap the issue). Suppose also that experience of color E would
arise from the occurrence of this representation (such an account is consistent with Lycan 1996). Thus, my experience of blue is somehow going to be
dependent upon the underlying representational machinery having been
selected for representing blue (or at least color, or at the very least some
capacity of seeing things) in the environment. Now, consider the following
scenario. We know that evolution works in a ramshackle way. Suppose that
an organism is born and because of a random mutation it can see a particular
shade of blue that is bluer than is perceivable by the other members of its
species—we'll call it deeper-blue. In this individual, this capability has not
yet been selected for or against, and so it has merely appeared via dumb
luck. But it seems common sense that there will be a phenomenal experience accompanying the exercise of this capability. It could even happen
that the ability is passed on in a subpopulation but never selected for or
against. This would happen, for example, if although there may be deeper-
blue things in the environment, none of them was ever of significant use or
harm. Is it then impossible to have a deeper-blue experience? If that were

so, how would we ever get any conscious experience? Unlike the twin arguments against teleofunctions (in which we are asked to imagine having an exact twin with a different history, or even no history), this scenario describes something like what actually must have happened: surely a capacity must occur in some individual of a species *before* it can be selected for or against. Thus, on an evolution-based teleofunctional theory of the supervenience base for phenomenal experience, an organism can have a kind of zombie capability (such as the capability to see deeper blue without having a phenomenal experience of deeper blue) because the capability has as yet no proper teleofunction.

There are several potential answers to this objection. One is that the ability to see deeper blue gets a teleofunction and thus a representational role in a derived way. Although I accept that there can be derived teleofunctions, I believe that derived teleofunction is the weak point of the etiological teleofunctional accounts, since it is unclear when such a claim is legitimate; but I will set this concern aside here. Another answer is that teleofunctions (and the ability to derive some kinds of teleofunction), and therefore consciousness, emerge gradually in a continuum (see Lycan 1987, 44). But neither of these answers is satisfactory, since the real perplexity is not the method of the bootstrapping, but that the bootstrapping happens at all. We have supposed that several generations of a subpopulation had the deeper-blue trait, and it was not selected for. Suppose now that deep-blue-colored predators appear on the scene, and so this subpopulation now has selection pressures in its favor as its deeper-blue–blind rivals are eaten up. The first group of generations having this trait and the latter group would have *no internal differences* that explain why in the latter but not the former there are the phenomenal experiences in question; rather, it would be a fact about the history and environment of the organism that determined this. Thus, phenomenal experience would spring out of contingent external environmental factors.

This problem applies not just to the claim that phenomenal experiences are representations, but also to any theory that they strongly supervene on teleofunctions where the teleofunctions are similarly specified. The recent history version of the etiological account has the same problem, as does the propensity version (Bigelow and Pargetter 1987), and the relational theory (Walsh 1996). Also, this problem may arise for some of the other versions of teleofunctions. For example, some teleofunctions might be specified in a historical account of learning. Thus Fred Dretske (1981), for example, exploits not evolution but rather the notion of a training period to explain some mental teleofunctions. A representation can get a functional role by having a training period in which certain correct associations are learned; then future associations are right or wrong inasmuch as they live up to the training period's cases. But if we were to use Dretske's approach to explain teleofunctions, we would have something like a bunch of brain reactions happening throughout an organism's life, but which become phenomenal conscious only after the end of some arbitrary training period. And similar kinds of problems arise for many explanations of causal co-variance under optimal conditions, depending upon how we explain optimal conditions.

The problem with these accounts lies with the nature of etiological teleofunctional explanation and related notions. The etiological theories primarily offer an account of how it can be legitimate to describe something as having a function. That is, they are not ontological[57] claims, but rather analysis of when it is appropriate to claim a thing plays a teleofunctional role. But, if a teleofunction is going to be posited as the supervenience base for (some aspect of) a phenomenal experience, then the theory of teleofunctions is providing not just an analysis or explanation, but also is identifying kinds for another theory. Taking etiological theories in this way leads to a very weird kind of externalism, as I showed above. (But since an etiological account of functional explanation alone does not entail an ontological claim, the fact that in the thought experiment we cannot call the ability to see deeper blue a teleofunction is not going to be a problem; we might just accept that the ability to see deeper blue does not have the kind of function that is etiologically specified until it is selected for or until it can serve to assist survival, since this will be how we define the relevant teleofunctions.) I think that some weird consequences are inevitable in a teleofunctional account of consciousness, but they can be less extravagant. The primary notion of teleofunction that needs to be clarified is that one specified in terms of the actual internal conditions of the organism; that is, the relevant teleofunctions need to be understood as occurrent, individual organic conditions.

Systematic Teleofunctions

There is an alternative approach to explaining some teleofunctions; instead of appealing to an etiology, it is possible to appeal to the organizational properties of the thing with the function. This is the systems-based approach. This approach has been less developed, perhaps because the view is more complex and so the demands of explaining it are great; but important defenses of the view are found in Gerd Sommerhoff (1950), Ernest Nagel (1977), and Gerhard Schlosser (1998). The approach can exploit the insights of the evolutionary account of teleofunctions, but remains local and quite natural in its effects.

The basic idea of the systems-based approach to explaining teleofunctions is that goal-directed behavior is a property of whole *systems*. We can think of an organism as a complex system that has certain capabilities which we identify as teleofunctions because they maintain certain features of the system. Prima facie, most organisms are adaptive and self-organizing complex systems. The notion of a self-organizing system is not, unfortunately, very easily defined. But for my purposes here, we do not need it to be. What matters instead is that, undeniably, such systems do exist, and that affective organisms are surely examples of them. This is most obvious when we consider homeostasis. The process of evolution produces systems which act in their environments in a way that maintains a stable range of values on many parameters of the organism: body temperature, water levels, physical integrity (e.g., some avoid being broken in two), and many others. These homeostatic functions are in part demonstrable in a simple empirical way. Given the opportunity to drink water, many organisms will do so in a way that maintains a range of the quantity of water in their bodies. Many organisms maintain a constant narrow range of body temperature, and many also, when given the opportunity to walk along a temperature gradient, will seek a place that allows them easy thermoregulation. And so on. Of course, all organisms depend upon their environment for stability on some dimensions. Thus, some organisms will eat too much if food is available in excess of what would normally be the case in their environment. Similarly, no organism that I know of can directly detect and avoid x-rays. Organisms also have limited abilities to respond; they can travel only a particular distance, or thermoregulate in a particular range of external temperatures, and so on. But within certain parameters, which should be expected to be close to those in which they evolved, organisms demonstrate homeostasis for much of their lives. There is no doubt an issue about what counts as a proper or normal set of such ranges for an organism, and one might worry that this will start the account back onto a historical and externalist track. But this can be avoided by the observations that the relevant parameters will be maintained only in a particular range which we can empirically identify (a rat heated to 10,000 degrees centigrade is not going to thermoregulate, or maintain its internal water levels, and so on); thus, we can empirically identify the ranges of environmental conditions in which the organism will succeed in various kinds of homeostasis. Conversely, we can know as an experimentally demonstrable fact that an organism will die if it does not stay in these ranges.

The primary difficulty confronting the systems-based approach is that the parameters that we identify as demonstrating the effects of teleofunctions need to be, to some degree, "orthogonal to" (i.e., independent of) each other (E. Nagel 1977, 273). This is because all kinds of rather trivial systems can be said to maintain state along dependent parameters. Ernest Nagel uses the example of a ball set in motion in a spherical bowl (274). Is its gyring trajectory toward rest teleofunctional? His answer is that this is a different kind of process since the laws of physics make all the relevant parameters tightly related. This may then seem a bit odd: we identify as having teleofunctions those systems that have components which operate not as a simple, but rather as a complex, application of laws of nature. As I shall repeat below, however, I don't think that this is a problem. Teleofunctional systems, and hence autonomous systems, come in degrees, and a ball moving in a bowl is a limit case of a system demonstrating negligible self-organization and autonomy. We should not shy away from the possibility that there is no clear division between complex autonomous systems, such as the homeostatic systems in organisms, and simpler physical ones.

And, for our purposes here, it is sufficient to note that the kinds of organisms that are our concern (those that have affects) are of more than sufficient complexity to meet this criterion.

Recently, Schlosser (1998; see also Christensen 1996) has offered a more general teleofunctional account which is systems based, and which provides a definition of teleofunctions that utilizes many of the insights of Larry Wright (1976) and others working to explore an etiological account. Schlosser argues that a "*functional* state or trait X is any state or trait of a complex system, which by generating another state or trait F (the *function* of X) is under certain circumstances necessary for its self-production" (305). The basic idea is that X and F occur in a complex system, and in a sense they are necessary for the generation of one another. Schlosser is concerned that the notion of "complex system" is very vague; in fact, it is playing a role like Ernest Nagel's notion of the "orthogonal" parameters: if X and F produce each other in a tight, trivial loop, then we are disinclined to think of F as a teleofunction. But if the relation between X and F is complex, then the teleofunctional ascription is more compelling. Again, we can set aside this issue with the observations that there is a continuum in nature of various degrees of complex systems, and that the biological systems that demonstrate basic emotions and other affects are undoubtedly complex. Another feature which is equally problematic is the time that such functions endure. Schlosser recognizes that the cycles of production must be more than one loop; and that we will think of a system as a homeostatic and therefore interestingly self-organizing system only if it is homeostatic for some amount of time. But this, too, is a matter-of-degree issue which, though requiring further analysis, poses no refutation of the view.

Thus, Schlosser offers the following account (315):

> F_c is a function of $X_c(t)$ iff:
> for a certain period of time $t_0 < t < t + x + y < t_0 + T$
> 1. $X(t)$ is directly causally necessary to establish $F(t+x)$ (under certain circumstances c_1);
> 2. $F(t+x)$ is indirectly causally necessary to establish $X(t+x+y)$ under certain circumstances c_2);
> 3. the causal relations between $X(t)$, $F(t+x)$, $X(t+x+y)$ are complex.

The time indexes are required to clarify that the causal relation between these states is correctly ordered; the reproduced states are instances of types.

Thus, consider a homeostatic process like the maintenance of internal water levels. In a primate, central nervous system osmoreceptors (kind X) detect cellular dehydration (teleofunction F), which can motivate the organism to drink water (see Rolls 1999, 205ff). We can say that the osmoreceptors have as a teleofunction the detection of cellular dehydration in order to stimulate rehydrating behaviors; these behaviors in turn are indirectly causally necessary for the reproduction of such osmoreceptors, since without sufficient hydration the organism would simply not be able to produce and maintain this neural subsystem.

One very significant advantage of this approach is that it is closer to how we typically ascribe biological teleofunctions. If we were to discover a new kind of mammal, for example, we would not be stumped to understand it, waiting until the evolutionary biologists placed it in evolutionary history and then told us why this or that organ or behavior evolved. We could just watch it in its environment, and working with some basic naturalist presuppositions (and we have many of them: all animals must eat something to gain energy sources, energy is necessary for life, high temperatures impede the biochemical processes of life, and so on), we could develop theories of what it was up to. This is how ethologists have always had to work, after all.

The Schlosser account is in part a kind of microetiological one, in which the reproduction of capabilities is the criterion used to identify their teleofunction. One might therefore argue that it is also strange that phenomenal experience would supervene on a system with a history. But the criterion is local in both space and time, and I consider this much less costly an explanation as a result. And the two explanations should actually not diverge very much. The etiological explanation of teleofunctions should be expected to yield a set of functions that is nearly coextensive with the systems-based account of teleofunction. They can diverge primarily when newer functions appear that would not yet have been selected for.

The hypothesis that I propose is that phenomenal experience strongly supervenes upon the systems-based teleofunctions of which we are aware— I will call these *a-teleofunctions*. My point in picking out these specific teleofunctions is a very simple one: we are not hard-wired to be able to be directly aware of the functioning of our livers, for example, and so although there are teleofunctions that it serves, these are not a-teleofunctions, and we have no phenomenal experience of them. Other teleofunctions are potentially a-teleofunctions but sometimes have effects that are too tiny or fast to generate awareness.

I have placed special stress upon homeostatic processes. I believe that homestasis yields the primary teleofunctions that constitute phenomenal experience. This is a view endorsed, for example, by Jaak Panksepp, who argues that "sensations generate pleasure or displeasure in direct relation to their influence on the homeostatic equilibrium of the body" (1998, 164). Panksepp gives an analysis of how the phenomenal experience of thirst can become so intense it is overwhelming (165ff), arguing that this is illustrative of how feeling is related to homeostatic drives. One objection to this view is that there are teleofunctions which are not homeostatic on the usual conception of this term; sexual behavior is a typical example, and we do clearly have phenomenal experiences associated with sexual drives and sexual activity. We could offer a compelling unified account of how things like sexual behavior can be *indirectly homeostatic*, where endogenous factors alter the system and set it on a course of behavior that can be thought of

as seeking a return to another state. Thus, lust would be like an endoge-
nously produced thirst, and sexual behavior like drinking. But I think that
we can pass over what may be a contentious issue, and just observe that
homeostasis provides the clearest, and perhaps the most important, cases
of the kind of systems-based teleofunctions upon which, when we are
aware of the process, phenomenal experience strongly supervenes.

The Puzzles Revisited

I can now show how this approach solves the four puzzles presented in the
last chapter.

Puzzle 1: Strong Supervenience and the Role of Phenomenal States

I have hypothesized that phenomenal experience strongly supervenes
upon the teleofunctions of various processes of which we are aware. Thus,
the phenomenal experience of a conscious instance of fear is inseparable
from the bodily changes that we experience as part of this emotion: the
motivation to flee, the change in heart rate, the shaking excitement of adrenaline. The phenomenal experience of joy, instead, will be completely different, and necessarily so; to change the phenomenal experience of joy with
that of fear, for example, would be to change the a-teleofunctions (and
hence all the relevant body states) from joy to fear. There is no room here
for inverted emotions. Experiences are not tokens in a representational
system that can be replaced by other tokens—they are not, like words,
wholly arbitrary—but rather, the experience is inseparable from the a-
teleofunctional events.

It is worth noting that this steers a plausible path between two extremes
that have plagued theories of phenomenal experience. One extreme was
the simple brute assertion that phenomenal experiences just are brain
states, without any reference to their teleofunctional role. Another extreme
is a functional account so broad that it allows for a variety of multiple
realizability arguments. Many philosophers have supposed that psychological properties were multiply realizable, and hence for some of these
philosophers this means that phenomenal experience also will be multiply
realizable. The intuition that compelled many was that psychological properties are teleofunctional, and presumably a Martian or a robot can have
capabilities that fulfill some of the same teleofunctions as are present in
humans. Hence, be it made of wholly different biological matter or of sili-
con chips, these functionally similar things can feel pain. A simplistic identity theory or some versions of strong supervenience are seen to be incompatible with this, since they would identify or tightly link pain, for
example, with something like one kind of neural event not had by Martians
or robots.

On the face of it, there is surely something right about the multiple realizability thesis, at least in some weak form. And as we have supposed here that phenomenal experiences strongly supervene on the teleofunctional roles of an organism's mental apparatus, we can grant that some degree of multiple realizability is therefore possible. But there is much objectionable about the debates that have revolved around this "problem." First, it is difficult to straighten out to what degree a teleofunctional role is independent of its realization. In natural systems, the actual functioning of a system is always going to be constrained and shaped in significant ways by the implementation. A teleofunction's implementation can exploit natural facts that would be hard or impossible to re-create in other natural systems. Thus, a teleofunctional description is not one that needs to be wholly distinct from the kind of description a reductive identity theory might give; made fine-grained enough, a functional description may not be multiply realizable at all.

Second, the intuition that robots or radically different aliens feel pains just as humans do is stated in a way that seems to reify pains into a single natural kind. But pain is an event, and events can be both reducible to physical stuff and be quite variable. Glossing over the variation within a class of events can trick us into accepting a false dilemma between a functional description that is highly amenable to broad multiple realizability, and a reductive one inconsistent with even weak notions of multiple realizability. This is because we are misled to treat a predicate for a phenomenal experience as something either determinately true or false in a straightforward way (talk about "qualia" can encourage this). But there really is no sense in which most event terms are like that. They are not well expressed as bivalent properties, but rather as something more like a collection of properties measured as magnitudes. A naturalistic theory of phenomenal experience is certainly not going to get anywhere looking for things like "red experience" that either obtain or do not obtain, period; just as we would never think to look for "body temperature" which obtains or does not obtain. Surely a blind spider does not have red experience, and surely a primate that can recognize red things as red has some kind of experience we might call red experience. There may be no clear division, and so no interesting sense in which there is a cutoff point, in between the having and lacking of red experience, just as there is no interesting sense in which there is a division between a hurricane and a large, circulating storm that has slightly slower wind speeds. There are all kinds of events which are real things out there in the world, which rightly fit into a scientific worldview, but which are not simple entities that either obtain or fail to obtain in every case. To insist that they all do leads to endless pseudoproblems.

The systems-based teleofunctional approach is consistent with this observation. Affective experience strongly supervenes on the teleofunctional role of that affect in the system of the organism. These systems are very complex, and there is no easy division between the teleofunctions that we can specify for different but similar kinds of such systems. Thus, for example, we should expect that species (i.e., kinds of systems) very close to us, such as other mammals, have some affective experiences negligibly different from our own, because their nervous systems are very similar to our own. Some organisms will have similar enough features that we can identify affects, but they will be different (not necessarily weaker or stronger, just different) inasmuch as the role (very finely differentiated) is different. There will be no easy answer to where the affect ends and something other, but like it, begins.

Puzzles 2 and 3: Explaining Distinctiveness and Intensity with the Homeostatic Intensity Hypothesis

The systems-based teleofunction theory provides a ready answer to the second and third puzzles, which were revealed by careful attention to the phenomenal experience of some emotions. A highly plausible hypothesis, amenable to empirical investigation, is what I will call the *homeostatic intensity hypothesis.*

The homeostatic intensity hypothesis has two elements, corresponding to the two puzzles. First, some affects and other states cause a great many changes in an organism. Rage and terror, for example, are not just a matter of some neurons in the language center firing away, as might be the case when we contemplate numbers; rather, many cortical and subcortical areas are stimulated. Very substantial physiological changes occur, and these in turn cause more changes in the brain and elsewhere in the nervous system. From a homeostatic perspective, rage and terror engage a great deal more of the organism's homeostatic teleofunctions than do, for example, contemplating a number or holding a belief. *The character, and hence distinctiveness, of a phenomenal experience is determined by the specific a-teleofunctions that constitute it.* Thus, thinking about 2 and thinking about 3 are going to be negligibly distinct phenomenal experiences because there are negligible differences in the kinds and numbers of a-teleofunctions that these events effect. Feeling rage and feeling joy are extremely distinct because they arouse many diverse a-teleofunctions.

Second, many of the parameters that are altered during some affects and other states admit of a range of alteration. Mild fear can differ from terror because of the degree of adrenaline that is released and the consequent degree of the changes this causes; changes in body temperature can be greater; muscle tension can increase; and so on. Thinking about inflation or 2 will cause some changes in some portions of the brain, but the changes will be relatively small. No matter how hard you think about 2, you are not going to involve much of your body in the process, and those functions that are involved will be altered relatively little. Thus, *the intensity of the phenomenal experience is determined by both the quantity of a-teleofunctions that are altered in the experience, and the magnitude of those alterations.* This is consistent with the fact that basic emotions seem particularly capable of a range of intensities; basic emotions, as given in the affect program theory, involve many distributed systems in the body and the alterations of these systems can admit of significant differences in magnitude, resulting in differing intensities of experience. The measure of intensity will be against baselines that are defined in terms of the stable homeostasis of the organism under normal conditions.

Puzzle 4: Representations and Teleofunctions

Finally, the systematic teleofunctions approach helps clarify the issue of what role representation plays in the account of consciousness as intentional state. Our problem was that although we might say a mood or pain is intentional, it seems highly unlikely that we need a "belief-desire system" for these experiences, and it can even be hard to see in what sense a phenomenal experience needs to be a representation: the physical changes that constitute the experience itself seem sufficient to explain the relevant features. The answer is that when our goal is to explain the nature of phenomenal experiences themselves, we can drop the notion of representation in the robust sense of a token that stands in a representational system for something else (which need not be present or even exist). And we can definitely reject any requirement that a propositional attitude be involved, or even a symbolic state (such as is required in linguistic theories of consciousness; e.g., Rolls 1999). Rather, phenomenal experiences strongly supervene on a-teleofunctions of the organism. This means that the nature of the experience is not constrained by or explained by representation except that any of these experiences *can be* a representation, and it must be taken as such in order for one to be aware of it, to remember it, to be able to report on it, and so on.

Panksepp has some observations about awareness that are relevant here. Panksepp notes that the coherent affects, intentions, and activity of split-brain patients strongly counsels against associating conscious awareness with any lateralized ability such as language, and rather suggests that the core of such awareness lies in subcortical affective and motor processes:

> These brain areas appear to be most likely sources for the primal neural mechanisms that generate affective states of consciousness. It will be argued that those primordial circuits may elaborate a fundamental sense of "self" within the brain. Although this is not a very skilled and intelligent self and its pervasive influence may often seem preconscious (especially when higher forms of consciousness have matured during ontogenetic development), it ultimately allows animals to develop into the intentional, volitional, and cognitively selective creatures that they are. It may do this in part by providing a basic body image that can control primitive attentional and intentional focus. (1998, 308)

This is a compelling approach, consistent with many of the claims I make here concerning autonomy. It also is consistent, to use the terminology introduced in chapter 2, with the claim that awareness is not necessarily propositional, nor symbolic, but is representational. A-teleofunctions should be understood in light of this: the awareness that is required to make these teleofunctions into a-teleofunctions is representational, and not necessarily symbolic or propositional.

Conclusion and a Clarification about Autonomy

Taking emotions into account suggests very fruitful emendations to the consciousness debate. The systems-based teleofunctional theory of consciousness is consistent with the claim that experience of an affect cannot be separated from the role of the affect, while escaping the pitfalls of the etiological accounts. It offers a solution, in the homeostatic intensity hypothesis, to the troubling difficulty of explaining qualitative and quantitative variations in experiences (variations that are explicitly revealed in the occurrences of basic emotions). Finally, attending carefully to the experience of emotions casts some light on the ambiguities inherent in the notion of "representation," and helps clarify the sense in which a phenomenal experience need be or can be representational.

The theory of systems-based teleofunctions, including homeostatic teleofunctions, offers a way to ground the notion of autonomy somewhat more. I have said that a system (e.g., an organism) is autonomous inasmuch as it pursues its own goals and maintains its integrity in ways that compensate for changes in the organism and in its environment. I can now clarify, adding that a system has autonomy to the degree that it has its own ends (which are directly or indirectly the products of systematic teleofunctions) and is able to pursue those ends and maintain its homeostasis, while adapting its strategies to alterations to its internal state or its environment. Generally, more autonomous systems will be more complex systems (although it does not follow that more complex systems are more autonomous; the history of AI provides plenty of examples of extremely complex systems with negligible autonomy). Autonomy can be understood in relation to a certain notion of flexibility: systems are autonomous to the degree that they use different strategies to maintain homeostasis and pursue their ends under varying conditions. As observed above, the division between autonomous and nonautonomous systems is not sharp. But there is nonetheless a very significant difference between negligibly autonomous systems, such as thermostats or our best robots, on the one hand, and highly autonomous ones, such as crickets or cats, on the other hand.

11

The Computational Theory of Mind

As both a modeling tool and an engineering program eager to learn from nature, AI has become an essential part of our endeavor to understand the mind. However, the inspiration that the computer has provided has been considered in neglect of basic emotions and other affects. It is my task in this chapter and the next to address in a preliminary way some of this oversight. In this chapter I will argue that a strict version of the computational theory of mind is untenable. The next will provide some speculations on what our best understanding of emotions could offer the engineering practice of AI.

The computational theory of mind has been a leading theory in the philosophy of mind; it has also been an inspiration for cognitive science. There are several versions, most of which are so weak in their formulation that they are tantamount to common sense and are widely accepted (e.g., the mind is a processor of information); but some stronger forms have taken the mind to be a computer of the kind described in classical AI: a manipulator of discrete symbols. This view coheres well with reductive and other forms of cognitivism about emotion. Although it is not as widely held today as it once was, this view is still influential, and it has not been properly criticized for its failure to explain or account for affects. Criticizing the view will also provide an opportunity to criticize a weaker sense of "cognitivism," expanding that notion now to include not only propositional attitude theories but also these symbolic ones.

Symbolic Computational Functionalism

Cognitive scientists and philosophers often distinguish levels of description appropriate to minds and brains. One such distinction is drawn between levels of processing dependence, where a lower-level process must be complete before the higher-level one can be, because the higher-level process is constituted by the lower-level ones. This is a notion common to computer science, where a high-level language can be constructed out of a lower-level language (think of a Scheme interpreter written in C). Another distinction in levels is made between appropriate theoretical levels, such as Daniel Dennett's distinction between the design stance and the intentional stance (1971), and Marr's distinction between computational, algorithmic, and hardware levels (1982) (see also Millikan 1990; Newell 1981). These levels are distinguished on the supposition that there are different theoretical vocabularies appropriate for each; for example, each level might have a corresponding science with its own taxonomy, such as computation with its symbols and states, and neural implementation with its neurons, neurotransmitters, and action potentials. These are called "levels" because there is often, though not always, a commitment that one is reducible to or supervenes upon another (and if the commitment for reduction is strong there may be no distinction in kind between processing dependence levels and theoretical levels). Scientists often circumvent coming down explicitly for one kind of reductive commitment or another, and simultaneously roughly respect these theoretical levels while also giving explanations which mix them. A model for word recognition processes, for example, might make reference both to semantic priming and the plausible neural structure and limitations of the sensory system(s) involved. However, other explanatory frameworks require that we carefully distinguish different theoretical levels, separating out the implementational from the semantic, the biological limitations from the logical ones. One such approach is the classical computational theory of mind, *symbolic computational functionalism* (for brevity, in this chapter I will use "computationalism" to identify this position). This theory has two very definite advantages. Since it treats minds as manipulators of discrete symbols, it readily allows for modeling (or implementation) in discrete logical structures and computer languages that have been a staple of twentieth-century philosophy of mind and computer science. For symbolic computational functionalism, a human mind may well be a deterministic finite state automata, which can thus in principle be fully described in a first-order logic. A second advantage is that the theory, being pitched at the level of symbol processing, is implementation independent. As we have already seen in the case of consciousness, there is broad intuitive appeal to the notion that different kinds of systems, such as robots or alien organisms, could have the same kinds of mental states, even if their physical structure were not much like our own (e.g., Putnam 1964, 1975).

The advantage of a simple implementation independence has not gone unchallenged. In a different context, Patricia Churchland and Terrence Sejnowski have argued that we might waste time and energy by ignoring lower theoretical levels:

Computational space is undoubtedly vast, and the possible ways to perform any task are probably legion. Theorizing at a high level without benefit of lower-level constraints runs the risk of exploring a part of that space that may be interesting in its own right but remote from where the brain's solution resides. (1992, 11–12)

Others, taking a more radical tack, have argued against representational theories of mind, one of which would be computationalism, on the grounds that representations do not earn us anything more in our best theories of mind than is already had in non-representational descriptions (Ramsey 1997; see also van Gelder 1995). Representations might even, as Rodney Brooks once argued, confuse things:

> When we examine very simple level intelligence we find that explicit representations and models of the world simply get in the way. It turns out to be better to use the world as its own model. . . . Representation is the wrong unit of abstraction in building the bulkiest parts of intelligent systems. (1991, 140)

To these objections the computationalist has responses. To the former, she might likely say that she is interested not in making a physiologically accurate model of the human mind, but rather in finding the essential features of any intelligent agent. (A compelling analogy for this case can be found with flight; for centuries it seemed only logical that we should try to emulate birds to create flying machines, but it was only when we developed a much more abstractly functional understanding of flight that we found success.) Or, in more traditional AI, one might go so far as to say she wants only to solve a problem, such as making a computer that can talk or recognize faces. In these cases, exploring the computational space need not be beholden to human physiological features. In the next chapter I will address why even AI as a purely engineering endeavor should be concerned with emotions; in this chapter, I am concerned with how well computationalism explains the intelligence of humans or other animals.

To the latter and more radical objection, that representation may be unnecessary or even misleading, the computationalist is certainly eager to respond with lengthy debate (e.g., Clark and Toribio 1994). Much of the work that has gone into representational theories of mind has been dedicated precisely to delineating when something is functioning as a representation, how such representations are fixed to their objects, how they are used in inference, and how they might be reduced to existing physical structures. At this early stage in the sciences of mind, there seems to be no known way to settle the debate between representationalists and anti-representationalists without begging the question.

However, the case for computationalism is more dubious when we acknowledge that there are mental phenomena that require, for a proper accounting, that we get below the level of symbol processing. Such phenomena show us that a computationalist theory of mind which hopes to have a sufficiently complete description of the mind is hoping in vain. Chief among these phenomena are some of the affects, including the basic emotions. These affects pose a problem to computationalism because by their very nature they act across the traditional levels of description that computationalists respect. Basic emotions are intentional, but can to a significant degree be disassociated from any propositional or symbolic contents; some of their role may be amenable to an abstract functional description of a cognitive kind, but they also have essential physiological elements; they can be associated with judgments and perceptions, but actually they can be shown to influence perception and judgment, and to be independent of, and in some senses prior to, complex kinds of perception and judgment. Basic emotions and other affects cast us back again and again into the problem of an integrated, embodied agency, something for which the symbolic computational functionalists do not yet have a good account.

I shall proceed by arguing that contemporary evidence strongly suggests that basic emotions and other affects influence perception, and do so at a subcognitive level; that although these affects are related to cognitive states of the kind that would characterize symbolic computational functionalism, the affects are separable from these states; that these affects have a complex and important role to play in memory; and that, given all these facts, affects are necessary for rational action. In conclusion, I shall argue that these features pose insurmountable problems for computationalism. Focusing on perception, memory, and rational action is advantageous because it is unlikely that any computationalist can escape these issues by reducing the size of her domain; that is, she cannot reasonably explain or model intelligent behavior without also modeling or explaining these things. I can make this point by reviewing evidence largely from cognitive psychology and neuroscience, some of which we have already seen in chapters 1 and 2, since such evidence is, in this case, perhaps the most substantial. However, the comments I make here could have been made by anyone who was comfortable with a few plausible claims about basic emotions and other affects (namely, they influence perception and memory, they are bodily, they are integral to rationality), based, perhaps, on one's own experience.

In this chapter, I shall construe "cognitivism" slightly more broadly than I do elsewhere in the book; I will take cognition to include both propositional attitudes and symbolic systems.

Emotional Congruence in Social Judgment and Perception or Categorization

We might begin a consideration of the relation between emotions and cognition by wondering whether for the computationalist emotions are, as AI researchers sometimes call it, symbolic or subsymbolic: that is, are the basic emotions, and other affects, symbolic processes of the kind that are typically taken to be cognitive, or are they processes occurring at a more fundamental level? This will in part depend upon whether the relevant affects follow cognitions, cognitions follow these affects, or the two can occur independently (I shall consider the possibility of reductive cognitivism in the next section). Although models that presume emotions follow cognition have been predominant for several decades, as we have already seen, the answer is that all three relations are possible in different kinds of cases.

The best theory of the relation of the basic emotions to propositional attitudes is weak content cognitivism, the view that these emotions often are, or are caused by, propositional attitudes (which, although entertained, need not be believed). But, as we saw, that some affects can be caused by mental states like beliefs and other propositional attitudes does not entail that all such affects are caused by beliefs and propositional attitudes, or that all affects are cognitive. Evidence was rallied in chapters 1 and 2 for this view, and included the mere exposure effects; neuroscientific evidence for separate affective and cognitive systems; that affects are phylogenetically ancient, and are shared with nonhuman animals; and that some affective behaviors need not be learned. This evidence and more reveals that some affects, including the basic emotions, can occur without the kind of cognitive contents that we would find typifying a cognitive theory of affects. I argued in passing in chapter 5 that many of these subcognitive affective abilities are not symbolic, and I will argue this point further here; this would show that they are not the kind of thing that a symbolic computational functionalist model of mind has the tools to explain.

But, setting aside for a moment whether a computational theory of mind can explain affects, we can ask whether such a theory *needs* to explain basic emotions and other affects. Perhaps the most important factors in such a consideration are the ways in which some affects can influence perception, judgment, and memory. Any computational theory of mind should explain how we make judgments about our perceptions and experiences, and how we use our memory. But a substantial and growing body of research gives evidence that these kinds of capabilities can be influenced in significant ways by basic emotions and other affects.

Much of this evidence is concerned with social judgments, that is, judgments that we make about other persons. These appear to be highly influenced by the affective state of the subject making the judgment. Much of this large body of research has been concerned only to show congruence of judgments along some one-dimensional measure, such as positive and negative "mood."[58] For example, Forgas and Bower (1987) used a bogus test to evoke in subjects either a sense of accomplishment or a sense of failure and rejection—the "good mood" or "bad mood"—and then tested the subject's judgments about a number of described characters. They found that subjects took longer to think about mood-consistent information, that they later had better recall of details that were consistent with the mood, that their errors in recall were biased by the mood, that the judgments about the characters were significantly influenced by their mood, and the speed at which those judgments were made was consistent with the mood. In other words, the moods of subjects influenced their social judgments about others in a number of ways, all of which revealed that people in a bad mood are more likely to judge others as bad, and in a good mood are more likely to judge others as good.

Thus, it appears that some affective states influence social judgments. Clearly, our judgments about others are not shaped entirely by our mood, but it does seem that it provides some direction to judgments, which may be very influential when we lack sufficient information of any other kinds. Ralph Erber (1991) found that mood influenced judgments when a person was described in both positive and negative terms. After invoking positive or negative moods in subjects by using stories, in an allegedly unrelated experiment subjects were told about individuals with both positive and negative traits, and then asked to rate the likelihood of certain behaviors. Being in a positive mood increased the likelihood of judgments consistent with the positive traits, and being in a negative mood increased the likelihood of judgments consistent with the negative traits. Joseph Forgas (1992) found that mood was more likely to influence our judgments about atypical or peculiar people. Both of these experiments suggest that the influence of mood is stronger in those cases where other judgment strategies are weakened because of ambiguity, lack of information, or failure of old categories to apply. Thus, affective state appears to influence these judgments both by increasing the likelihood of congruent conclusions, but also perhaps in other ways. One emerging theory is that a positive affective state increases the likelihood that a subject will judge that some particular falls under a category—as if positive affective state led to more generous reasoning (Isen and Daubman 1984; Isen, Daubman, and Nowicki 1987; Isen, Niedenthal, and Contor 1992; Schwarz and Bless 1991).

Given either possibility, the leading model of affective influence on judgment or perception are semantic activation networks, in which emotions and other affects excite, and increase the likelihood of judgments with, consistent semantic categories. If this is the case, then emotions and other affect should be expected to influence other kinds of judgment or perception. This is consistent with the fact that priming has been observed for affective stimuli. Priming occurs when a stimulus facilitates in some way the perception or categorization of another stimulus. Priming has been demonstrated for affectively laden terms. For example, subjects may be asked to evaluate a term as having either a positive or negative affect. If the term is preceded by a term that has the same affective value, the time of the decision making is reduced; that is, preceding (what the researchers consider) a positive term with a positive term makes the decision faster, and preceding a negative term with a negative term has the same effect (e.g., Hermans, Houwer, and Eelen 1994). The "prime," or first stimulus, can have this effect even if presented very briefly. Thus, affective priming is best understood as the influence of automatic affective evaluations that are probably occurring at all times, and that can expedite other, including cognitive, affective evaluations. This influence, furthermore, may occur across modalities; for example, for some people affectively valenced smells can prime word recognition (Hermans, Baeyens, and Eelen 1998).

Emotions might in turn influence such primary cognitive processes as perception. Again, this too seems common sense. If someone is home alone, frightened, she may mistake her running cat as a danger and leap back in shock. If one is in love, her friends might accuse her of seeing the world through rose-colored glasses. If someone is depressed, she may continually interpret events in a negative way. And so on. This phenomenon, if it does occur, is called *emotional congruence in perception*. "Emotional congruence" is the term for the tendency of cognitive processes (such as perception, or how we categorize perceptual experiences) to agree along some dimension with emotional state. Unfortunately, the intuitively appealing notion of emotional congruence has been somewhat difficult to demonstrate in the laboratory. However, some recent experiments have provided empirical evidence of emotional congruence in perception or in categorization.

Many experiments that failed to show emotional congruence in perception used models in which emotions and tested stimuli were categorized as positive and negative. Niedenthal, Setterlund and Jones (1994) criticized these approaches as being too impoverished to capture the actual influence of emotions, and offer as an alternative a categorical model. Thus, instead of expecting that so-called positive emotions facilitate the recognition of so-called positive stimuli, one should instead investigate what effect, say, sadness has on the perception of generally sad stimuli. (Note that this categorical view is consistent with the affect program theory.) Working with the categorical approach, Niedenthal and her colleagues (see also Niedenthal and Setterlund 1994) were able to offer a clear demonstration of emotional congruence in word perception. They studied emotional influences crossmodally, using music to evoke the affective state and testing for word recognition or gender facial recognition (where the pictures of faces were expressing affect), thereby avoiding problems of other semantic interference that could result from using words to both evoke and test an affective influence. Using music to induce either a sad or a happy state, and then having subjects perform a lexical decision task (in which they must, as quickly as possible, identify words as words and nonwords as nonwords), they found that happy subjects were able to recognize happy words more quickly than sad subjects, and that sad subjects were quicker to recognize sad words. Similar results were found when subjects were tested in recognizing the gender of faces that displayed either a sad, happy, or neutral expression: sad subjects were faster at recognizing the gender of sad faces, and happy subjects faster as recognizing the gender of happy faces. These results offer some important preliminary evidence for emotional congruence in perception. They have also been repeated and refined in Niedenthal, Halberstadt, and Setterlund (1997), where some facilitation based upon emotional congruence was also shown for word-naming. These experiments leave some ambiguity about whether the actual influence is on perception, or rather on some kind of categorization. But under either interpretation, they demonstrate some significant influences of emotion on short-term processes of the kind that a cognitive, and in particular a computationalist, theory of mind will want to explain.

Many of these results strongly suggest that emotions and other affects influence perception in a way that is not necessarily conscious. Niedenthal and Cantor (1986) were able to show that judgments and recall of individuals portrayed in photographs were more likely to be positive when the individual's pupils were dilated—something about which the subjects are presumably wholly unconscious (that is, they need not be able to report, "we prefer this person because his pupils are dilated"). Kitayama and Howard (1994) have argued that some affective influence on perception can be understood as preconscious arousal or amplification of some stimuli. Given the other kinds of evidence that emotions and other affects can be unconscious, it is likely that any affective effects would not need to be conscious. And even if the effects are conscious—say, in the sense that the agent can report upon the effect—they still do not cohere well with a reductive or doxastic cognitive theory of mind in a way that is going to facilitate a symbolic computational functionalist account. Note that music and even odors have been used as evokers of mood. As I have already mentioned, theories like reductive cognitivism do not even have a glimmer of a hope of explaining the affective influence of music; the same would be true of a reductive cognitivism based not on propositional attitudes but on symbols.

Granted, then, that a computational theory of mind should have to account for the effects of some emotions and other affects upon perception and judgment, then computationalism is confronted with a serious problem. If emotions and other cognitive states can be subcognitive but can influence cognition, then they both fall outside of the symbolic computational model, and they influence the very kinds of things it aims to explain. Furthermore, the influence of emotions in these cases does not seem to be a discrete change as would be the case if some alteration was made in the logical rules of a logical inference system. Instead, it seems to be a continuous change in the probability that something will be perceived or categorized as one of two or more alternatives. Symbolic computational functionalism, inspired by an image of the mind as an combinatorial engine, is just not the right kind of structure to model or re-create these kinds of behaviors.

One alternative for the computationalist might be to weaken the symbolic model in a way that maintains the notion that minds are primarily manipulators of discrete symbols, but which allows for such continuous changes. This would be to weaken computational functionalism so that it is consistent with the network models that best explain these effects (e.g., Bower 1981). Connectionist networks are not strictly models of a symbolic computationalist kind. In a semantic network there are nodes that have discrete representational values, but this is not necessary. Representations can be distributed through the nodes or in the connections between them, and the activation of nodes can be of continuous values, as can the "weights" of the connections between the nodes which determine how the nodes will inter-relate. These models treat the effect of affects on perception as activation spreading from an emotional node to related semantic nodes and increasing their own activation. In chapter 6, I endorsed a similar model of emotional influence of cognitive contents in fictions; there, I considered the possibil-ity that semantic contents with emotional connotations could activate emo-tions. These semantic models are just the other direction of such activation: affects could activate semantic contents with affective content or connotations (and the relevant connections in these models are often sym-metric).

As I noted, it is not clear that a semantic activation model really is a symbolic computational model of a kind consistent with symbolic compu-tational functionalism; but setting this issue aside, if this kind of model is taken as a model of what emotions *are,* there is a problem. Such an ap-proach faces a dilemma: in order to truly explain the effects of emotions and other affects, it forces a rejection of the implementation independence that characterizes symbolic computational functionalism. This is because, in the psychological theories, the connectionist model is meant to describe the effects of some emotions, not to be a model of emotions. Prima facie, such models place emotion and the other nodes on the same level. To treat basic emotions and other affects as categories in a semantic activation model means that they are, from a purely cognitive position, structurally indistinct from any other broad cognitive category, such as "game" or "un-interesting." Yet surely not all such categories are properly called basic emotions. What separates basic emotions and other affects from these other categories are the host of other phenomena that accompany these affects, such as the somatic body responses, central nervous system patterns of activation, paradigmatic behaviors, and so on. What then becomes the pressing issue is the relation between these two things: the cognitive, se-mantic aspects of the affect and the subcognitive passion. Cognitive scien-tists who use the semantic activation models are only seeking to describe the possible semantic effects of emotion upon perception, if such effects are properly described as being categorizing; cognitive scientists are typi-cally willing to mix the theoretical levels and consider that the emotional nodes in the connectionist model will be part of other networks, such as networks that model or represent somatic activities of emotion. The com-putationalist, with her commitment to purity of levels, is forced into main-taining a distinction between the fully cognitive, mental emotion running in parallel to a bodily—and therefore external to the mind and the compu-tational theory itself—reaction or correlate to the emotion. Such a model cannot be complete, therefore; and the computationalist is at a loss to ex-plain anything like emotional congruence in perception or categorization, unless she is willing to include in the model such implementation-dependent details as characterize affects.

Affective Influences on the Formation and Recall of Memories

Basic emotions and other affects also can influence memory. There is a large body of literature concerned with how moods, in particular elation and depression, can influence memory (for review see Blaney 1986). Two kinds of effects are believed to occur in this regard: state dependence, in which the memories of a subject are expected to be influenced by what the subject learned when previously in that mood; and mood congruence, in which some information is more likely to be recalled or stored given the subject's mood. These effects can also be part of the influence of affects on judgments, given that judgments will often require the recall of memories. Although there is substantial evidence for both state dependence and mood congruence, the results are often very difficult to interpret, and sometimes even contradictory. For this reason, we will consider clearer influences here.

First, it should be noted that some affective conditioning is a kind of learning. For example, fear conditioning is itself a kind of learning and therefore a kind of memory formation. Throughout our lives, when painful and traumatic experiences occur, we can be conditioned to associate other stimuli with those experiences. These are memories that arise because of, and which can themselves stimulate the reoccurrence of, emotions. And, if there are other kinds of affective conditioning, these also would require some kind of memory formation.

But substantial research also shows that declarative memory—our memory of such things as words, pictures, events, and so on—is also directly influenced by emotions. Our most dramatic memories of emotional experiences—so-called flashbulb memories (Brown and Kulik 1977)—are not necessarily accurate (Neisser and Harsch 1992), although they are definitely more vivid. But there is nonetheless substantial evidence, from both human and nonhuman animal studies, that emotion facilitates some kinds of memory formation. Exciting research is uncovering the neural underpinnings of some of these effects. These findings reveal that for some emotions, particularly fear, the "storage of memory for emotionally arousing events is modulated by an endogenous neurobiological system which is normally inactive in nonemotionally arousing learning situations, but which becomes active in emotionally stressful learning situations to insure that the strength of memory for an event is, in general, proportional to its importance" (Cahill 1997, 238). Thus, adrenal hormones are released when animals, including humans, are in a stressful situation. It has long been known that the administration of adrenal hormones after some kind of learning task can aid the formation of memories, and that various techniques for blocking the activity of these hormones can inhibit memory formation (see Roozendaal, Quirarte, and McGaugh 1997). Since these effects happen only if the hormone or its blocker are administered shortly after a learning task, the hormones appear to be actually facilitating the formation of memories.

It is thought that these effects arise in part because of effects upon the amygdala, a nucleus now well known to play a central role in fear conditioning and perhaps other kinds of affective processes; but it is also clear that the amygdala is not itself the storage place of the emotional memories, but rather is necessary to their formation (McGaugh et al. 1993).

A fascinating recent study with humans reveals that these findings can be shown for such processes as the recall of stories (Cahill et al. 1994). Subjects were given an injection of either a placebo, or propranolol (which inhibits some effects of adrenal hormones), one hour before viewing a series of slides that were accompanied by a story. One story had a very affective content (in which the character is in a car accident and badly injured, dismembered, and sent into surgery) and one with neutral content (in which the character just views with interest some of the things at his father's workplace). Subjects who had the propranolol injection did not remember the affective story as well as did those who had a placebo; but they did remember the affectively neutral story as well as did the placebo subjects. The results dramatically suggest that some affective experiences improve memory formation through a mechanism triggered by these stress hormones.

Some interesting preliminary evidence suggests that the extended body plays an important role in these effects of emotion upon memory. Radnitz and colleagues (reported in Cahill 1997, 244) have found that, among veterans, quadraplegics are significantly less likely than paraplegics to have post-traumatic stress disorder. One compelling theory of how post-traumatic stress disorder arises is that the patients in question have suffered an extremely stressful experience that has, through the kinds of mechanisms just described, fostered the formation of extremely intrusive and vivid memories. If the peripheral influences of the whole body can result in a greater degree of stress hormones, which in turn facilitate a vivid "flashback," then this result regarding quadraplegics coheres well. Baseline levels of norepinephrine and epinephrine are both lower in quadraplegics than in paraplegics and normals.

To capture the effects of basic emotions and other affects on memory, the symbolic computational functionalist faces problems similar to those observed above. These effects show that some affective states, such as stress and fear, which need not be conscious, facilitate the formation of some memories and perhaps also some kinds of recall (such as the "flashback"). Given that the basic emotions are not reducible to propositional attitudes, and that their influence in these cases arises from processes that are continuous and diffuse, any account of their influence on memory formation or recall is going to mix the processing levels and so eliminate implementation independence. These effects are also not going to be well modeled as discrete symbolic states; at best, the computationalist could argue that they are symbolic states with continuous magnitudes. Thus, both the advantage (implementation independence) and the elements (discrete symbolic states) of a computational approach would be lost.

Affect and Rationality

The basic emotions and other affects have important roles to play in rationality and rational action. In chapter 5, I reviewed ways in which basic emotions can be said to play a part in a rational order, and also some ways in which they may facilitate rational action. If these emotions or other affects influence perception, judgment, or memory, then they will certainly affect in substantial ways the rational decision making and actions of any agent. Here, it would be useful to review some of the evidence that affects, perhaps including some basic emotions, play necessary roles in normal rational behavior. First and foremost is the point, already made, that we have no reason to believe that other general motivational states (e.g., desires) can fill in for basic emotions. In any case, where the basic emotion motivates rational behavior, we require additional evidence before we can grant that the basic emotion is unnecessary for that kind of rational behavior. Second, I have reviewed some evidence consistent with this. The most vivid examples came from the studies of patients with frontal lobe damage by Antonio Damasio and his colleagues (Damasio, Tranel, and Damasio 1990; see also Damasio 1994), and by Edmund Rolls and his colleagues (1994); these provide some illustration of the importance of affect to rationality (see chapters 2 and 8). Thus, even though some of these patients showed no significant cognitive deficits, such as loss of the conceptual capabilities that cognitivists associate with affect and that computationalists take to be the essence of thought, they could show profound deficits in rational decision making and action. As Damasio aptly puts it, "We might summarize [EVR's] predicament as *to know but not to feel*" (1994, 45).

There is also some interesting evidence that cognition can sometimes *reduce* the utility of decision making! In a series of related articles Timothy Wilson and colleagues (Wilson and Schooler 1991; Wilson, Hodges, and LaFleur, 1995; Wilson et al. 1993; Wilson and LaFleur 1995) have uncovered evidence that when subjects are asked to articulate their reasons for their preferences,[59] they sometimes change their preferences in ways that they later regret. There is a significant body of research on the possible disadvantages of introspection; for example, one study (Schooler and Engstler-Schooler 1990) showed that when subjects verbalized their memory of faces or other stimuli, they were less likely than controls to recognize the faces later. Wilson and his colleagues expanded this area of research by demonstrating that introspecting at length, such as making lists of pro and con reasons for choosing among options, can lead to choices that the decision maker later sees as inferior to the offered alternatives. This is compellingly consistent with the view that subcognitive affects give value to alternatives and give reason a scale to measure against; and some kinds of cognitive deliberation via introspection can interfere with and even impair the proper function of these affects.

A Note about Embodiment

Philosophers and cognitive scientists sometimes use the terms "embodiment" or "embodied cognition" for the idea that cognitive and other mental processes are in some necessary way connected to the extended body of the agent. Recognition of embodiment has been an important element of many critiques of the computational view of mind; for example, traditionally symbolic computational functionalism fell into the trap of needlessly trying to represent in symbols many elements of motor control that are explicable simply in terms of the way the body of the organism is constructed (see Clark 1996). But some issues of embodiment also arise for affects. For example, Damasio's explanation of the role of affect in rationality, arising from his study of EVR, is his *somatic marker hypothesis.* On this theory, affective bodily reactions act as one kind of indicator for the value of an option. For example, "When [a] bad outcome connected with a given response option comes into mind, however fleetingly, you experience an unpleasant gut feeling" (1994, 173). These somatic markers then help a person decide between courses of action. On this view, the body acts as a theater for the affects. Damasio's somatic marker hypothesis is consistent with a strong claim for embodiment, since it would make the role of the extended body a necessary feature of human cognition. But the somatic marker hypothesis is controversial, for the same reasons that any neo-Jamesian theory is controversial (e.g, see Rolls 1999, 70–73). Many of the theories of emotion in philosophy, early natural science, and folk psychology share an association of emotions with the extended body, in distinction from the mind, or even the brain, alone. The reason for this might plausibly be said to be the phenomenological evidence. Whereas language use, mathematical reasoning, and planning about the future seem to be skills that require little contribution from the whole body, the heat of anger or the ache of despair seem to be centered right in the pit of one's chest. Williams James captured this sense acutely when he wrote:

> If we fancy some strong emotion, and then try to abstract from our consciousness of it all the feelings of its bodily symptoms, we find we have nothing left behind, no "mind-stuff" out of which the emotion can be constituted, and that a cold and neutral state of intellectual perception is all that remains. (1950, 451)

However, many have argued that there is a separate mental or cognitive aspect of the emotion, distinct from the bodily passions. In his own theory of passions, Descartes gave an early and clear statement of this kind of position. He distinguished between passions and emotions. Emotions can be "internal" to the soul, but are usually accompanied by correlated passion in the body. For these passions, he readily gave explanations of their corresponding bodily states, which are caused when the brain sends different amounts and kinds of animal spirits to different parts of the body (e.g., 1985,

363). In Descartes's own theory we see tensions which still remain between the embodied states of passion and the mental or cognitive features of the affect. We still are often saddled with a dual-explanation theory of this kind. Reductive cognitivists, as we have seen, often dismiss the bodily reactions that accompany an emotion as unnecessary epiphenomena of the emotion; and doxastic cognitivists often treat them as necessary by definition but not relevant to the role of emotions.

It is possible, of course, to steer a reasonable course between James and Descartes. We can do this by first recognizing that the extended body can play significant roles in affects and therefore in cognition, but that these roles are sometimes unnecessary. This establishes both that embodiment is important, but also recognizes the valid criticisms of a Jamesian position (e.g., the time taken to cause a somatic response, and then to detect it, is too slow for some affective reactions). Thus, the somatic marker hypothesis does not need to be the sole explanation of how affects assist cognition. That is, suppose that EVR's deficits arise not because of his failure to cause somatic reactions, but rather because the lost orbitofrontal cortex was directly necessary for the kind of reasoning in question. It could still be the case that the kinds of somatic reactions that occur in a normal are potentially, even if slowly and imperfectly, influential on reasoning of the relevant kind, in those individuals; and that EVR could have a deficit also because he lacks this. And if this is correct, then the somatic excitation of the extended body can and does play some role in cognition. That is, there may be two or more tracks: a direct neural track through which affects operate on cognition (and this would presumably require orbitofrontal structures since their ablation produces some relevant deficits), and an indirect track that excites somatic states which in turn alter cognition. Another possibility is that somatic excitation, and other effects of affects on the extended body, are part of the overall intensity of the affect, so that the effect of these affects upon cognition would be significantly influenced by the extended body. This is consistent with the results concerning memory and post-traumatic stress disorder discussed above (and also in Hohmann 1966). Thus, it is highly plausible that the extended body plays some role, even if not a necessary one, in directly influencing cognition by way of influencing or acting in consort with affects. Explaining any such role will require at the very least a significant expansion in the computationalist program. The logical manipulation of symbols is not a plausible approach at all to understanding how this influence could operate.

Finally, another, more general, point regarding embodiment is that a proper account of the body of the organism will be necessary to explain the functions of affects and many other mental states. This is a consequence of the hierarchical view of mind; but it also is tantamount to a platitude. Any organism of sufficient complexity to be active in its environment will have abilities—such as motor control, perceptuomotor integration, and affects (including basic emotions with accompanying motor programs)—that evolved to utilize (and evolved in conjunction with) the genotype's body form. And this diachronic perspective translates into a synchronic one when we recognize that many affective states will have the extended body as an essential referent for many instances: pain, pleasure, thirst, hunger, any occurrent motor program, and many other motivational states will activate, arise from, or at least refer to states of the extended body. How this general consideration can translate into practical considerations is something I will consider in the next chapter.

Conclusion

Symbolic computational functionalism is confronted with a series of problems. If some affects operate sometimes independently of cognition, computationalism can at best model them as separate and parallel processes that can influence and be influenced by cognition. Because of the commitment to implementation independence, the kind of bodily features accompanying basic emotions and other affects must be treated as external, and perhaps then even contingent and unnecessary, by a computational theory. Computational theories of mind are as a result naturally compelled toward a view shared with some forms of cognitivism: a view that separates emotions of the mind and the contingent, usually parallel, passions of the body. Integrating these two is a serious problem; and yet this integration is necessary to explain the role of the emotion. Furthermore, computationalism cannot well account for the effects of some basic emotions and other affects on perception or categorization. Even expanding computationalism to allow for some connectionism will fail, since we have noted that treating affects as semantic categories makes them indistinct from other cognitive categories of similar generality. And, whereas rationality would certainly be a feature of mind for which the symbolic computational theory of mind would have to account, it is unclear how, if at all, it can account for this role of affect. Again, computationalists can allow for emotions to operate as categories, sorting out depressing contents from happy ones, and so on. But in patients like EVR, the ability to articulate such categorizations is present, but seems impotent to influence their reasoning in appropriate ways.

Symbolic computational functionalism, as a theory of human or other animal minds, is inadequate. This result is also evidence against the stronger forms of implementation independence.

12

Affective Engineering

Both the philosophy and the sciences of mind have much to learn from the short history of AI. AI sometimes clarifies conceptual mistakes in a way that is particularly compelling. Trying to make a system that simulates or actually instantiates an intelligent behavior is a very rigorous test of a theory of that behavior. The results can be, and have been, very revealing. But our best understanding of basic emotions and other affects also have much to offer AI. There is no doubt that work in AI has met with much more failure than success, when we consider the blissfully optimistic predictions that have long characterized the pronouncements from workers in the field. Attempts to overcome some of the limitations that AI has faced would benefit from an approach that takes affect seriously. In this way, even the most practically oriented AI—what we might call GOHAI, Good Old Hacking AI—has something to learn from affect. In this chapter, I will review some of the lessons of this kind. I will understand AI to include not just symbolic computational functionalism, but also connectionism, genetic algorithms, electrical and other (e.g., neuromorphic) kinds of engineering, robotics, and other approaches when they are united under the goal of engineering systems capable of autonomous behavior. The stress on autonomous behavior is necessary for reasons I have articulated before, but also because the goal of AI is to re-create not only intelligent behaviors of the kind typically taken to be cognitive, like human speech, but also the kind of independence exercised by most animals. Autonomy is, and should be treated as, the central problem of AI, just as with the philosophy of mind.

Traditionally, AI researchers have in practice wholly neglected emotions and other affects while in principle being open to them. Presumably one reason for this has been that the tools of classical AI were specifically designed for modeling and creating symbol manipulators. With LISP and its dialects, and a valuable variety of logics, it is not clear where, if anywhere, affect might fit in. This has also meant that most of the AI work on emotions has been wholly consistent with reductive cognitivism. And this tendency toward a default cognitivism when, if ever, basic emotions are considered is amplified by the fact that typically an AI project lacks anything remotely corresponding to a body. Robotics has been more difficult, and far more costly, than programming alone, and so has trailed behind programming in AI projects (but robotics is growing cheaper and more powerful now at a rate that may soon make it widely accessible, and we can expect it to become an essential part, if not the core, of AI in the future).

To explore both what AI can learn from our best understanding of affects, and also perhaps how this understanding can be improved by AI, it will be useful at the outset to distinguish two broad kinds of ways that affect and AI can be integrated. I will call these *shallow affective engineering* and *deep affective engineering.* The term "shallow" is not meant to be a disparagement, but rather to draw attention to the fact that this kind of engineering focuses on re-creating or exploiting some few features of affects without actually seeking to instantiate affects themselves; in contrast, deep affective engineering seeks to actually create affective systems as an engineering strategy. My primary concern here is with the possibility of deep affective engineering, but I will survey some applications of shallow affective engineering.

This division, and my discussion here of affective engineering, is founded on the presumption that either the affect program theory is true, or at least that some affective capabilities are inherited biological capabilities and that reductive cognitivism and closely related kinds of cognitivism are false. This is an important qualifier because some AI researchers have believed that emotions emerge or arise out of the capabilities that constitute intelligence. For example, Marvin Minsky (1985) argued that emotions arise from simple affects or preferences that can compete and play complex roles in cognitive systems. Affects are for him "varieties or types of thoughts, each based on a different brain-machine that specialized in some particular domain of thought" (163). These can act together and against each other in increasingly complex ways, and from this emotions will result. On this view, basic emotions are neither a problem for AI nor are they something that needs to be hard-wired in to be present: they just emerge from a complex cognitive system. I will not discuss this view here except to note that the scientific evidence rules against it. The arguments against it would be analogous to the arguments against reductive and doxastic cognitivism, social constructionism, and symbolic computational functionalism. At least for the basic emotions, the inherited and biologically based, and not the emergentist, view is the more supported by the findings of biology and other relevant sciences.

Shallow Affective Engineering

Early examples of AI projects that exemplify working within the constraints of symbolic classical AI include PARRY and BORIS. Kenneth Colby's PARRY program (1974, 1981) was one of the first notable AI programs concerned, if only indirectly, with emotion. Reminiscent of the

ELIZA program, PARRY was a program that interacted via communication over a computer terminal. PARRY was designed by Colby to respond like a (presumably human) person with paranoid schizophrenia, and thus "discoursed" in a way that seemed to show exaggerated affect. A similar program was BORIS (Dyer 1982), a story analyzer that could answer some questions about affects as they related to the story analyzed. In these and similar cases, affects are treated as nothing more than structures of symbols, or even predispositions to certain terms and phrases. As such, they of course fit well into a reductive or doxastic cognitivist (including symbolic computational functionalist) model.

Like these early programs, most uses for shallow affective engineering entail developing systems that can simulate the appearance of, or can "recognize" and respond to, basic emotions; and most of them are primarily concerned with facilitating human-computer interaction. In a recent book, Rosalind Picard offers an extensive and insightful review of a number of such uses and suggests many others (1997). She observes that systems that could simulate the appearance of emotions would be of use in improved text-to-speech programs, the creation of virtual actors, and other entertainment uses; and systems that recognize and categorize emotions of their users would allow for better monitoring of consumer feedback, games or other kinds of entertainment that change to reflect mood, recording systems that focus upon things of affective interest to the user, systems that learn user preference, and other uses.[60]

One example of a project that has come some distance in some of these directions has been Clark Elliott's affective reasoner (AR) project. Like many shallow affective engineering projects, Elliott uses the Ortony, Clore, and Collins (1988) model of the cognitive structure of emotions. This model can directly be translated into a symbolic computational system, and so provides a ready structure that AI researchers can adapt and use. AR is a program that utilizes both AI and multimedia components, and can listen to users through speech recognition software and respond by way of music, speech, and a changing projection of a simple face that emulates emotional expressions (Elliott 1998). By changing parameters in the underlying adaptation of the Ortony, Clore, and Collins model, characters can be portrayed who have the appearance of their own emotions and temperament, and appear more credible as agents with which the user can interact (Elliott 1994). This same structure is used both to present, and in a sense create, stories; the system is used to analyze a report of some kind, and then present that report with the appropriate affect. Other research on creating credibly emotional agents of this kind has been done by W. Scott Neal Reilly (1996).

As these examples suggest, the potential entertainment uses are the aspect of affective engineering now being most actively pursued, often with industry support; and it is with agents that this research is now most active. In this context, "agents"[61] refers to programs, as opposed to robots, that demonstrate some autonomy; as such, work on agents is a kind of AI in which the goal is programs, including programs that may be "mobile" in

the sense that they can move between machines. (This terminology sometimes gets blurred, however; for example, "agents" can be taken to refer to
devices which serve their users in some way that demonstrates autonomous activity, such as helping the user with some task without having to be
instructed to do so.) Danny Hillis, one the pioneers of computer engineering and AI, and now a vice president of research and development at Walt
Disney Imagineering, recently argued that one of the primary tasks confronting the development of entertainment agents was "a computable science of emotion" (reported in Elliott 1998). This is an area of use where we
can expect shallow affective engineering to accomplish much in the future.

I should note that, given the complexity of the relationship between the
social or cognitive role of emotions and their subcognitive aspects, it is
unlikely that these kinds of applications—in which the relation between
discourse and emotional expressions is central—would directly benefit in
the near term from a pursuit of deep affective engineering. That is, for these
projects, the kind of model that Ortony, Clore, and Collins offer is probably
the best place to start. The subcognitive structures of emotions and their
relations to cognition is going to be extremely complex. At present, we do
not understand it sufficiently well to offer a theory amenable to computer
simulation. But if the cognitive structure of emotions is sufficiently clear
and consistent, so that a model of it alone is sufficiently reliable, then any
researcher aiming to simulate only these kinds of responses would best—
indeed, would have to—use such a model.

Other uses that shallow affective engineering might satisfy are not directly related to discourse and emotional expression or to human-computer
interaction; we need only take inspiration from the kind of roles that emotions serve and exploit those strategies. For example, emotions suggest that
one effective strategy for overcoming extreme decision complexity (which
can arise whenever choosing a course of action via inferences may be an
interminable or unreliable strategy) is to have a set of reliable schemes for
activity (such as, in the case of humans: flee, fight, reject/expel, jump back
and observe). Also, emotions and other affects, since they can occur more
quickly than cognitive judgments, suggest the strategy of using fast responses to important but quickly occurring events; thus, a plane that comes
too near to another plane might be programmed to automatically steer away
until the pilot is able to assess the situation and respond. And, as the importance of autonomous software agents grow, we may be able to learn from
the socioeconomic role of emotions. For example, agents will have to compete for scarce resources. We might decide that those agents that use too
many resources should be "punished" by other agents—such as reducing
their access to servers—so that a more equitable distribution can be
achieved. In such a case, agents could be designed to be recognizable to
other agents, to have a social memory of other agents, and to use strategies
that are inspired by angry behaviors and that help ensure more equitable
distributions (like those behaviors discussed in chapter 5). These are just

brief suggestions; my point is that shallow affective engineering has many other places to look for applications.

Deep Affective Engineering

There is little or no work extant in AI that can be called deep affective engineering. But the affect program theory reveals that a rich notion of affects could usefully be incorporated into the most basic design of an autonomous system. The principal argument for undertaking deep affective engineering is what I will call the *biomorphic argument.* The first premise is the simple observation that nature does a vastly better job at creating autonomous systems than we have ever come close to doing. This alone is reason to turn to biology for guidance on how to engineer autonomous systems. After all, our theories and prejudices may or may not provide a viable approach, but nature surely has one—or rather, has millions of kinds, in fact. We would be wise to learn from real autonomous systems, including real cognitive ones, to find answers. Another premise is that biology reveals that in addition to being much less successful than nature, we are very, very inefficient in our approaches when compared to real organisms. A watch, a cellular telephone, even an oven today may have hundreds of thousands, even millions, of transistors in it, drawing very significant amounts of power. But these units still need to be set, dialed, or monitored. In contrast, an ant has a few hundred neurons, uses a tiny fraction as much power, but successfully navigates and acts in its world in a robust, adaptive, dependable way, using flexible strategies. Our best work in AI can only aspire to imitate some few features of an ant's capabilities and accomplishments with what appears to be many more resources; evolution is vastly superior at engineering efficient autonomous systems than have been humans. Finally, the idea of starting with pure symbol or proposition manipulation, as modeled by a symbol manipulating language, and getting autonomous behavior out of this, has been a failure; furthermore, it reveals very deep prejudices about the mind—such as the cognitive autonomy fallacy— that are conceptually confused, unrealistic, and inconsistent with our best scientific understanding. From these premises, arising from observations of nature's success and our failures, we can conclude with some confidence that AI would be much better served to turn to biology, and away from a rationalistic psychology, for its answers.

Biology tells us that affect is ubiquitous and effective. All the mammals, and many other species, have at least a few of the basic emotions. Other kinds of affects or motivation-related states, such as pain, hunger, and so on, are present in all but the simplest of animals. In contrast to the ubiquity of affect as a capability of autonomous behavior, for the vast majority of species we have no reason to believe that their successful autonomy arises from drawing inferences from believed propositions or manipulating internal symbols in a syntactic system. Affects are therefore one successful strategy for having an autonomous system, whereas propositional inference and related kinds of symbol manipulation are at best capabilities used by humans in only some of their autonomous behaviors.

The cognitive autonomy fallacy is the idea that cognitive skills (like the ability to entertain, and infer from, propositions and to manipulate discrete symbols) enable autonomy; this fallacy in part arises because of the erroneous belief that motion control and related kinds of subcognitive behaviors are inflexible mechanical activities, the answers to immediate "biological imperatives." The corollary prejudice is that cognitive capabilities, particularly the ability to entertain propositions and to use them to guide action, are the source of truly flexible behaviors. Again, it is here that the lessons of AI are most revealing. We learn that the truly difficult and elegant accomplishments of nature are not logical inference or playing chess, but rather are the ability to integrate motion control and perception into a competent performance of activity in the world. Note that programs like ELIZA and Elliott's impressive accomplishments with the AR project are relatively straightforward successes in the simulation of the kind of discourse that surrounds our understanding of emotional situations and use of affect terms. But we still have nothing by way of a successfully autonomous system that could move about in a realistically complex environment, including fleeing from threats or attacking rivals. In this regard, the prejudices about what is and is not flexible and complex are strikingly backward.

What then are the lessons that affect, and in particular the basic emotions, can offer AI? Perhaps the most interesting thing is a revised view of the mind. In pursuing practical approaches to the engineering of extremely complex systems, a change in perspectives can yield very significant changes in practice. Thinking of an intelligent system not as a symbol manipulator, but as foremost a passionate engine, is such a new perspective. Careful attention to affects reveals that a mind is a host of affective capabilities that can act as schemes for valuation (dividing things and events in the world into the fearful, the infuriating, the joyous, and so on); that are constantly, even if only in tiny degrees, present as motivations vying with each other to result in actions (like vectors in a space of action possibilities); and that these ubiquitous affects underlie effective action and intelligent reasoning by giving valence to opportunities. On top of these and other affective capabilities, propositional attitudes or symbol processing seem almost an afterthought. Furthermore, the biomorphic approach, coupled with a rudimentary understanding of the evolution of intelligence, suggests an approach to engineering in which the artificial evolution, or perhaps even just the ontogeny, of artificial autonomous systems should recapitulate some aspects of some examples of phylogeny. We should start with effective motor capabilities, develop and modify these into flexible action paradigms and motivations, which in turn (when they can be run but disconnected or otherwise suppressed) can ground the ability to make appraisals, and this ultimately underlies the beginnings of rationality.

But I can be more specific, and outline a few lessons that emotions can offer as inspiration to deep affective engineering. These speculative suggestions for future engineering and research can also act as a summary of some of the practical lessons suggested by the view of minds as passionate engines, and therefore I shall gather them under mnemonically useful slogans.

1. *Motion before emotion, action before abstraction.* Action is fundamental to autonomy and intelligence—being autonomous or intelligent is, of course, the capability for some kinds of action. Our strategies for coping with the world largely are motivations and action programs. Our best hypothesis about the genesis of some basic emotions and other affects is that they evolved first as inheritable behaviors and coordinated bodily changes that facilitate behaviors. This suggests a radically different approach to engineering autonomy. Instead of creating a symbol-manipulating intelligence, which then sends messages to actuators, we should begin by evolving, training (under which I mean to include unsupervised learning), or (worst case) directly programming effective action programs that can be elicited by and cope with commonly confronted tasks. These action programs can later serve as schemes for actions, as evaluative categories that underlie evaluative judgments, and as motivational systems.

Also, placing motion control before—and as underlying—cognitive skills is consistent with the hierarchical view of mind, according to which motion control is itself often handled by systems that are potentially independent of cognitive skills. This is supported, for example, by recent research on humans and animals that indicates that there are two potentially independent neural tracks that service visual perception: one concerned with utilizing visual information directly for motor activity, the other utilizing visual information in service of various cognitive skills. Ungerleider and Mishkin (1982) identified two visual systems in the cerebral cortex of monkeys: a ventral and a dorsal stream. Subsequent research has found that the dorsal stream is activated by both motion control and visual stimulation; also, lesions in the areas of the dorsal stream in primates result in deficits in visually guided behavior (see Goodale 1998). Evidence is mounting that the two streams are specialized:

> Both streams . . . transform visual information into motor output. In the dorsal stream, the transformation is direct: visual input and motor output are essentially "isomorphic" with one another. In the ventral stream, however, the transformation is quite indirect: the relationship between input and output is "propositional," and takes into account previous knowledge and experience. The ventral stream helps us identify goals and plan actions; the dorsal stream programs and controls those actions. (Goodale 1998, R491)

Similar kinds of evidence can be found for other organisms. For example, experiments have been performed in which portions of the optical tracts of frogs are "rewired." In some of these preparations, confronted with a visual task that requires a choice, the frog chooses the wrong side. However, confronted with a visual task that requires it to leap, the frog acts properly. This strongly suggests that there are two separate visual tracks here also: one directly integrated with motion control, the other servicing more representationally rich decision making (Ingle 1973, 1980, 1982). Such separate tracks can also provide a very powerful explanation of some instances of blindsight, in which brain damage results in a subject being unable to report upon his visual stimuli, but being still able to take some significant actions in regard to it (see Goodale and Milner 1995). Further evidence has been found in humans subjects, both damaged and normal. For example, some humans with strong forms of agnosia, resulting in the inability to properly recognize and categorize objects, can demonstrate quite normal abilities to integrate visual information with motor control. And in normal subjects, special experiments can reveal such dissociations, such as in the difference between motor reactions and perceptual reports when reaching for perceptual illusions. Milner and Goodale also rightly observe that our distant ancestors, which lacked anything like our cognitive capabilities, had to successfully integrate vision and motion control, but did not have to recognize and categorize objects with the same power that we do; this is consistent with the notion that the visual motor system is phylogenetically older than, and remains neuroanatomically partially independent of, perceptual and other highly cognitive vision capabilities.

2. *Control decisions, and decision complexity, by having rich categories of appraisals.* Related to the idea of beginning with motor programs is an approach to the problem of the computational complexity of the sensory environment by way of using appraisals. I have argued that a parsimonious way to understand appraisal and its relation to action is to understand appraisals as affects or representations that reliably activate affects. This allows us to explain how some evaluations motivate. It also makes appraisals more complex and structured since their fundamental forms will correspond to particular kinds of affects. Furthermore, our best understanding of rationality now entails both conceptual reasons and empirical results revealing that these complex natural affects are essential to rationality and rational action. The conceptual reasons include the fact that no system of inference alone explains why we would value one thing over another; we need to explain differences in, and different kinds of, evaluations to get a system capable of logical inference to actually perform something. Our empirical reasons include the kind of striking results demonstrable on subjects with ventral frontal lobe damage. These findings reveal that a subject with above average intelligence and all the kinds of capabilities that this entails and that constitute a significant degree of the inferential capabilities of rationality can demonstrate consistently irrational behavior (irrational

even by their own evaluation); and that the best explanation of this irrationality is a failure in affective capabilities. Thus, the vaulted capabilities that allow us to speak, draw inferences, and so on, are, when in the service of rational action, dependent upon and are phylogenetically posterior to independent affective capabilities. Adaptive activity must not only precede intelligent abstract thought in evolutionary development; it is doubtful that there can be anything like intelligent rational behavior divorced from at least the possibility of, if not the development through, action and affect.

This means that autonomous systems will continually depend upon appraisals—something often called "hot representation"—which occur continuously, quickly, and without the necessity of conscious awareness. There can be something quite unaffective about contemplating a mathematical concept or staring at the very familiar. But much of representation is not so cold, since many stimuli create in us an appraisal; and the potential to have subcognitive occurrences of affects yields the possibility of fast subcognitive appraisals. Even when we are consciously and cognitively engaged in contemplating a stimulus, we can have affective reactions as revealed by measurable physiological changes of which we may be wholly unaware. We are continually drawing and utilizing a host of representations of our environment, and many of these are charged with affective force. These appraisals not only underlie valuations and so are necessary for decision making, but they influence cognition in other ways. We saw that there is compelling, if still controversial, evidence for emotional congruence in perception and in the recall of memories; and direct and increasingly well-understood effects of affects on memory formation.

These results show that affect underlies decision making. It is also plausible that affects provide a strategy to reduce decision complexity.[62] An organism's fundamental problem in analyzing sensory information is that there is too much of this information. One strategy that biological organisms use is to do as much processing as possible at lower processing levels, including even in the sensory system itself (an insight exploited by neuromorphic computation; see Mead 1989; Douglas Mahowald, and Mead 1995). Another strategy can be to appraise information and retain attention only for that information which is of value (i.e., of affective interest). Thus, continuously occurring fast and subcognitive appraisals may serve to cut down on the complexity of the perceptual environment for the organism, which is confronted always with the problem that it takes in more information than it can use and so must filter out the salient in order to succeed.

3. *Subcognitive systems are smart.* Subcognitive affects can play roles which are impressively complex. I have focused on the role that subcognitive systems play in motor control and argued that this is crucial to autonomy. But subcognitive systems perform other tasks; it is a serious error to assume that only propositional or conscious representational systems are capable of impressive feats of recognition and categorization. One striking example illustrating this is reported by S. Z. Rapcsak and colleagues (1998).

They studied a patient with frontal lobe damage who, when shown pictures of both famous and unfamiliar faces as stimuli, made many false recognitions and misidentifications of the faces in verbal reports. However, *his autonomic body reactions, as measured by skin conductance, discriminated between unfamiliar and familiar faces as a normal person would.* In other words, the cognitive abilities that make him able to report his beliefs about the pictures were prone to very significant errors because of his frontal lobe damage, but his affective bodily reaction remained accurate. The subcognitive affective systems were more accurate than his cognitive ones.

4. *Bodies, not minds, are autonomous.* Embodiment is important for the several reasons discussed in the last chapter. Chief among these is that the extended body evolved in consort with our affective capabilities and our motor control capabilities; for both, the extended body is the primary target of activity since it is the body which must respond to actuating neural systems. From an engineering perspective, this means that the body should come into the development of perceptuomotor control and affect at the earliest possible stage. A related point, well understood by engineers, is that the physical body offers its own solutions (and problems); for example, one might not have to represent and enable certain goals for an actuator because the physical nature of the actuator might naturally lead to those goals (thus, tension in a limb can result in a particular position being a default one, which is returned to whenever actuators are turned off). That is, bodies are direct and practical solutions. Extended bodies are part of the implementation of many capabilities, many of them subcognitive, that create autonomy. Some of these features are basic functional features, such as the way perceptual organs are organized, or the existence of opposable thumbs.

Neural systems exploit embodiment also by representing the extended body. Our brains, for example, have several maps of the body, including a motor map and a somatosensory map that are side by side. These maps, and other kinds of representations of the body, play important roles in our cognitive capabilities and even in perception. One interesting example of such effects arises from the behavior of some hemi-neglect patients. Individuals with brain damage to the parietal lobe can sometimes display a behavior in which they ignore half of their visual field. This hemi-neglect can be demonstrated not only for perceived visual scenes, but also even for recalled visual scenes, and hemi-neglect patients generally do not realize that they are ignoring half of their visual field (they don't think of themselves as partially blind, for example, and resist strategies to overcome their deficit). These features strongly suggest that we actually form some kind of map of our visual field first, and then attend to its features. But, interestingly, a hemi-neglect patient will perform better at identifying the occurrence of a stimulus in the neglected region when his body (but not his head; thus his visual field remains unchanged) is turned 20 degrees toward the neglected region (Karnath, Christ, and Hartie 1993; Karnath, Schenkel, and Fischer

1991). This strongly suggests that the brain's maps of the body, or at least some representations of the orientation of the body, play important roles in how the mind represents the world, facilitating the guidance of action and of action plans by the capabilities that our bodies give us.

5. *Subcognitive parallel processing.* Many affective processes can operate independently of conscious awareness, and independently of, or in parallel with, the kinds of capabilities that are taken to constitute "high" cognition. That we show unconscious and subcognitive reactions to many stimuli also suggests that we may often have several motivational inclinations at once. Successfully autonomous systems like ourselves are therefore doing a great deal of parallel processing. However, this parallel processing is not likely an interruptive behavior, as some have argued. That emotional actions can sometimes be disruptions to planned activities has led some to suggest that emotions just are disruptions of action. Aaron Sloman and Monica Croucher (1981), for example, argue that robots will have emotions because emotions will be necessary constraints upon the motivational systems of robots. They offer a theory of emotions as interruptions, disturbances, and departures from the usual rational symbolic "motivational" system of an intelligence. This theory is explicitly a form of reductive cognitivism, and they apply it to human emotions:

> It is possible, in human beings, for the anger to produce physical dis-turbances. However, if X satisfied enough cognitive conditions he could rightly describe himself as being very angry, despite not having the physical symptoms. The anger could be strong, insofar as it con-stantly intruded into his thoughts and decisions, and insofar as he strongly desired to make Y suffer, and suffer a great deal. (1981: 200)

What is of interest in their approach is that they identify emotions as irrup-tions in the context of AI and robotics. Herbert Simon made very similar proposals (1967), arguing that emotions should be seen as interrupts in a serial processing system. The intuition underlying this approach may be the observation that conscious, cognitive processing seems to operate, at least for many tasks, in serial.

Those unfamiliar with computer architecture and operating systems may miss that the notion of interrupt is an important part of computer engineer-ing. Since most computers have (at the time of this writing, at least) only one central processing unit (CPU), but several users may want to use that computer, or one user may want to do several things at once, operating systems and the CPU architecture typically allow for "interrupts," in which for some very short period of time one active process that is using the CPU is stored and stopped, another process is taken out of memory and run on the CPU, then is stored and stopped, and the original or another process is restored. In such a case we say that the first process "interrupted" the sec-ond. Since this happens very quickly, it can simulate parallel processing for the purposes of the generally slower user. It can also be a technique for having more important tasks pre-empt less important tasks; and, it can lead to more CPU usage because waiting processes can be interrupted. So, from the perspective of a programmer or engineer, the idea that emotions are interrupts suggests a standard kind of implementation. However, this standard implementation of interrupts would not capture what is happening in an organism's affective states, since it would essentially mean that the emotion was a process that occurs only when the interrupt is initiated, and the initiation of the interrupt itself would be a symbolic process (explaining why these theories are consistent with reductive cognitivism). Instead, what we have in real biological systems is the possibility for a host of affective states, which we can think of as vectors in a motivational state space, any of which can override another if the motivated actions are inconsistent and if some relative threshold of activation is crossed. Advantages to the parallel approach include that the system in question is constantly processing affective responses, and is correspondingly always in a state of preparation relative to this.

6. *Partial parallel and vertical integration.* The complex evolutionary heritage of our brains has not resulted in either serially operating functional modules, nor solely independent functional modules. I have already noted that affective processes can happen in parallel, and in a way independent of cognition; parallel integration (including resolution between divergent motivations) is therefore sometimes necessary for certain kinds of tasks (as in, choosing how to act). But there is also a kind of vertical integration that occurs. We can identify processes, such as basic emotions, that cut across what appear otherwise to be the levels of historical development and functional complexity. Fear can range from something as simple as an unconscious reflexive response triggered by mere stimuli, to a response motivating action in relation to a concrete object in the world, up to complex cognitive processes motivating a complex response to a possible future state of affairs. The syndrome itself can be defined at various levels, but to capture the richest view of it we need to see that it is a thing of varying complexity. That is, basic emotions and other affects are, to varying degrees depending upon the particular occurrent instance, vertically integrated. This vertical integration is incompatible with symbolic computational functionalism and reductive and doxastic cognitivism because it requires that many of our activities are significantly influenced by, even dependent upon, some processes that clearly are not best described as symbol manipulating or as constituted out of propositional attitudes. In the case of basic emotions, this vertical integration is also essentially related, one should note, to something like the affect program theory, since on a reductive cognitive theory, for example, there would be no basic emotion there independent of cognition to be integrated with cognition.

13

Conclusion

Passionate Engines

I have made a broad, preliminary review of what our best scientific and philosophical understanding of basic emotions and other affects can tell us about some fundamental problems in the philosophy of mind and artificial intelligence. I have raised more questions than I have answered, but I have shown that we can no longer practice the philosophy, or the science, of mind without due consideration to what roles the basic emotions and other affects play. I closed the last chapter with a review of what I thought the general, practical lessons of affects are for attempts to engineer autonomous systems. In this chapter, I consider those themes that arose repeatedly throughout this book but for which I have not yet had opportunity to give a full treatment: the issue of naturalism in the philosophy of mind, the onto-logical implications of affects, and the cognitive autonomy fallacy.

Naturalism and the Mind

One of the ironies of contemporary philosophy of mind is that a host of related views which were often taken as saving the rich variety of mental phenomena ended up being the most simplistic, reductive ways of under-standing the mind. To draw attention to this, I have used interpretationism as one of my primary examples in this book, for it has been said that one of the concerns that most motivates an interpretationist account of mind is a conviction that in some sense we require our folk-psychological view of ourselves. As Stephen Stich has put it, intentional systems theory seems motivated by the belief that

> if we had to renounce folk psychology, we should probably have to reject the notions of personhood and moral agency as well. But to do this is to plunge into the abyss, since the concept of personhood stands at the very center of our conception of ourselves and our place in the universe. (1983, 242)

This may indeed be right; but unfortunately, the interpretationists treat folk psychology as a rational discourse of attribution of beliefs and desires that is warranted on instrumental grounds. As we have seen here, this fails to explain emotional actions and so to predict, explain, or reduce the relevant basic emotions. This failure points toward a failure in the interpretationist notion of what is salvageable in folk psychology by rational attributions. Folk psychology is not belief-desire psychology alone, nor does it take the mind to be constituted by B-D rationality. The existence of basic emotions and emotional actions is a brute fact about human beings. Ironically, the interpretationist account begs us to sweep basic emotions under the rug, and if this account is meant to save a rich folk psychology, this is nothing less than a *reductio ad absurdum* of the position, since it does to a very large class of action and mental states what a science of mind is claimed to threaten to do. Basic emotions are an essential part of us, including an essential part of how we understand ourselves and construct our personal identities; we recognize that they are as much a brute fact of the mind as are vision or imagination. The very idea that we could explain our actions without reference to basic emotions and other affects is troubling for the very reason that many may fear that explaining human beings without belief and desire is troubling: it seems we would not be the same beings without them. In a sense, it is fair to say that were our emotions somehow eliminated, the very referent of "we" would change. Our mental lives are much richer than just combinations of belief and desire impelled along by game theory; and it is naturalist views of the mind, clinging closely to what we discover through scientific study, which provide vastly more complex and satisfying portraits of our mental landscapes. Interpretationism is hardly alone in having these problems; similar kinds of errors are implicit in the many theories that fall prey to the cognitive autonomy fallacy.

But the primary fault for the simplistic conception of naturalism that clouds these debates lies with naturalists; analytic philosophy has long adopted a peculiar notion of physics as the model of what a science of mind should be like, and expected an impoverished reduction of mental phenomena to simple axioms. Many of the views that characterize contemporary philosophy of mind are predicated on these prejudices. For example, such very different approaches as Paul Churchland's eliminativism and Donald Davidson's interpretationism arise because of a common acceptance of the claim that a scientific theory of mind cannot account for beliefs and some other mental states; in this regard, the two theorists differ only in that one concludes that we therefore have to get rid of them altogether, and the other tries to escape by holding that these "states" are just explanatory posits. It is beyond the mandate of this book to refute the arguments that science cannot account for beliefs and other mental states; but we can note in this regard that the progress of sciences are equally likely, if not much more likely, to enrich and expand upon an unscientific notion as they are to eliminate it. Paul Churchland has rightly pointed out that in the progress of sciences some concepts are just dropped as wrong; a favorite example in this regard is the concept of phlogiston. But for every case where the progress of science has eliminated something, we can find many more cases where it has introduced or embraced a whole gaggle of concepts that would not have previously seemed legitimate or even have been imagined. An example can be found in early mechanics. Newton was so indoctrinated with the view, popular in his time, that physical events had to be explained in terms of the impact of rigid bodies that he confessed discomfort with the "occult force" of gravitation, since it requires action at a distance. Yet today, fields are a standard part of the worldview that even the most die-hard reductive physicalist would fight to maintain. The same can be said for many other scientific advances. Consider the exploding ontology of chemistry in relation to the predecessor psuedoscience of alchemy: one might rightly say that we had to eliminate the four elements, since there really were no such four elements; but in place of them we have now more than a hundred. Just so, the sciences of mind are more likely to find an ever greater variety of phenomena and thus of natural kinds, and along the way to embrace and expand upon some of our folk psychological posits, as they are to yield a simple reduction to some few principles or an elimination.

Finally, it is ever more evident that biology, not physics, should be the model of a proper science of mind. A mind is more like a rain forest than a collection of rigid bodies, and it requires a natural history to be understood, not a few simple laws and a few basic elements in simple relations. We have seen numerous examples of this so far in this book. Instead of grouping emotions into some overarching class of belief-desire nexuses or logical relations to beliefs and desires or even various social roles, we have seen that affects are so vast and varied that a naturalist would be well advised to focus on just a few of them at a time. The scientific evidence points toward there being pancultural and biologically based emotions, but nowhere is the picture simple. Some of these basic emotions result in a variety of coordinated and complex bodily responses and behaviors. They likely have distributed underlying neural structures (that is, no one emotion center is expected). They are shaped by culture and cognition to varying degrees into rich and varied possibilities. Nowhere is our scientifically informed picture one of a reduction to some simple principles. And there are surprises: for example, I have argued for two inversions of the commonsense views. First, that some affect programs include motor programs, and so it is the suppression of emotional actions, not the actions themselves, that is primarily in need of explanation on the affect program theory. Second, that belief is secondary and (phylogenetically and developmentally) posterior to the entertaining of content as a cognitive elicitor of emotions.

Nor should the view of the science of mind as natural history be taken to be an endorsement of simplistic adaptationism (see Gould 1978). It is not hard to think of important roles that the basic emotions could play, and therefore to tell a "just so" story of how they evolved. Which roles truly were selected for will only be revealed, if at all, by future empirical research. But the naturalist approach is not just evolutionary, nor need it be adaptationist. In chapter 6, I considered the possibility that the ability to emote for fictions was a consequence of our evolved abilities to entertain contents, so that our emoting for fictions arises from a gap between this ability and our learned or developed ability to mark some of these contents as warranting belief and others as not so warranting. If so, the ability to emote for fictions is perhaps wholly without any survival value, but rather is a side effect of another useful ability. Suppose this were true; it is, as far as we know now, as likely a story as any other. Who among us would trade her own mental life with someone who was able to separate out the fiction from the report in such a way that she would never emote for a fiction—say, a person whose warrant-marking system was so efficient that she could without effort (that is, automatically and unconsciously) sort the contents into those warranted and those unwarranted and emote only for the former? I suspect few if any. This happy accident has become part of what we are, and plays extremely complex and subtle roles in our cultures. Here our mental lives are best understood via a natural history of human minds, not by some simplistic reductionist physicalism, instrumental evolutionary psychology, or rationalistic interpretationism. What matters to us in this case—the ability to pity and fear for Lear—is not the kind of thing that would find an interesting reduction with these approaches. And yet, it is consistent with, and its origin and local (that is, within the individual) function is best explained by, physicalist and evolutionary approaches. The naturalism neither eliminates nor simplifies; it adds and complicates.

My point here is quite general: under the examination of naturalism, phenomena do not fade into nothing, but are revealed rich and strange. The prejudice that naturalism results in simplistic explanations and the elimination of supposed phenomena is unfounded. More often naturalism results in a complex, expansive understanding of phenomena; and historically it has always been vastly richer than the non-naturalist alternatives of philosophers. This realization is thrust upon us when we examine the basic emotions, because they are numerous, complex, and fail to obey the kind of divisions drawn down by the opponents, or even the self-proclaimed friends, of naturalism.

Affects, the Mind-Body Problem, and the Role of Cognition

Because some emotions integrate features typically placed on two sides of a purported divide between rational agency and brute mechanics, the basic emotions prevent one kind of answer to the mind-body problem as it is concerned with mental content, rationality, and rational action. This is the kind of answer that seeks to separate out mental contents and the active participation of minds in some rational order—e.g., a Kantian "space of reasons"—from the deterministic material realm, by appealing to supposed failures of some kinds of scientific reduction, or even just of a scientific accounting.

These findings thus touch upon the ontology of mind. Interpretationism is again a useful and influential example. The reason that Davidson offers for his claim that there are no psychophysical laws is that the mental is interpreted given certain background assumptions, and so fails to be the kind of thing that can be reconciled properly with the physical given the background assumptions we make to understand the physical:

> There are no strict psychophysical laws because of the disparate commitments of the mental and physical schemes. It is a feature of physical reality that physical change can be explained by laws that connect it with other changes and conditions physically described. It is a feature of the mental that the attribution of mental phenomena must be responsible to the background of reasons, beliefs, and intentions of the individual. . . . [W]hen we use the concepts of belief, desire, and the rest, we must stand prepared, as the evidence accumulates, to adjust our theory in the light of considerations of overall cogency: the constitutive ideal of rationality partly controls each phase in the evolution of what must be an evolving theory. (1980c, 222–223)

But this argument presupposes the fundamental posits of intepretationism (I take it that Daniel Dennett, given his claims about the irreducibility of some of the patterns revealed from the intentional stance [e.g., 1993e, 22ff] holds a form of anomolous monism also), namely that mental contents are interpreted and not real entities, and that the ascription of them by way of interpretation is a holistic attribution constrained or constituted by particular assumptions about rationality. Equivalently, another defense of this position is that ideals of rationality constitute beliefs, and that these ideals cannot be realized in a physical system that has a nonintentional description. But we have no reason, other than a wish to accept this kind of anomalist view, to accept this view of belief.[63]

The import of affects here is that we can readily show, as I did in chapter 3, that there are roles for affects in action that make a scientific explanation (such as the affect program theory) in part able to predict the outcome,[64] whereas the interpretationist approach cannot. Basic emotions, and other affects, constrain the kinds of interpretative strategies that are reasonable to such a degree that claims about the indeterminacy of interpretations fail to be compelling; and furthermore, these constraints must, at least in part, be describable in physical terms. In other words, we observe type-specific psychophysical laws at work.

The ontological implications need not be for an impoverished reductionism; rather, it is interaction for which we must account. Thus, we might still ultimately discover that some kind of nonreductive naturalism (on some understanding of "nonreductive") is the best approach to explain minds. As is more and more the consensus among philosophers of science, and, as I argue briefly above, the sciences are already so rich in their approaches that it is unlikely that anything like the strong kinds of reduction that worried past philosophers are today relevant. Also, there are possibilities for in-principle reductions that cannot be demonstrated because of issues of mathematical complexity; these possibilities can yield a kind of emergence which is still not pluralistic in some strong senses of pluralism. And regardless of whether a reduction of the mental to the physical is in practice or even in principle possible, we have no reason to expect that a reduction of, say, concepts in an individual mind, or the social role of propositions in a collection of minds, would be useful. Finally, there is the perennial problem that it is difficult to specify in any nonarbitrary way what counts as the base in any sweeping claims for global reduction (the notion of what is physical, for instance, has continually changed), making broad notions of reduction often moot. What matters, instead, is being able to describe, understand, and predict *interactions* between events or states that are described in successful sciences. The lesson of the failure of interpretationism is that a theory of mind will have to be capable of accounting for rich (and type-specific) interactions among various levels of mental organization, such as those between the physiology of a body and the rational thoughts that may guide it.

The Cognitive Autonomy Fallacy

These considerations about ontology are related to the issue of what constitutes autonomy. For many philosophers and for some psychologists, to be an autonomous agent requires that one can behave in a way that can properly be said to be caused by mental contents like propositional attitudes. Cognition is taken to be the source of a flexibility in behavior that is synonymous with self-control, self-regulation, free will, spontaneity, and related notions. These theorists are of course free to define autonomy any way they want to, and philosophers are generally careful about the applications of this kind of definition and consistent in their use of it; but defining autonomy in this narrow way leads to fundamental conceptual confusions, if we want to integrate our best scientific understanding of behavior with our cognitive theories. In fact, this narrow definition of autonomy coheres with the cognitive autonomy fallacy and usually is an expression of prejudices that constitute it. This fallacy arises when we wrongly assume that cognitive capabilities are the underpinnings of autonomy (construed as I have done so in this book). Although the cognitive autonomy fallacy is as common to psychologists, AI researchers, and other scientists (but often for different reasons) as it is to philosophers, clarifying the nature of the fallacy is most easily done by examining it in a philosophical context. Thus John McDowell has written:

In mere animals, sentience is in the service of a mode of life that is structured exclusively by immediate biological imperatives. That is not to imply that the life is restricted to a struggle to keep the individual and the species going. There can be immediate biological imperatives that are at most indirectly connected with survival and reproduction: for instance, the impulse to play, which is found in many animals. But without falling into that kind of restrictiveness, we can recognize that a merely animal life is shaped by goals whose control of the animal's behavior at a given moment is an immediate outcome of biological forces. A mere animal does not weigh reasons and decide what to do. . . . [Its life] can be no more than a succession of problems and opportunities, constituted as such by those biological imperatives.

When we acquire conceptual powers, our lives come to embrace not just coping with problems and exploiting opportunities, constituted as such by immediate biological imperatives, but exercising spontaneity, deciding what to think and do. (1994, 115)

This passage reveals some of the indefensible claims that underlie an instance of the cognitive autonomy fallacy. Nonhuman animals cannot in any significant sense be separated out from humans by way of any limitation on behavior such as is described here. First, there is much behavior that is not given to "immediate biological imperatives." Birds build nests long before they have young to raise, spiders build webs, beavers build dams. The utility of these constructions is not immediate; they are potentially useful in the future. We can of course insist that these are responses to biological imperatives, but then we can also make the same claim about human behavior. Second, the notion that we demonstrate this mystifying power of "spontaneity" which nonhuman animals lack is unfounded.[65] A chimpanzee using a stick to dig up termites must choose which stick to use and which holes to poke it into. A bird looking for nest material must also choose between resources. We have no reason to believe that these choices are the operation of "biological imperatives," whereas our own behavior is not. Third, most of what we do is not best explained by way of reference to our cognitive capabilities alone, and much needs no reference to them. Which is to say, most of what we do is surely motivated by the same kind of capabilities that we share with nonhuman animals. Does a father who loves and cares for his child really have the distant future in mind when he does so, for example? Is his behavior constrained by inference as he reasons though categorical imperatives? We can do these things, but they explain only a fraction of our activity. Although this father may take notes to help him plan for the college education that is fifteen years down the road, or value his child as a potential adult, or worry if his treatment of his child can consistently be a universal law, his love and motivation is simultaneously as immediate and unclouded as any "biological imperative." Similarly, most of our normal coping with the world is not a chain of inferences or the exercising of any other kind of unambiguously cognitive capability, but rather is found in the kind of skills we share with other nonhuman animals: walking, reaching, a fast and unreflective grasp of the emotional state of others, and so on.

Thus, the notion of "biological imperatives" being used here is simply not useful. Indeed, it is difficult to know what the phrase could really mean. Given that those behaviors that do not serve survival or procreation can be caused by "biological imperatives," and given that nonhuman animals can do things that are useful only for delayed potential gains (such as nest building), what is left to this notion? All that is left is a way to refer to causes of behavior in nonhuman animals; and, in addition to creating the deception that something more substantial is at issue, such a terminological distinction is groundless. If we are trying to develop a theory of autonomy, using this approach would be as useful as basing a theory of circulation on a division between hearts in human versus hearts in nonhuman animals. The correspondingly narrow way of understanding autonomy, because of these conceptual difficulties to which it leads, does not cohere with our best understanding—nor even with a basic understanding—of human and nonhuman behavior. Only the broader notion of autonomy is a useful, or even a significant, way to understand this flexibility demonstrated by some organisms.

As already noted, it is here that the failures and successes of AI are instructive. In AI, the highly cognitive is usually easiest to model or engineer, and is by far the most brittle. The activities displayed by real organisms which present the greatest engineering challenge and reveal the greatest flexibility are motor control and its integration with perception. Any first-semester freshman computer science student can program a calculator in an afternoon; if she is talented or closer to graduation, she can program a decent chess-playing program, or a text-based interaction program like ELIZA or PARRY. But the best engineers and programmers in the world, working together for years, cannot yet come close to re-creating the competence of motor control exercised by a cricket. And perturb a calculator program (change the syntax of one line, reduce the power to the computer, break one "key" of the input), and it will almost certainly fail to function. Just so, conscious human reasoning, highly prone to drawing invalid conclusions, also can be easily misdirected into inferential errors (Nisbett and Ross 1980). But push against a standing cricket and it can lean to compensate for the shifting of its mass; put it in a wind tunnel and it can dynamically alter its motion to compensate for the force; tear off a front leg and its walking gait changes dynamically to compensate.

Perhaps we are easily misled into believing that the kind of cognitive capabilities that constitute cognitive rationality, for example, alone yield flexibility because it is in the exercise of these kinds of capabilities that some aspects of some of our actions come under the influence of beliefs, including social mores and other cognitive elements necessary to social organization, and because these are the things we value most highly as deliberating, planning, and social animals. And since deliberation and planning are cognitive tasks using such capabilities as the formation of propositions, the use of these propositions in inferences, and so on, we equate—or, it may be more accurate to say that we implicitly define—voluntary action with action that is generated as a result of, and in satisfaction of specifications stated by means of, such capabilities. But fixating on these capabilities, even if they are what is special about our kinds of minds and also about human organization, makes us extremely susceptible to a deceptive picture of autonomy and, as a result, of the ontology of mind and body. We believe that it is in the realm of cognition—or, worse, in the realm of cognitive contents, in "the space of reasons"—that all autonomous activity happens, and that all else is brute simple mechanics. In other words, the cognitive autonomy fallacy arises because we can fail to understand that we single out the cognitive *just because* it is cognitive.

This is not to deny that our cognitive abilities are special. They allow us to organize a society in ways otherwise impossible. They allow logic and science and art. They allow us to record the past and speculate about and plan for the more distant future. They allow us to formulate explicit questions of purpose and reflect upon our own purposes. Perhaps what is most unique is that they enable us to create whole "worlds" of mental contents (e.g., the referents of nominalized predicates, such as triangularity; and also fictional worlds), in which our conceptual contents are things with which we are (in some sense) concerned. Finally, of course, these cognitive abilities are extremely effective; they make us the terror of the "mere animal" world, for example. But though these abilities make us human, they do not transform us into beings with some non-natural or anomalous or secondarily natural ability of "spontaneity" (unless "spontaneity" just has the trivial meaning of having our kinds of cognitive capabilities; which would have the same problems, discussed above, as the trivial meaning of "biological imperatives"). The point is that many nonhuman animals reveal a great deal of autonomy, so much so that they differ from us only in lacking the cognitive skills in question. Understood in this broad way, we must note that nonhumans animals can show as much or almost as much autonomy as humans, and that we have little reason to think of the cognitive abilities that humans have as anything but one among many strategies for autonomy. Thus, having cognitive skills is special; but it does not entail anything more than having cognitive skills. There are all kinds of other strategies that nature has for autonomy and adaptation, and many of them are not cognitive but are still extremely successful, robust, and adaptive. Cognition—understood as the ability to entertain and utilize (e.g., draw logical inferences from) propositional attitudes, and perhaps as the ability to be guided by B-D or cognitive rationality—is neither necessary nor sufficient for autonomy.[66]

A better understanding of emotions and emotional action reveal some of the deceptions implicit in the cognitive autonomy fallacy because some emotions stretch across the implicit "divide": they are bodily and cognitive; they are passive (i.e., sometimes resistant to cognitive control) and active; they are had by nonhumans and humans; they influence and can be influenced by cognition. What some emotions reveal is that there are no easy answers to the mind-body problem as it arises in terms of content, rationality, and rational action to be found in singling out cognition as special by way of appealing to anomalous states, emergent patterns, or second natures. The plausibility of interpretationism and other similar programs rests on ignoring the affective dimension of autonomy—a dimension that we have no reason to believe is unnecessary, and very many reasons to believe is necessary, to what it is to have a mind.

Conclusion

Our best understanding of the basic emotions and other affects counsels broad but significant differences in how we conceive of mind and therefore attempt to explain it. They reveal to us that autonomy, not cognition, is the starting place for explaining the special abilities that organisms have. Autonomy, at least in the terrestrial organisms from which we must learn, is largely constituted through representational acumen, affects, and perceptuomotor control. The kind of abilities that constitute the special human abilities of cognition, such as language, can provide increased autonomy, but they are not the wellsprings of autonomy. The proper function of these abilities is dependent upon representational abilities, affects, and perceptuomotor control. Along with this functional dependency comes a hierarchical functional organization of the brain's systems: there are not only functional modules, but also a hierarchy of such modules, with some dependent upon others, and with affect and perceptuomotor control near the foundation of this hierarchy. That is, affects and perceptuomotor control are the foundation upon which autonomy, and then cognition, is built; and this is perhaps even reflected in the hierarchical arrangements of brain anatomy. Ultimately, affects remind us in specific, demonstrable ways that the body and mind, passion and action, are inseparable. This means that as we make progress in the science of affects, it becomes evident that "anomalous" views of mind and a host of related nonreductive positions must be abandoned along with highly cognitive views of mind consistent with the cognitive autonomy fallacy. But this is no loss: the natural world is far richer than these views ever allowed, and the passionate engine of mind is the richest thing in this world.

Notes

1. The term *basic* has sometimes been associated with the view that all emotions are constructed out of some combination of the basic emotions. I do not endorse this view. However, I continue to use the term because all the alternative terms are traditionally even more loaded. *Primitive, fundamental, innate,* and so on are also potentially deceptive.

2. I consider a functional account (at least in the sense I use the term here) to be consistent with a type-reduction account.

3. See Niedenthal, Setterlund, and Jones (1994) and Niedenthal, Halberstadt, and Setterlund (1997) for examples, explanations, and criticisms of the problems that can result from the application of such models of emotion as they relate to emotional congruence in perception. Their adoption of a categorical model of emotions is consistent with the affect program theory as opposed to these one- or multidimensional appraisal theories and related theories.

4. My concern, in making this distinction, is not with the role that context dependency may play (for example, a sense of "disposition" that is sometimes used by neuroscientists), but rather to clarify an ambiguity in the use of emotion terms. As I also explain below, this is closely related to an issue about whether our use of emotion terms entails that there is a measurable body state or rather is just a way of talking about the likelihood of certain kinds of behavior (and which may or may not require such a measurable body state that constitutes a motivation during, or just before, the occurrence of that behavior).

5. I will not discuss temperament in this book. It is a difficult and interesting topic. See Steinmetz 1994.

6. As I'll explain in chapter 3, the interpretationists can be said to hold a position like this, as long as the contrary notion of there being a correspondence between desire and an actual body state is understood sufficiently strongly (as it must be for any realistic naturalism about affects and their role in mind). Similar issues arise for various defenses of internalism, as I will discuss in chapter 8.

7. These distinguishing features are tilted toward philosophers in that they include relation to cognitive content—and, in particular, the question of whether an affect is a propositional attitude or a similar kind of complex cognitive state. But these features are similar to those used by many scientists, such as in Frijda 1986 (see 1–4).

8. This is largely my failing; I am not familiar with this literature, and also do not know how to respond to the many objections that it can raise. For example, a social constructionist might hold that some emotions are as long-or short-lived as they are because this is what is considered appropriate in that culture. Or some differences in duration could be products of other defining features of emotions and thus secondary in importance to those features. And so on.

9. I will not discuss this experiment, which is often taken to show that autonomic responses are insufficiently complex to specify emotions. A number of criticisms have effectively shown that this experiment does not establish this. See Damasio 1994, Gordon 1987, Griffiths 1997, LeDoux 1996, Levenson 1992.

10. For example, in Ekman, Levenson, and Friesen 1983, both happiness and anger were found to result in an increase in heart rate and in temperature. Although both increased dramatically more for anger than for happiness, one might question whether weak anger would appear like an intense happiness on these two measures alone.

11. My target here is to get at a notion like Chalmers's notion of *psychological consciousness* (1996, 25–26). I prefer the term "working" since it explicitly separates the concept from any specific body of theory. My criterion here that the state be reportable is much stronger than Chalmers would require, however; I will weaken this in chapter 9.

12. Ben-Zeev argues, "It is meaningless to say that an agent is unaware of, or misidentifies, his feelings." Instead, he writes "An unconscious emotion then is usually one about whose nature the agent is not clear, but is aware of many of its components" (1987, 401). If we applied this reasoning to our discussion, alexithymia would be a matter not of failing to identify feelings, but rather failure to identify the affect from which they arise. I shall remain agnostic about this; I take it to be an empirical question— although there may be a conceptual issue in clarifying what "identifying one's feelings" is. Here, we need only the weaker case of failing to recognize the emotion as what it is.

13. For a dated but useful review of related research of nonhuman primate facial expression, see also Chevalier-Skolnikoff 1973.

14. Stating that the action is a consequence of the program can be a little deceptive, since the action is not separable from the program; a car's engine can idle while the car sits still (the analogous case to not acting on the program) but the activity of speeding along in the car cannot be separated from the running of the engine (the analogous case to the action program being uninhibited and leading to action).

15. But there remain substantive empirical and conceptual issues about what the relevant inhibition is. It may be that a combination of things, some best called inhibition, others best called redirection, others disconnection, are involved in an occurrent action program not resulting in emotional action. There is also a conceptual issue about whether these can ultimately be distinguished in a robust way. Here I will not hypothesize about which, if any, of these alterations of emotional function is operating, and will use "inhibition" as a broad term to cover all of them.

16. I believe that the arguments that I will make that refer to type-specific function and eliciting conditions (these arguments occur in chapters 5 through 8) could be made with the weaker supposition merely that there are some type-specific functions and eliciting conditions. However, such arguments would be convoluted and lack any intuitive appeal, and I believe

that these hypotheses regarding function and eliciting conditions are surely close enough to the truth to be appropriate.

17. To avoid the kind of confusion that is invited by the term *intentionality* throughout the text I will use the terms *volition* and *volitional* in the place of the terms *intention* and *intentional* when referring to the relevant kinds of actions.

18. Here I use the colloquial phrasing "afraid of the rabid dog," but the reductive and doxastic cognitivists about emotions are going to be concerned with propositional forms (e.g., "Eric is afraid that the rabid dog will attack him"). My arguments will still stand if we rewrite all the sentences containing emotion terms into plausibly corresponding propositional forms. I will return to this issue in chapter 5, however, and reveal that it is quite important.

19. If we assume that Karen is capable of overcoming her fear, this example is of the most obvious kind of B-D inconsistent action: akratic actions for which it is right to say that emotion provided the motivation for the action.

20. I do allow, below, for the possibility that under some theories of desire Eric can have desires that are consequences of his emotion and that are additional to the set listed here, or even that the emotion may count as a desire. For reasons I explain—namely, that these desires require the emotion—these are not relevant exceptions to the supposed case.

21. It is important to note that the normal folk psychological notion of intending is not reducible to belief and desire (see Brand 1984, 121–27), but even if it were, the problem would stand: by supposition the emotional actions in question would then have the relevant kind of belief and desire as cause or constituent, and yet they are not predictable.

22. *Akrasia* is the Greek term for weakness of the will, and an akratic action is one which someone undertakes even if they know it is better for them not to do so.

23. Data is a character appearing on the television show *Star Trek: The Next Generation* who lacks emotions. I opine, contrary to some views, that such an organism is possible. One complication is that heuristics may be practically necessary, and one effective heuristic may be emotions of the kind discussed here (I return to this theme in chapter 12). But this is not a problem for the argument, since positing such a heuristic is to posit something additional to belief and desire, which goes some way toward making our point.

24. I do not believe that there is a generic motivational state corresponding to the philosopher's notion of desire, and the supposition that there is such a state may in part be why irrealist views like interpretationism seem plausible accounts of motivation (I discuss this in chapter 8); but since the interpretationists assume that there is such a state, or rather that the concept is an appropriate one to explain human action, I have granted their use of "desire" here and shown that even granted as is, the concept fails to account for emotional actions. But if desires are merely ascribed explanations, then under some descriptions, emotions can be counted as constituting some desire or desires; and if one supposes that there are some motivational states which are under some conditions quite like the generic notion of desire, then it is still possible that such a state would accompany an instance of a basic emotion. Thus, if one insists upon utilizing posits of generic desires, they can still be used along with the notion of the basic emotions.

25. Instead, it would seem that the closest thing to such a mistake would be the very approach endorsed by Lutz. At its best, her approach sees emotion terms not as referring to physical states but as concepts used to do certain things. The naturalist would see this as an approach that will lose the rich natural phenomena—a richness that itself will play an important role in the culture—in search of a sterile language game that the natives supposedly play. At its worst, her approach reveals a fundamental confusion of concept and its object: e.g., "emotions are cultural concepts" (Lutz 1988a, 413).

26. We might say of some child, "he plays that he is a firefighter." Two things make this inapplicable here. First, this is somewhat like saying the child pretends that he is a fireman, and presumably requires cognitive abilities lacking in a rat. That is—second, and more important—"play" here must refer to Panksepp's concept, in which it is a basic emotion, not a pretending state.

27. I have included here sadness and joy, which I have not discussed before. Though I suspect that they are basic, I offer no defense of the position that they are covered by the affect program theory. I include them here because it seems difficult to produce a plausible sentence of English that has joy or sadness as directed at a concretum, and so they are of interest as examples.

28. This echoes Clark's "007 principle"; see Clark 1989, 64ff.

29. Related to the view that basic emotions require or are propositional attitudes may be the traditional confusion that a mind must model all of its world before it can act in it. For an overview and critique, see Clark 1996, especially pp. 35ff.

30. It is possible that a cognitive instance of a basic emotion could be caused by one proposition or propositional attitude but have a different one for its object (the example of displaced emotions, discussed in chapter 2, could involve such cases). This would not, however, be normal (in a teleofunctional sense of "normal"). In this book, I will pass over such dissociations, and consider only those cases where the content that is one of the causes of a cognitive instance of a basic emotion is also part of its object.

31. Theories that Nissenbaum considers include Hume 1951, Kenny 1963, A. Rorty 1980a, Solomon 1977, Arnold 1960, and Wilson 1972. A more recent endorsement of all emotions having a common form of object directedness is found in de Sousa (1990).

32. I will not discuss music here, so I pass over several issues. One issue is that it is always possible for the cognitivist to claim that music generates affects but not basic emotions. This seems to me a plausible defense. Another is to claim that music does generate basic emotions, and these emotions have propositional content or otherwise complex cognitive contents that are somehow in the music. This I find extremely implausible. See Budd 1985 for a review of some of the philosophical theories trying to tackle these issues.

33. Recall that, typically, a reductive cognitive theory of emotion might reduce emotions to beliefs and desires, or a doxastic cognitive theory might hold that not only certain beliefs but also certain desires are necessary and sufficient for a kind of emotion. Thus, as I am here concerned with the relevant beliefs only, I can assume without loss of relevant generality that the desires and other relevant states of the subjects are relevantly the same in the various contrasting cases.

34. Thus, if ϕ is the fictional operator, and S_i is a story i (which may be a portion of another story), we might put this point by observing that: $\phi(\phi(S_i)) \rightarrow \phi(S_i)$.

35. I have a vivid memory of playing with a young cousin (I was perhaps eight, my cousin approaching five) on our grandmother's bed, pretending it was a lifeboat. We were lost at sea, our ship had crashed. My cousin asked, "What happened to my parents?" "They were eaten by sharks," I told him. He promptly began to howl in despair, which summoned my grandmother and aunts.

36. As noted before, there is an ambiguity in the term "belief." In one sense, we might say that a cat has beliefs; this is the same sense in which we can say that the child believes all contents. But this is weaker than is required for many of our cognitive skills, and for the exercise of abilities satisfying traditional notions of rationality, which require that one recognize what makes a belief worth believing. That is, believed contents are those recognized as warranting a kind of commitment. Thus, one way to answer the contentious issue of whether nonhuman organisms have beliefs (as opposed, say, to being capable only of simpler representational states) might be answered by stipulating that belief in a rich sense requires warrant. Some nonhuman animals might under some conditions be said to entertain propositional contents (represent situations or states of affairs as such), but it may be that humans alone have notions of warrant that they can apply and so can have beliefs of the kind that can be beholden to standards of B-D rationality.

37. The seeker of emotions can also exploit these subcortical pathways. A bungee jumper who is convinced of the soundness of the bungee cord will still feel exhilaration close to terror jumping off of a bridge. Similarly, a mountain climber attached by rope to a secure hold above cannot fall to her death as she scales the cliff; but nonetheless the tremendous drop below will be very stimulating.

38. This is essentially the reverse of some of the semantic networks used to explain emotional congruence in perception or memory: in those networks, an emotion stimulates a whole category of related elements; here, we suggest that the related elements stimulate the emotion. This is consistent with many variations of semantic networks, where such connections are often symmetric.

39. A neuroscientist once told me a nasty practical joke sometimes undertaken in labs: point a decorticate cat at an unsuspecting person, and then pinch its tail. Instead of turning to attack the source of the pain, the cat attacked whatever was in front of it.

40. But, as noted before, extinguished fear conditioning appears not to be unlearned but rather in some sense suppressed, since the conditioning can be reinstated more quickly and can even spontaneously reappear.

41. An interesting example here is the many civic movements started by the parents of children killed or murdered: these include movements that brought about changes in drunken-driving laws and in prison sentencing. The parents seek changes that perhaps would have saved their children, knowing of course that it is too late for them. Their anger in part motivates them to work for changes that would improve the social system in which they participate. Such acts are excellently clear examples of altruism.

42. An instance of this arises in Blackburn's notion of emotional ascent (see 1998, 9).

43. Blackburn (1998, 61ff) argues that such cases are not counterexamples to internalism because they are parasitic upon internalism and presuppose that internalism is normal. This follows if we understand practical judgments, and especially ethical judgments, as appeals to affects, and we understand values as expressions of affects. However, my arguments here are consistent with an expressivist view like Blackburn's, since we can still limn the relations between practical judgments and motivations, even if we do it by looking at abnormal cases.

44. A debate that touches upon both moral psychology and the philosophy of mind is whether our understanding of others is primarily in the form of a theory of their own mental states, or is primarily given to us by way of simulating their mental states. Of course, we may well do both things. But if our understanding of each other in part explains moral motivation, one view is clearly superior to the other. That is, we have no reason to believe that a theory of another person's mental states will motivate me to respect those mental states. But if I simulate another person's mental states, then I can have a direct motivation to respect them in the relevant way. For example, if my understanding of another person's fear of something is given to me by simulating that fear, then I could be motivated by that simulation not to be the cause of that fear. That is, imagine I have a passenger in the car who is very afraid of fast driving; if my way of understanding this is to simulate the fear of fast driving, I am directly motivated not to drive fast. The psychopaths would simply fail to model the affects of other minds sufficiently; if so, their sometimes extremely violent behavior would be made possible by their inability to simulate the affects of others, and so to be motivated by them.

45. I can set aside as irrelevant the many such statements (e.g., "that is infuriating," "that is terrifying") that would not be emotional judgments because they are proclaimed in a dispositional sense or a colloquial sense. The dispositional sense is evident when one says that something is terrifying, referring to some event long past, and for which one is now unmoved. The colloquial sense is evident when we call something "terrifying" when we merely find it mildly frightening, or "infuriating" when we find it just annoying. That is, we sometimes use emotional judgment terms weakly, without any real claim about our own state. Both uses are derivative upon the meaning of the terms in their occurrent and sincere use (for otherwise the terms would be deprived of their dispositional and informal senses).

46. *Qualia* is the philosopher's term for the phenomenal properties of instances of experience.

47. I do not endorse the idea that there is a prior intension which is pretheoretic. But something like prior intension is a necessary element of the view in question, and so I will admit the distinction here for the sake of argument. For those who think that all concepts are theory laden, or who otherwise object to the distinction, then "prior intension" can be taken to mean something like the intension of the concept as given in folk psychology or at least as given in some theory other than the theories in question.

48. Thus Lycan 1987 has a chapter titled, "Color as a Paradigm Case of *Quale*." Lycan 1996 continues this approach: "Take phenomenal color as a paradigm case of quale" (69). Chalmers writes, "In addressing the philosophical mysteries associated with conscious experience, a simple color sensation raises the problems as deeply as one's experience of a Bach chorale" (1996, 11)—and presumably as deeply as fury or terror. Jackson's fa-

mous "colorblind Mary" argument is of course only about color (1982). And so on.

49. There may not be a linear spectrum of any aspect of affects as there is for an aspect of color, but to illustrate this point I need only for these two affects to motivate actions that are distinct and typically incompatible.

50. Obviously, such arguments are not conclusive. But since our prior intension of the concept of emotional experience is functional, the concept of emotional consciousness has a unity where the concept of perceptual consciousness seems to allow of a division. Prima facie, this shifts the burden of proof to the epiphenomenalist or the token role theorists for these cases. The person who believes that emotional experience plays a functional role need not explain why the phenomenal experience of an emotion and the function of the emotion are distinct because we do not ever treat them as if they are. And, since it would furthermore take additional justification to show why phenomenal experience of an emotion is different from phenomenal experience of other kinds, I have shifted the burden of proof for phenomenal experience as a whole.

51. Paul Churchland (1989a 31–33) briefly discusses a different form of this problem.

52. Here also the question about how strong a representational account needs to be is crucial. For example, for Paul Churchland, the answer might be that there is no significant difference between the representational and causal account. A token role theory might only require reliable co-variance, and causation surely gives this. If this is too weak for representation, maybe we should eliminate the stronger notion of representation.

53. The notions of weak and strong supervenience, and much if not most of our contemporary understanding of supervenience, comes from Jaegwon Kim (see 1993a, 1993b). The definitions of weak and strong supervenience used here are variations on Kim 1993b (80–81).

54. Phenomenal experiences are events, so the use of properties in the definition of supervenience can be somewhat awkward; however, when required we can replace "property" with "event" in all the definitions to describe the corresponding form of supervenience.

55. We need to index the experience to this world to be able to refer to alternative colors that get called the same. That is, when we refer to a green or red experience in another world, we mean what are called "a green experience" and "a red experience" in this world, since they may be identified differently in that world.

56. There are three important complications we can pass over. First, I assume that natural laws can explain everything relevant to the questions we will be asking, and it is to these natural laws (some perhaps yet undiscovered) that we refer when we specify natural possibility. Second, there are subtle technical issues concerning negative facts (for an excellent analysis see Chalmers 1996, 32–89; and for some relevant discussion see also Kim 1993d). Third, that I will mean natural possibility by "possibility" and its cognates entails that some of the claims made below are not so strong as they may sound if we forget this. For example, I deny the *natural possibility* of a zombie world, but this is consistent with, for example, Chalmers's claim that the zombie world is *logically possible* (a claim I neither endorse nor deny). Again: I am not claiming to solve the hard problem, but rather to explore some relations between phenomenal experience and the functional role of some conscious affects.

57. Ontology is that branch of metaphysics which is concerned with questions of what kinds of things there are.

58. Here differences in terminology arise. I have not used *mood* in a way that is necessarily consistent with the use of the term in the literature under review here. Also, in chapter 1 I rejected the idea that affects fit well into categories like positive versus negative. However, since our purpose here is only to show how affects can influence primary cognitive processes, these differences need not concern us. Demonstration of a significant influence along such an impoverished measure would be sufficient for my argument here.

59. Note that such articulations of reasons have in the past been used by cognitive scientists to provide algorithms that they supposed the subjects were using to make their decisions; and these kinds of algorithms were often taken to be the starting place for the symbolic computational functionalist to design an AI system.

60. If I understand her correctly, Picard is open to the idea of deep affective engineering, but erroneously believes that such a thing can be had through the approaches of shallow affective engineering.

61. In philosophy, *agent* can be a technical term for something that behaves with intentionality, and in particular for something that behaves by way of being motivated by beliefs, desires, or other intentional states. In this chapter, I use the term in the sense it is used by AI, and use *system* to include (but not be limited to) agents in the philosophical sense.

62. Important in this regard is de Sousa's argument (1987, 172ff) that emotions are one solution to the frame problem in AI.

63. For Davidson, "it is necessary that there be endless interlocked beliefs. The system of such beliefs identifies a thought by locating it in a logical and epistemic space" (Davidson 1984, 157). But do people really find beliefs intelligible only as logically related to other beliefs? I find the idea incredible, just as I find it implausible that no organism can hold just a few beliefs, some in isolation from the others. There is a false dilemma drawn again and again in recent philosophy of mind, between all mental states being wholly independent of each other, at one extreme, and radical holism where they are all inseparable, at the other. There is no reason to see either alternative as likely, and it is clearly false to conclude that the negation of one implies the assertion of the other.

How much an instance of a kind of mental state requires other mental states is an empirical matter (if only because the natures of the mental states in question are not yet well understood). This of course means that the interpretationist can deny that such considerations apply to this issue; for example, one might claim that the mode of understanding beliefs described above is special and not about what people really do; but then, why are we even considering it as part of a theory of mind?

64. Since I believe that a teleofunctional account can have a role in a naturalist theory, I do not require that such an explanation be nonintentional—but a teleofunctional account need have nothing to do with inference, nor with a holistic network of beliefs, nor with irreducible norms of rationality.

65. In terms of the free will problem, I deny that the problem is any different for humans than it is for other animals. Humans have, instead, additional abilities and so additional kinds of controls over their behavior, but these are as natural as those other abilities that are shared with nonhuman animals. For the record, I do agree that our reflective conceptual abili-

ties provide us with special abilities and burdens; perhaps most important, they make humans the kind of beings who can question their own purpose.

66. These observations may strike at the heart of the history of post–WWII analytic philosophy, when Quine (1953), Sellars (1997), Wittgenstein (1953) and their followers—including Davidson and Dennett—coupled the linguistic turn in philosophy to a coherentism or holism, largely as a result of their attacks on some features of some forms of empiricism. I would argue that these views also arose because of a far too simplistic conception of what naturalism allows of our theories, and of what naturalism can be expected to explain and fail to explain or eliminate. These philosophers are constantly tempted by the idea that mental states are just expressions of the exercise of language. Although the motivations for these views largely arose out of epistemological concerns, most of the accompanying theories of mind can fruitfully be understood as extreme instances of the cognitive autonomy fallacy.

Bibliography

Arnold, M. B. 1960. *Emotion and personality*. New York: Columbia University Press.

Averill, James R. 1974. An analysis of psychophysiological symbolism and its influence on theories of emotion. *Journal for the Theory of Social Behaviour* 4 (2): 147–190.

———. 1980a A constructivist view of emotion. In *Theories of emotion*. Vol. 1 of *Emotion: Theory, Research, and Experience*, ed. Robert Plutchik and Henry Kellerman. New York: Academic Press.

———. 1980b Emotion and anxiety: Sociocultural, biological, and psychological determinants. In *Explaining Emotions*, Ed. Amelie Oksenberg Rorty, 37–72. Berkeley: University of California Press.

Bard, P. 1928. A diencephalic mechanism for the expression of rage. *American Journal of Physiology* 84:490–515.

Bazzett, H. C., and W. G. Penfield. 1922. A study of the sherrington decerebrate animal in the chronic as well as the acute condition. *Brain* 45:185–265.

Bechara, A., Antonio R. Damasio, Hanna Damasio, S. Anderson. 1994. Insensitivity to future consequences following damage to human prefrontal cortex." *Cognition* 50:7–12.

Bennett, Jonathan. 1989. *Rationality: An essay towards an analysis*. Indianapolis: Hackett.

Ben-Zeev, Aaron. 1987. The nature of emotions. *Philosophical Studies* 52: 393–409.

Bigelow, John, and Robert Pargetter. 1987. Functions. *Journal of Philosophy* 84 (4): 181–196.

Blackburn, Simon. 1998. *Ruling passions: A theory of practical reasoning*. New York: Oxford University Press.

Blaney, P. 1986. Affect and memory: A review. *Psychological Bulletin* 99: 229–246.

Block, Ned. 1995. On a confusion about a function of consciousness. *Behavioral and Brain Sciences* 18:227–287.

Boorse, C. 1976. Wright on functions. *Philosophical Review* 85:70–86.

Boruah, Bijoy H. 1988. *Fiction and emotion: A study in aesthetics and the philosophy of mind*. Oxford: Clarendon Press.

Boucher, J. D., and M. E. Brandt. 1981. *Judgment of emotion: American and Malay antecedents. Journal of Cross-Cultural Psychology* 12:272–283.

Bower, Gordon H. 1981. Mood and memory. *American Psychologist* 36: 129–148.

Braitenberg, Valentino. 1984. *Vehicles: Experiments in synthetic psychology.* Cambridge: MIT Press.

Brand, Myles. 1984. *Intending and acting: Toward a naturalized action theory.* Cambridge: MIT Press.

Brandom, Robert. 1994. *Making it explicit: Reasoning, representing, and discursive commitment.* Cambridge, Mass.: Harvard University Press.

Brink, David O. 1989. *Moral realism and the foundations of ethics.* Cambridge: Cambridge University Press.

Brooks, Rodney. 1991. Intelligence without representation. *Artificial Intelligence* 47:139–159.

Brown, R., and J. Kulik. 1977. Flashbulb memories. *Cognition* 5:73–99.

Budd, Malcolm. 1985 *Music and the emotions: The philosophical theories.* London: Routledge & Kegan Paul.

Cahill, Larry. 1997. The neurobiology of emotionally influenced memory. In *Psychobiology of Posttraumatic stress disorder*, Ed. Rachel, Yehuda and Alexander C. McFarlane, 238–246. New York: New York Academy of Sciences.

Cahill, Larry, Bruce Prins, Michael Weber, and James L. McGaugh. 1994. β-adrenergic activation and memory for emotional events. *Nature* 371:702–704.

Calvino, Italo. 1993. Tutto in un punto. In *Le Cosmicomiche*. Milan: Arnoldo Mondadori Editore S.p.A.

Cannon, W. B., and S. W. Britton. 1924. Pseudoaffective medulliadrenal secretion. *American Journal of Physiology* 72:283–294.

Chalmers, David John. 1995. Facing up to the problem of consciousness. *Journal of Consciousness Studies* 2:200–219.

———. (1996) *The conscious mind: In search of a fundamental theory of consciousness.* New York: Oxford University Press.

Cherniak, Christopher. 1986. *Minimal rationality.* Cambridge: MIT Press.

Chevalier-Skolnikoff, Suzanne. 1973. Facial expression of emotion in non-human primates. In *Darwin and Facial expression*, Ed. Paul Ekman, 11–89. New York: Academic Press.

Christensen, Wayne. 1996. A complex systems theory of teleology. *Biology and Philosophy* 11:301–320.

Churchland, Patricia S., and Terrence J. Sejnowski. 1992. *The computational brain.* Cambridge: MIT Press.

Churchland, Paul M. 1989a. Functionalism, qualia, and intentionality. In *A neurocomputational perspective*, 22–46. Cambridge: MIT Press.

———. 1989b *A neurocomputational perspective*, Cambridge: MIT Press.

Clark, Andy. 1989. *Microcognition: Philosophy, cognitive science, and parallel distributed processing.* Cambridge: MIT Press.

———. 1996. *Being there: Putting brain, body, and world together again.* Cambridge: MIT Press.

Clark, Andy, and Josefa Toribio. 1994. Doing without representations? *Synthese* 101 (3):401–431.

Cleckley, H. 1941. *The mask of sanity.* St. Louis: Mosby.

Clore, Gerald L. 1994. Why emotions are never unconscious. In *The nature of emotion: Fundamental questions* Ed. Paul Ekman and Richard J. Davidson, 103–111. New York: Oxford University Press.

Cocchiarella, Nino. 1995. Conceptual realism as formal ontology. In *Formal ontology*, ed. R. Poli and P. Simons. Dordrecht: Kluwer Academic Press.

Cohen, L. Jonathan. 1992. Rationality. In *A companion to epistemology*, Ed. Jonathan Dancy and Ernest Sosa, 415–420. Cambridge, Mass: Blackwell.

Cohon, Rachel. 1993. Internalism about reasons for action. *Pacific Philosophical Quarterly* 74:265–288.

Colby, K. M. 1974. *Artificial paranoia*. New York: Pergamon Press.

———. 1981. Modeling a paranoid mind. *Behavioral and Brain Sciences* 4: 515–50.

Cytowic, Richard E. 1998. *The man who tasted shapes*. Cambridge: MIT Press.

Damasio, Antonio. 1994. *Descartes' error*. New York: Grosst/Putnam.

Damasio, Antonio R., Daniel Tranel, and Hanna Damasio. 1990. Individuals with sociopathic behavior caused by frontal damage fail to respond autonomically to social stimuli. *Behavioral Brain Research* 41 (1990): 81–94.

Dancy, Jonathan. 1993. *Moral reasons*. Cambridge, Mass: Blackwell.

Davidson, Donald. 1963. Actions, reasons, and causes. *Journal of Philosophy* (60) 23:685–700.

———. 1976. Hume's cognitive theory of pride. *Journal of Philosophy* 73 (13):744–757.

———. 1980a. *Essays on actions and events*. New York: Oxford University Press.

———. 1980b. How is weakness of the will possible? In *Essays on actions and events*, 21–42. New York: Oxford University Press.

———. 1980c. Mental events. In *Essays on actions and events*, 207–227. New York: Oxford University Press.

———. 1984. Thought and Talk. In *Inquiries into truth and Interpretation*, 155–170. New York: Oxford University Press.

Deigh, J. 1994. Cognitivism in the theory of emotions. *Ethics* 104:824–854.

Dennett, Daniel C. 1971. Intentional Systems. *Journal of Philosophy* 63 (4): 87–106.

———. 1981. *Brainstorms*. Cambridge: MIT Press.

———. 1991. *Consciousness explained*. Boston: Little, Brown.

———. 1993a. *The intentional stance*. Cambridge: MIT Press.

———. 1993e. True believers. In *The intentional stance*, 13–42. Cambridge: MIT Press.

———. 1993d. Three kinds of intentional psychology. In *The intentional stance*, 43–68. Cambridge: MIT Press.

———. 1993b. Making sense of ourselves. In *The intentional stance*, 84–101. Cambridge: MIT Press.

———. 1993c. Mid-term examination. In *The intentional stance*, 339–350. Cambridge: MIT Press.

Descartes, René. 1985. *The philosophical writings of Descartes, volume I*. Trans. John Cottingham, Robert Stoothoff, and Dugald Murdoch. New York: Cambridge University Press.

de Sousa, Ronald. 1987. *The rationality of emotion*. Cambridge: MIT Press.

Douglas, Rodney, Misha Mahowald, and Carver Mead. 1995. Neuromorphic analogue VLSI. *Annual review of Neuroscience* 18:255–281.

Dretske, Fred. 1981. *Knowledge and the flow of information*. Cambridge: MIT Press.

Dummett, Michael. 1981. *Frege: Philosophy of language*. 2nd ed. Cambridge, Mass: Harvard University Press.

Dyer, M. C. 1982. *In depth understanding. A computer model of integrated processing for narrative comprehension*. Cambridge: MIT Press.

Eibl-Eibesfeldt, Irenäus. 1973. The expressive behavior of the deaf-and-blind-born. In *Social communication and movement*, ed. M. von Cranach and I. Vine. New York: Academic Press.

———. 1989. *Human ethology.* New York: Aldine de Gruyter.

Ekman, Paul. 1980. Biological and cultural contributions to body and facial movement in the expression of emotions. In *Explaining emotions*, ed. Amelie Oksenberg Rorty, 37–72. Berkeley: University of California Press.

———. 1988. The universality of a contempt expression: A replication. *Motivation and Emotion* 12:303–308.

———. 1993. Facial expression and emotion. *American Psychologist* 48: 384–392.

———, ed. 1973. *Darwin and facial expression.* New York: Academic Press.

Ekman, Paul, and Richard J. Davidson, eds. 1994. *The nature of emotion: Fundamental questions.* New York: Oxford University Press.

Ekman, Paul, and Wallace V. Friesen. 1971. Constants across cultures in the face and emotion. *Journal of Personality and Social Psychology* 17:124–129.

———. 1975. *Unmasking the face.* Englewood Cliffs, N.J.: Prentice Hall.

Ekman, Paul, Robert W. Levenson, and Wallace V. Friesen. 1983. Autonomic nervous activity distinguishes among emotions. *Science* 221: 1208–1210.

Ekman, Paul, E. R. Sorenson, and Wallace V. Friesen. 1969. Pan-cultural elements in facial displays of emotions. *Science* 164:86–88.

Elliott, Clark. 1994. Multi-media communication with emotion-driven "believable agents." In *AAAI technical report for the spring symposium on believable agents*, 16–20. Stanford, Calif.: AAAI.

———. 1998. Hunting for the Holy Grail with "emotionally intelligent" virtual actors. *SIGART Bulletin* 9 (1): 20–28.

Erber, Ralph. 1991. Affective and semantic priming: effects of mood on category accessibility and inference. *Journal of Experimental Social Psychology* 27:480–498.

Ervin, Frank R., and John Martin. 1986. Neurophysiological bases of the primary emotions. In *Biological foundations of emotion*. Vol. 3 of *Emotion: Theory, research, and experience*, ed. Robert Plutchik and Henry Kellerman, 145–170. New York: Academic Press.

Esteves, Francisco, Ulf Dimberg, Arne Ohman. 1994. Automatically elicited fear: Condidtioned skin conductance responses to masked facial expressions. *Cognition and emotion* 8 (5): 393–413.

Falk, W. D. 1986. "Ought" and motivation. In *Ought, reasons, and morality: The collected papers of W. D. Falk,* 21–41. Ithaca, N.Y.: Cornell University Press.

Fish, D. R., P. Gloor, F. L. Quesney, A. Oliver. 1993. Clinical responses to electrical brain stimulation of the temporal and frontal lobes in patients with epilepsy. *Brain* 116:297–414.

Fodor, J. A. 1983. *The modularity of mind: An essay in faculty psychology.* Cambridge: MIT Press.

———. 1990. *A theory of content and other essays.* Cambridge: MIT Press.

Forgas, Joseph P. 1992. On mood and peculiar people: Affect and person typicality in impression formation. *Journal of Personality and Social Psychology* 62 (5):863–875.

Forgas, Joseph P., and Gordon H. Bower. 1987. Mood effects on person-perception judgments. *Journal of Personality and Social Psychology* 53 (1): 53–60.

Frank, Robert H. 1988. *Passions within reason: The strategic role of the emotions.* New York: W. W. Norton.

Frijda, Nico H. 1986. *The emotions.* New York: Cambridge University Press.

Fulcher, J. S. 1942. Voluntary facial expressions in blind and seeing children. *Archives of Psychology* 38:272.

Gazzaniga, Michael S. 1970. *The bisected brain.* New York: Appleton-Century-Crofts.

Gazzaniga, Michael S., and Joseph E. LeDoux. 1978. *The integrated mind.* New York: Plenum.

Gloor, Pierre. 1990. Experiential phenomena of temporal lobe epilepsy. *Brain* 113:1673–1694.

Godfrey-Smith, Peter. 1994. A modern history theory of functions. *Nous* 28 (3): 344–362.

Goodale, Melvyn A. 1998. Visuomotor control: Where does vision end and action begin? *Current Biology* 8:R489–R491.

Goodale, Melvyn A., and A. David Milner. 1995. *The visual brain in action.* New York: Oxford University Press.

Gordon, H. W., and R. W. Sperry. 1968. Lateralization of olfactory perception in the surgically separated hemispheres of man. *Neuropsychologia* 7:111–120.

Gordon, Robert. 1987. *The structure of emotions.* New York: Cambridge University Press.

Gould, Stephen Jay. 1978. Sociobiology: The art of storytelling. *New Scientist* 80:530–533.

Gray, J. A. 1991. The neuropsychology of temperament. In *Explorations in temperament: International perspectives on theory and measurement,* ed. J. Strelau and A. Angleitner, 105–128. New York: Plenum.

Greenspan, Patricia S. 1988. *Emotions and reasons: An inquiry into emotional justification.* New York: Routledge.

Griffiths, Paul E. 1989. The degeneration of the cognitive theory of emotion. *Philosophical Psychology* 2 (3): 297–313.

———. 1990. Modularity and the psychoevolutionary theory of emotion. *Biology and Philosophy* 5 (2): 175–196.

———. 1993. Functional analysis and proper functions. *British Journal of the Philosophy of Science* 44:409–422.

———. 1997. *What emotions really are: The problem of psychological categories.* Chicago: University of Chicago Press.

Hamilton, Vernon, Gordon H. Bower, and Nico H. Frijda, eds. 1988. *Cognitive perspectives on emotion and motivation.* Boston: Kluwer Academic Publishers.

Hare, R. D. 1965. Temporal gradient of fear arousal in psychopaths. *Journal of Abnormal Psychology* 70:442–445.

———. 1966. Psychopathy and choice of immediate versus delayed punishment. *Journal of Abnormal Psychology* 71:25–29.

Harré, Rom, 1986a. An outline of the social constructivist viewpoint. In *The Social Construction of Emotions* New York: Basil Blackwell.

———, ed. 1986b. *The social construction of emotions.* New York: Basil Blackwell.

Harré, Rom, and Grant Gillett. 1994. *The discursive mind.* Thousand Oaks, Calif.: Sage Publications.

Hebb, D. O. 1946. Emotion in man and animal: The intuitive processes of recognition. *Psychological Review* 53:88–106.

Hermans, Dirk, Frank Baeyens, and Paul Eelen. 1998. Odours as affective-processing context for word evaluation: A case of cross-modal affective priming. *Cognition and Emotion* 12 (4): 601–613.

Hermans, Dirk, J. De Houwer, and Paul Eelen. 1994. The affective priming effect: Automatic activation of evaluative information in memory. *Cognition and emotion* 8:515–533.

Hill, W. F. 1978. Effects of mere exposure on preferences in nonhuman mammals. *Psychological Bulletin* 85:1177–1198.

Hohmann, George W. 1966. Some effects of spinal cord lesions on experienced emotional feelings. *Psychophysiology* 3 (2): 143–156.

Hume, David. 1951. *A treatise on human nature.* Ed. L. A. Selby-Bigge. Oxford: Oxford University Press.

Ingle, D. 1973. Tow visual systems in the frog. *Science* 181:1053–1055.

———. 1980. Some effects of pretectum lesions on the frog's detection of stationary objects. *Behavioral Brain Research* 1:139–163.

———. 1982. Organization of visuomotor behaviors in vertebrates. In *Analysis of visual behavior,* ed. D. Ingle, M. A. Goodale, and R. J. W. Mansfield, 67–109. Cambridge: MIT Press.

Isen, Alice M., and K. A. Daubman. 1984. The influence of affect on categorization. *Journal of Personality and Social Psychology* 47:1206–1217.

Isen, Alice M., K. A. Daubman, G. P. Nowicki. 1987. Positive affect facilitates creative problem solving. *Journal of Personality and Social Psychology* 52:1122–1131.

Isen, Alice M., Paula M. Niedenthal, and Nancy Cantor. 1992. An influence of positive affect on social categorization. *Motivation and Emotion* 16 (1): 65–78.

Izard, Carroll E. 1971. *The face of emotion.* New York: Appleton-Century-Crofts.

Jackson, Frank. 1982. "Epiphenomenal qualia." *Philosophical Quarterly* 32:127–136.

James, William. 1950. *The principles of psychology, volume II.* New York: Dover.

Jordon, Michael I., and David A. Rosenbaum. 1989. Action. In *Foundations of cognitive science,* ed. Michael I. Posner 727–767. Cambridge: MIT Press.

Kagel, John R., and Alvin E. Roth, eds. 1995. *The handbook of experimental economics.* Princeton, N.J.: Princeton University Press.

Karnath, H. O., K. Christ, and W. Hartje. 1993. Decrease of contralateral neglect by neck muscle vibration and spatial orientation of trunk midline. *Brain* 116:383–396.

Karnath, H. O., P. Schenkel, and B. Fischer. 1991. Trunk orientation as the determining factor of the "contralateral" deficit in the neglect syndrome and as the physical anchor of the internal representation of body orientation in space. *Brain* 114:1997–2014

Keltner, D. 1995. Signs of appeasement: evidence for the distinct displays of embarrassment, amusement, and shame. *Journal of Personality and Social Psychology* 68:441–454.

Kemper, T. D. 1987. How many emotions are there? Wedding the social and the autonomic components. *American Journal of Sociology* 93:263–289.

Kenny, A. 1963. *Action, emotion, and will.* London: Routledge.

Kim, Jaegwon. 1993a. Concepts of supervenience. In *Supervenience and mind,* 53–78. New York: Cambridge University Press.

————. 1993b. "Strong" and "global" supervenience revisited. In *Supervenience and mind*, 79–91. New York: Cambridge University Press.

————. 1993c. *Supervenience and mind: Selected philosophical essays.* New York: Cambridge University Press.

————. 1993d. Supervenience as a philosophical concept. In *Supervenience and mind*, 131–160. New York: Cambridge University Press.

King, H. E. 1961. Psychological effects of excitation in the limbic system. In *Electrical Stimulation of the Brain,* ed. D. E. Sheer, 477–486. Austin: University of Texas Press.

Kirk, R. 1974. Zombies versus materialists. *Aristotlean Society (supplement)* 48:135–152.

Kitayama, Shinobu, and Susan Howard. 1994. Affective regulation of perception and comprehension: Amplification and semantic priming. In *The heart's eye*, ed. Paula Niedenthal and Shinobu Kitayama, 41–65. San Diego: Academic Press.

Kitcher, Philip. 1993. Function and design. In *Midwest Studies in Philosophy*, no. 18, ed. Peter French, Theodore Uehling Jr., and Howard Wettstein, 379–397. Notre Dame, Ind.: University of Notre Dame Press.

Kunst-Wilson, W. R., and R. B. Zajonc. 1980. Affective discrimination of stimuli that cannot be recognized. *Science* 207:557–558.

Lamarque, Peter. 1981. How can we fear and pity fictions? *British Journal of Aesthetics* 21 (4): 291–304.

Lane, Richard D., Geoffrey L. Ahern, Gary E. Schwartz, and Alfred Kaszniak. 1997. Is alexithymia the emotional equivalent of blindsight? *Biological Psychiatry* 42:834–844.

Lane, Richard D., and Gary E. Schwartz. 1987. Levels of emotional awareness: A cognitive-developmental theory and its application to psychopathology. *American Journal of Psychiatry* 144:133–143.

Lane, Richard D., Lee Sechrest, Robert Reidel, Victoria Weldon, Alfred Kaszniak, and Gary E. Schwartz. 1996. Impaired verbal and nonverbal emotion recognition in alexithymia. *Psychosomatic Medicine* 58:203–210.

Lazarus, Richard. 1991. *Emotion and adaptation.* New York: Oxford University Press.

LeDoux, Joseph E. 1984. Cognition and emotion: Processing functions and brain systems. In *Handbook of cognitive neuroscience*, ed. Michael S. Gazzaniga 357–368. New York: Plenum Press.

————. 1996. *The emotional brain: The mysterious underpinnings of emotional life.* New York: Simon & Schuster.

Levenson, Robert W. 1992. Autonomic nervous system differences among emotions. *Psychological Science* 3 (1): 23–27.

————. 1994. "The search for autonomic specificity." In *The nature of emotion*, ed. Paul Exman and Richard J. Davidson, 252–257. New York: Oxford University Press.

Levenson, Robert W., Paul Ekman, Wallace V. Friesen. 1990. Voluntary facial action generates emotion-specific autonomic nervous system activity. *Psychophysiology* 27:363–384.

Leventhal, Howard. 1984. A perceptual-motor theory of emotion. *Advances in experimental social psychology, Volume 17.* New York: Academic Press.

Lewis, David. 1988. Desire as belief. *Mind* 97 (387): 323–332.

————. 1996. "Desire as Belief, II." *Mind* 105 (418): 303.

Lorenz, Konrad. 1984. *The foundations of ethology.* New York: Springer-Verlag.

Lutz, Catherine A. 1988b. *Unnatural emotions: Everyday sentiments on a Micronesian atoll and their challenge to Western theory.* Chicago: University of Chicago Press.

———. 1988a. Ethnographic perspectives on the emotion lexicon. In *Cognitive perspectives on emotion and motivation,* ed. Vernon Hamilton, Gordon H. Bower, and Nico H. Frijda, 399–419. Boston: Kluwer Academic Press.

Lycan, William G. 1987. *Consciousness.* Cambridge: MIT Press.

———. 1996. *Consciousness and experience.* Cambridge: MIT Press.

MacLean, Paul D. 1990. *The triune brain in evolution: Role in paleocerebral functions.* New York and London: Plenum Press.

Marks, Joel. 1982. A theory of emotion. *Philosophical Studies* 42:227–242.

Marr, D. 1982. *Vision.* New York: W. H. Freeman.

Martin, J. B., and R. Pihl. 1985. "The stress-alexithymia hypothesis: Theoretical and empirical considerations." *Psychotherapy and Psychosomatics* 43:169–76.

McDowell, John. 1994. *Mind and world.* Cambridge, Mass: Harvard University Press.

———. 1998. Are moral requirements hypothetical imperatives? In *Mind, value, and reality,* 77–94. Cambridge, Mass: Harvard University Press.

McGaugh, James L., Ines B. Introini-Collison, Larry F. Cahill, Claudio Castellano, Carla Dalmaz, Marise B. Parent, and Cedric L. Williams. 1993. Neuromodulatory systems and memory storage: Role of the amygdala. *Behavioral Brain Research* 58:81–90.

Mead, Carver. 1989 *Analog VLSI and neural systems.* Reading, Mass.: Addison-Wesley.

Mele, Alfred. 1995. Motivation: Essentially motivation-constituting attitudes. *Philosophical Review* 104:387–423.

———. 1996. Internalist moral cognitivism and listlessness. *Ethics* 106: 727–753.

Miller, R. E., W. F. Caul, and I. R. Mirsky. 1971. Communication of affects between feral and socially isolated monkeys. *Journal of Personality and Social Psychology* 7:231–229.

Millikan, R. G. 1984. *Language, thought, and other biological categories.* Cambridge: MIT Press.

———. 1990. Truth rules, hoverflies, and the Kripke-Wittgenstein Paradox. *Philosophical Review* 99 (3): 323–353.

———. 1993. *White Queen psychology and other essays for Alice.* Cambridge, MIT Press.

Milner, A. David, and Melvyn A. Goodale. 1995. *The visual brain in action.* Vol. 27 of *Oxford Psychology Series.* Oxford: Oxford University Press.

Minsky, Marvin. 1985. *The society of mind.* New York: Simon & Schuster.

Nagel, Ernest. 1977. Teleology revisited. *Journal of Philosophy* 74 (5):261–301.

Nagel, Thomas. 1970. *The possibility of altruism.* Princeton, N.J.: Princeton University Press.

———. 1979. What is it like to be a bat? In *Mortal questions.* Cambridge: Cambridge University Press, 165–180.

Nash, Ronald Alan. 1989. Cognitive theories of emotion. *Noûs* 23:481–504.

Nathanson, Stephen. 1985. *The Ideal of Rationality.* Atlantic Highlands, N.J.: Humanities Press.

Neander, K. 1991. Functions as selected effects: The conceptual analyst's defense." *Philosophy of Science* 58:168–184.

Neisser, Ulric, and Nicole Harsch. 1992. Phantom flashbulbs: False recollections of hearing the news about *Challenger*. In *Affect and accuracy in recall: Studies of "flashbulb" memories*, ed. Eugene Winograd and Ulric Neisser. New York: Cambridge University Press.

Nemiah, J. C., and P. E. Sifneos. 1970. Affect and fantasy in patients with psychosomatic disorder. In *Modern trends in psychosomatic medicine, vol. 2*, 26–34. New York: Appleton-Century-Crofts.

Newell, Allen. 1981. The knowledge level. *AI Magazine* (summer): 1–20.

Niedenthal, Paula M., and Nancy Cantor. 1986. Affective responses as guides to category-based inferences. *Motivation and Emotion* 10 (3): 217–232.

Niedenthal, Paula M., Jamin B. Halberstadt, and Marc B. Setterlund. 1997. Being happy and seeing "happy": Emotional state mediates visual word recognition. *Cognition and Emotion* 11 (4): 403–432.

Niedenthal, Paula, and Shinobu Kitayama, eds. 1994. *The heart's eye: Emotional influences in perception and attention*. San Diego: Academic Press.

Niedenthal, Paula M., and Marc B. Setterlund. 1994. Emotion congruence in perception. *Personality and Social Psychology Bulletin*, 20 (4): 401–411.

Niedenthal, Paula M., Marc B. Setterlund, Douglas E. Jones. 1994. Emotional organization of perceptual memory. In *The Heart's Eye*, ed. Paula Niedenthal and Shinobu Kitayama, 87–113. San Diego: Academic Press.

Nisbett, Richard, and Lee Ross. 1980. *Human inference: Strategies and shortcomings of social judgment*. Englewood Cliffs, N.J.: Prentice Hall.

Nissenbaum, Helen Fay. 1985. *Emotion and focus*. Stanford, Calif. Center for the Study of Language and Information.

Nussbaum, Martha. 1987. The Stoics on the extirpation of the passions. *Apeiron* 20:129–177.

———. 1990. Narrative emotions. In *Love's knowledge*. New York: Oxford University Press.

Öhman, Arne. 1988. Preattentive processes in the generation of emotions. In *Cognitive prespectives on emotion and motivation*, ed. Vernon Hamilton, Gordon H. Bower, and Nico H. Frijda, 127–144. Boston: Kluwer Academic Publishers.

Öhman, Arne, U. Dimberg, and F. Esteves. 1989. Preattentive activation of aversive emotions. In *Aversion, avoidance, and anxiety*, ed. T. Archer and L. G. Nilsson, 169–193. Hillsdale, N.J.: Lawrence Erlbaum.

Öhman, Arne, and Joaquim J. F. Soares. 1993. On the automatic nature of phobic fear: Conditioned electrodermal responses to masked fear-relevant stimuli. *Journal of Abnormal Psychology* 102 (1): 121–132.

———. 1994. "Unconscious anxiety": Phobic responses to masked stimuli. *Journal of Abnormal Psychology* 103 (2): 231–240.

Ortony, Andrew, Gerald Clore, and Allan Collins. 1988. *The cognitive structure of emotions*. New York: Cambridge University Press.

Panksepp, Jaak. 1982. Toward a general psychobiological theory of emotions. *Behavioral and Brain Sciences* 5: 407–467.

———. 1998. *Affective neuroscience: The foundations of human and animal emotions*. New York: Oxford University Press.

Papciak, A. S., M. Feuerstein, J. A. Spiegel. 1985. Stress reactivity in alexithymia: Decoupling of physiological and cognitive responses. *Journal of Human Stress* 1: 135–42.

Patrick, Christopher J., Bruce N. Cuthbert, Peter J. Lang. 1994. Emotion in the criminal psychopath: Fear image processing. *Journal of Abnormal Psychology* 103 (3): 523–34.

Picard, Rosalind. 1997. *Affective computation.* Cambridge,: MIT Press.

Plutchik, Robert. 1980. *Emotion: A psychoevolutionary synthesis.* New York: Harper & Row.

————. 1994. *The psychology and biology of emotion.* New York: Harper-Collins.

Plutchik, Robert, and Henry Kellerman. 1986. *Biological foundations of emotion.* Vol. 3 of *Emotion: Theory, research, and experience.* New York: Academic Press.

Port, Robert F., and Timothy van Gelder, eds. 1995. *Mind as motion: Explorations in the dynamics of cognition.* Cambridge: MIT Press.

Putnam, Hilary. 1964. Robots: Machines or artificially created life? *Journal of Philosophy* 61: 668–691.

————. 1975. The nature of mental states. In *Mind, language, and reality.* Vol. 2 of *Philosophical papers.* Cambridge: MIT Press.

Quine, Willard van Orman. 1953. Two dogmas of empiricism. In *From a logical point of view.* Cambridge, Mass: Harvard University Press.

Radford, Colin. 1975. How can we be moved by the fate of Anna Karenina? In supplementary vol. 40 of the *Proceedings of the Aristotlean Society,* 67–80.

Ramsey, William. 1997. Do connectionist representations earn their explanatory keep? *Mind and Language* 12 (1): 34–66.

Rapcsak, S. Z., A. W. Kaszniak, S. L. Reminger, M. L. Glisky, E. L. Glisky, and J. F. Comer. 1998. Dissociation between verbal and autonomic measures of memory following frontal lobe damage. *Neurology* 50 (5): 1259–1265.

Reilly, W. Scott Neal. 1996. *Believable and social emotional agents.* Ph.D. dissertation, Carnegie Mellon University.

Rescher, Nicholas. 1988. *Rationality.* Oxford: Oxford University Press.

Rinn, W. E. 1984. The neuropsychology of facial expression: A review of the neurological and psychological mechanisms for producing facial expressions. *Psychological Bulletin* 95: 52–77.

Rolls, Edmund T. 1999. *The brain and emotion.* Oxford: Oxford University Press.

Rolls, Edmund T., J. Hornak, D. Wade, and J. McGrath. 1994. Emotion-related learning in patients with social and emotional changes associated with front lobe damage. *Journal of Neurology, Neurosurgery, and Psychiatry* 57: 1518–1524.

Roozendaal, Benno, Gina L. Quirarte, and James L. McGaugh. 1997. Stress-activated hormonal systems and the regulation of memory storage. In *Psychobiology of posttraumatic stress disorder,* ed. Rachel Yehuda and Alexander C. McFarlane, 247–258. New York: New York Academy of Sciences.

Rorty, Amelie Oksenberg. 1980a. Explaining emotions. In *Explaining emotions,* ed. Amelie Oksenberg Rorty, 103–126. Berkeley: University of California Press.

————, ed. 1980b. *Explaining emotions.* Berkeley: University of California Press.

Rorty, Richard. 1997. Introduction to *Empiricism and the philosophy of mind*, by Wilfrid Sellars, 1–12. Cambridge, Mass.: Harvard University Press.

Rosaldo, Michelle. 1980. *Knowledge and passion: Ilongot notions of self and social life*. New York: Cambridge University Press.

Roth, Alvin E. (1995a) Bargaining experiments. In *The handbook of experimental economics*, ed. John R. Kagel and Alvin E. Roth, 253–348. Princeton, N.J.: Princeton University Press.

——. 1995b. Introduction to experimental economics. In *The handbook of experimental economics*, ed. John R. Kagel and Alvin E. Roth, 3–110. Princeton, N.J.: Princeton University Press.

Schachter, S., and J. E. Singer. 1962. Cognitive, social, and physiological determinants of emotional state. *Psychological Review* 69: 379–399.

Scherer, K. R., and Paul Ekman, eds. 1984. *Approaches to emotion.* Hillsdale, N.J.: Lawrence Erlbaum.

Scherer, K. R., and H. G. Walbott. 1986. How universal and specific is emotional experience? Evidence from 27 countries on five continents. *Social Science Information* 25: 1–14.

Scherer, K. R., H. G. Walbott, A. B. Summerfield, eds. 1986. *Experiencing emotion: A crosscultural study.* Cambridge: Cambridge University Press.

Schlosser, Gerhard. 1998 Self-re-production and functionality: A systems-theoretical approach to teleological explanation." *Syntheses* 116: 303–354.

Schooler, J. W., and T. Y. Engstler-Schooler. 1990. Verbal overshadowing of visual memories: Some thing are better left unsaid. *Cognitive Psychology* 22:26–71.

Schwarz, Norbert, and Herbert Bless. 1991 Happy and mindless, but sad and smart? The impact of affective states on analytic reasoning. In *Emotion and social judgments*, ed. Joseph P. Forgas, 55–72. New York: Pergamon Press.

Scruton, Roger. 1974. *Art and imagination: A study in the philosophy of mind.* London: Methuen.

Seligman, M. E. P. 1971. Phobias and preparedness. *Behavior Therapy* 2: 307–320.

Sellars, Wilfrid. 1997. *Empiricism and the philosophy of mind.* Cambridge, Mass.: Harvard University Press.

Shaffer, Jerome A. 1983. An assessment of emotion. *American Philosophical Quarterly*, 20 (2): 161–73.

Siegel, R. A. 1978. Probability of punishment and suppression of behavior in psychopathic and nonpsychopathic offenders." *Journal of Abnormal Psychology* 99: 430–439.

Sifneos, P. E. 1972. *Short-term psychotherapy and emotional crisis.* Cambridge, Mass.: Harvard University Press.

Simon, Herbert A. 1967. Motivational and emotional controls of cognition. *Psychological Review* 74(1): 29–39.

Singer, J. A., and P. Salovey. 1988. Mood and memory. *Clinical Psychology Review* 8: 211–251.

Skinner, B. F. 1953. *Science and human behavior.* New York: Macmillan.

Sloman, Aaron, and Monica Croucher. 1981. Why robots will have emotions. Proceedings of the International Joint Conference on Artificial Intelligence Vancouver.

Solomon, Robert C. 1977. *The passions: The myth and nature of human emotion.* Garden City, N.Y.: Anchor Books.

Sommerhoff, Gerd. 1950. *Analytical biology.* New York: Oxford University Press.

Steinmetz, Joseph E. 1994. Brain substrates of emotion and temperament. In *Temperament*, ed. John E. Bates and Theodore D. Wachs, 17–46. Washington, DC: American Psychological Association.

Stich, Stephen (1983) *From folk psychology to cognitive science: The case against belief.* Cambridge: MIT Press.

Stocker, Michael. 1979. Desiring the bad. *Journal of Philosophy* 76: 738–753.

———. 1987. "Emotional Thoughts." *American Philosophical Quarterly* 24 (1): 59–69.

Stocker, Michael, and Elizabeth Hegeman. 1996. *Valuing emotions.* New York: Cambridge University Press.

Tassinary, Louis G., and John T. Cacioppo. 1992. Unobservable facial actions and emotion. *Psychological Science* 3 (1): 28–33.

Taylor, Charles. 1964. *The explanation of behavior.* London: Routledge & Kegan Paul.

Tomkins, Silvan. 1962. *Affect, imagery, consciousness. Vol. 1. The positive affects.* New York: Springer.

———. 1963. *Affect, imagery, consciousness. Vol. 2. The negative affects.* New York: Springer.

Tye, Michael. 1995a. *Ten problems of consciousness: A representational theory of the phenomenal mind.* Cambridge: MIT Press.

———. 1995b. What what it's like is really like. *Analysis* 55 (2): 125–126.

Ungerleider L. G., and M. Mishkin. 1982. Two cortical visual systems. In *Analysis of visual behavior*, ed. D. J. Ingle and M. A. Goodale, 549–586. Cambridge: MIT Press.

van Gelder, Tim. 1995. What might cognition be if not computation? *Journal of Philosophy* 7: 345–381.

Walsh, D. M. 1996. Fitness and function. *British Journal of the Philosophy of Science* 47: 553–574.

Walton, Kendall L. 1978. Fearing fictions. *Journal of Philosophy* 75 (1): 5–27.

———. 1990. *Mimesis as make-believe: On the foundations of the representational arts.* Cambridge, Mass: Harvard University Press.

Weston, Michael. 1975. How can we be moved by the fate of Anna Karenina? (Reply to Colin Radford). Supplementary vol. 49 of the *Proceedings of the Aristotlean Society,* 81–93.

Williams, Bernard. 1981. Internal and external reasons. In *Moral luck*, 101–113. Cambridge: Cambridge University Press.

———. 1995. Internal reasons and the obscurity of blame. In *Making sense of humanity and other philosophical essays,* 35–45. Cambridge: Cambridge University Press.

Wilson, J. R. S. 1972. *Emotion and object.* Cambridge: Cambridge University Press.

Wilson, Timothy D., Sara D. Hodges, and Suzanne J. LaFleur. 1995. Effects of introspecting about reasons: Inferring attitudes from accessible thoughts, *Journal of Personality and Social Psychology* 69 (1): 16–28.

Wilson, Timothy D., and Suzanne J. LaFleur. 1995. Knowing what you'll do: Effects of analyzing reasons on self-prediction. *Journal of Personality and Social Psychology* 68 (1): 21–35.

Wilson, Timothy D., Douglas J. Lisle, Jonathan W. Schooler, Sara D. Hodges, Kristen J. Klaaren, and Suzanne J. LaFleur. 1993. Introspecting about reasons can reduce post-choice satisfaction. *Personality and Social Psychology Bulletin* 19 (3): 331–39.

Wilson, Timothy D., and Jonathan W. Schooler. 1991. Thinking too much: Introspection can reduce the quality of preferences and decisions. *Journal of Personality and Social Psychology* 60 (2): 181–192.

Wittgenstein, Ludwig. 1953. *Philosophical investigations.* New York: Macmillan.

Wright, Larry. 1973. Functions. *Philosophical Review* 82: 139–168.

———. 1976. *Teleological explanations: An etiological analysis of goals and functions.* Berkeley: University of California Press.

Yanal, Robert J. 1994. The paradox of emotion and fiction. *Pacific Philosophical Quarterly* 75: 54–75.

Yehuda, Rachel, and Alexander C. McFarlane, eds. 1997. *Psychobiology of posttraumatic stress disorder.* Vol. 821 of the *Annals of the New York Academy of Sciences.* New York: New York Academy of Sciences.

Zajonc, R. B. 1968. Attitudinal effects of mere exposure. *Journal of Personality and Social Psychology Monograph* 9 (2): 1–28.

———. 1980. Feeling and thinking: Preferences need no inferences. *American Psychologist* 35 (2), 151–175.

Zajonc, R. B., S. T. Murphy, and M. Inglehart. 1989. Feeling and facial efference: Implications of the vascular theory of emotion. *Psychological Review* 96:395–416.

Index

action
  akratic, 63, 227nn19, 22
  arational, 58–59, 66–67
  B-D consistent, 51–52, 144
  B-D inconsistent, 51–52, 227n19
  B-D independent, 51–52
  B-D post-functional, 51–53
  emotional, 26–27, 46, 51–67, 95–98,
    129–130, 213, 216, 223, 226n15,
    227n24
  expressive, 52, 58, 128
  irrational, 58–59, 66–67
  programs. *See* motor programs
  relational, 12, 23, 27, 96–97, 100, 101,
    151
  volitional, 51, 58, 64–65
Adrenalin, 65, 182, 184, 197
affect, 5–9
  ascribed, 9
  bivalent, 7–8, 153–154
  as dispositions, 8–9
  monodimensional, 7–8, 153–154
  occurrent, 8–9
  temporal duration of, 10, 226n8
affect program, 24–28, 45, 80, 83–84, 86,
    110, 217
affect program theory, 3–29, 44, 45, 47,
    66, 69–70, 83–85, 86, 87–88, 95,
    103, 110, 118, 128, 131, 147, 151,
    153, 184–185, 193, 204, 207, 214,
    217, 225n3, 228n27
agent, 205–206, 232n61
AI, 22, 33, 122–123, 186, 187–215, 220,
    222
alexythemia, 13–14

anger, 5, 7, 22, 28, 40, 64–65, 72, 73, 77,
    84, 123, 130–131, 229n41
  functional role of, 29, 98, 132, 133,
    152–53
  physiological state of, 11, 184–185,
    226n10
anthropology (and social construction-
    ism), 71–76
anti-representationalism, 189
appraisal, 7, 25, 32, 43, 74–75, 81, 153–
    154, 210–211, 225n3
Arnold, M. B., 228n31
ascriptivism, 6, 9, 49, 54–55, 61–64,
    144, 227n24
autonomy, 22–23, 113, 122–123, 137,
    178–182, 186, 203, 207, 207–208,
    209–214, 221–224
Averill, James R., 69, 70, 74–75, 79–
    82

Bard, P., 39
basic emotions. *See* emotions, basic
Bazzett, H. C., 39
Bechara, A., 140
belief-desire consistency. *See* action, B-
    D consistent
belief-desire rationality, 40, 62, 65, 66,
    120–123, 127–128, 131, 166
belief-desire system, 40, 65, 166, 168,
    185, 216
Ben-Zeev, Aaron, 226n12
Bennett, Jonathan, 121
Bigelow, John, 175, 177
biomorphic argument, 207–208
Blackburn, Simon, 152, 229n42, 230n43

DATE DUE
